THE
TEREZIN DIARY OF
GONDA REDLICH

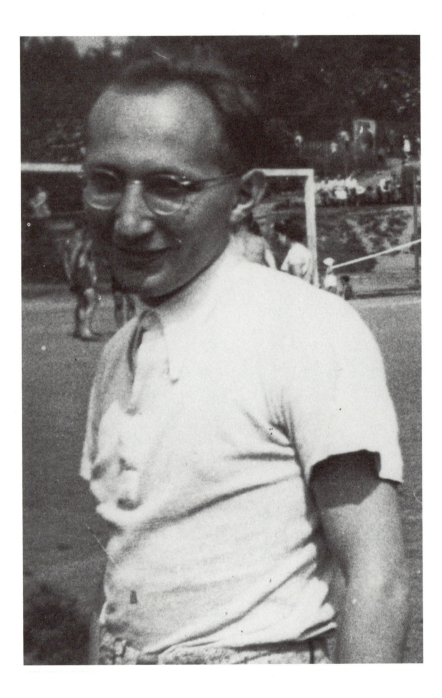

THE
TEREZIN DIARY OF
GONDA REDLICH

Saul S. Friedman, Editor

Laurence Kutler, Translator

Foreword by Nora Levin

THE UNIVERSITY PRESS OF KENTUCKY

Frontispiece: Gonda Redlich (courtesy Beit Theresienstadt)

Library of Congress Cataloging-in-Publication Data

Redlikh, Egon, 1916–1944.
    [Hayim ke-ilu. English]
    The Terezin diary of Gonda Redlich / Saul S. Friedman editor ;
Laurence Kutler, translator ; foreword by Nora Levin.
    p.   cm.
    Translated from the Hebrew.
    Includes bibliographical references and index.
    ISBN 0–8131–1804–2 (non-acidic recycled paper) :
    1. Terezin (Czechoslovakia : Concentration camp) 2. Holocaust,
Jewish (1939–1945)—Czechoslovakea—Personal narratives.
3. Redlikh, Egon, 1916–1944. 4. Czechoslovakia—Ethnic relations.
I. Friedman, Saul S., 1937–   . II. Title.
D805.C9R4313 1992
940.53'18'094371—dc20   92–11357
                                                      CIP

Contents

Foreword

The careful, preparatory work that often preceded the most destructive Nazi actions against Jews during the Holocaust was conspicuously missing during the first deportations "to the East" from Stettin in February 1940 and from other parts of Germany in October–November 1941. Both Reinhard Heydrich and Heinrich Himmler were impatient to have the Jews in the Third Reich disappear, but they did not want them killed in Germany. Consequently, these earliest deportations were swift, chaotic, and impossible to conceal. Later deportations required legal rationalizations of all kinds, definitions, categories, property disposal, and areas to be cleared for destruction. For old people who could not conceivably be considered dangerous to the Reich, for disabled and decorated war veterans, and for so-called prominent Jews whose disappearance might provoke embarrassing inquiries from abroad, Heydrich created a special ghetto in Theresienstadt, Czechoslovakia, about thirty-five miles from Prague. Letters from Czech and German Jews ordered to go to Theresienstadt speak of "taking a trip," of households "shrinking bit by bit," of the great pity that "we cannot travel together."

Theresienstadt was promoted not only as a special place for old Jews who "could not stand the strain of resettlement" but also as a "model ghetto," thus strengthening the myth that Jews were being transferred to places where they could survive. Actually, at a meeting held on October 10, 1941, in Hradcany Castle in Prague, involving Heydrich and Adolf Eichmann, Theresienstadt is referred to as a transit camp for the Jews of Bohemia and Moravia. At the Wannsee Conference on January 20, 1942, it is mentioned as a destination for German Jews. This "model ghetto" was to become a concealed funnel for Auschwitz and a death hole for many thousands of German, Czech, and Austrian Jews who were transferred there with Nazi-fabricated illusions and hopes. By May 1945, there were only 17,000 Jews who survived out of the 140,000 deported. Of the 15,000 children, a bare 100 survived.

At the October meeting, there was a sinister reference to living conditions in Theresienstadt: "The Jews will have to construct their homes underground," Heydrich said. At a subsequent news conference, he warned that "Judaism constitutes a racial and cultural danger to the peoples of Europe" and that measures taken were part of a step-by-step policy leading to the final goal (*Endziel*). Heydrich, of course, knew that the "final goal" was physical annihilation, but Jews did not. Nazi deceptions also played on the Jewish desire for autonomy and on Zionist dreams of a national reawakening. When the Nazis announced that an "autonomous Ghetto" would be set up in the Protectorate of Bohemia-Moravia, Jewish community leaders in Prague received the news with a certain feeling of relief. Jews would be spared the horrors of Poland and could, it was believed, remain in contact with fellow Czechs. Moreover, Jacob Edelstein, the head of the first Council of Elders (*Ältestenrat*), was a strongly committed Zionist, as were other members and Edelstein's successor, Dr. Paul Eppstein, thus strengthening the deception that Theresienstadt would have a Zionist character. Indeed, Eichmann spoke of it as a small-scale "Zionist experiment for a future Jewish state"—a phrase weirdly used in the quite surrealistic report of the International Red Cross, written several months after the liberation of Auschwitz, where most of the ghetto's victims had been murdered.

The Zionist and autonomous nature of Theresienstadt was also promoted by Dr. Siegfried Seidl, Eichmann's agent in Prague and the future SS head in the ghetto. Seidl ordered the Prague Jewish community to set up a work team, the *Aufbaukommando*, to prepare the ghetto-camp, and many Czech youths who volunteered were active and ardent Zionists. Much energy, hopefulness, and travail were expended in upbuilding the decrepit and squalid barracks of the old Czech fortress town of Terezin, but life in the "model ghetto" swiftly destroyed lingering illusions, and the prisoners soon realized that they were in a struggle for survival.

Edelstein had been made aware of Nazi treachery early. In the autumn of 1939 he had been ordered to Nisko (the Lublin "Reservation") in Poland to accompany a transport of Jewish men from Moravia and saw firsthand the brutal reality that lay behind Nazi "resettlement" plans. Later, in March 1941, Edelstein met with leaders of Dutch Jewry in the *Joodse Raad* and warned them of the danger of annihilation facing European Jews. Yet, although he and his family had emigration certificates for Palestine, Edelstein chose to share the fate of other Czech Jews and, as a Zionist, to uphold the chalutzic ideal whereby "the positive must be extracted from the negative in order to create new sources of life for the community." He wanted to create a "night shelter" so that survivors, especially Jewish youth, would be prepared for future productive work. By establishing industries and factories needed for the Nazi war effort, he hoped that a remnant of this youth could be saved—not an altogether foolhardy hope since thousands did survive until August 1944.

We are familiar with the influence and importance of the Zionist leadership and the Hechalutz movement in Theresienstadt through informative essays by Shlomo Schmiedt, a Hechalutz leader who lived in the ghetto for two years, and by the Holocaust scholar Dr. Livia Rothkirchen, as well as through articles that have appeared in the Israeli press from time to time and survivors' testimony. Hechalutz leaders and members were particularly effective in involving Jewish children and youths, many highly assimilated, in meaningful Jewish and cooperative group activities: study groups, disciplined physical exercise, holiday celebrations, and performances in Hebrew. Instructors tried gallantly to uphold old values while battling against a dissolving community and dissolving standards. For as long as they could hold out, they and the children also forged strong bonds of comradeship, mutual help, and special help to the aged and hungry.

These holding actions were strongly criticized by H. G. Adler in this massive sociological work *Theresienstadt, 1941–1945* published in 1955 in German. He characterized the ghetto as a *Zwangsgemein-schaft*—a forced or coercive society—but although the work is a mine of information and source material, it was written from an anti-Zionist point of view. Adler faults Edelstein and the whole Zionist position to hold on and hold out as long as possible in what we know was a sealed, no-exit crisis that had no precedent. To ask of this leadership, as Adler did, to prepare "an alternative plan appropriate for the new conditions" was to ask the impossible. To what degree conditions in Theresienstadt were impossible is set forth in dense detail in the diary of Egon Redlich, now available for the first time in English.

In Prague, Egon "Gonda" Redlich and Fredy Hirsch worked at the Zionist Youth Aliyah School. It was only natural that they would continue in these efforts after they were transferred to Theresienstadt. Redlich arrived in the ghetto sometime in December 1941 and began his diary entries January 1, 1942. They continued until August 2, 1944, but a second diary for his son Dan was started on March 16, 1944, and continued until October 6, 1944.

In 1982, Beit Theresienstadt, located in the Givath Chayim kibbutz in Israel, together with Beth Lochamei Hagetaot, published a Hebrew version edited by writer Ruth Bondy. The first English edition of the diaries has been translated by Dr. Laurence Kutler and richly annotated by Dr. Saul Friedman. We now know with terrifying clarity that no Jew, no human being, could have been prepared for the limitless Nazi hells to come—surely not one of Gonda Redlich's background. Yet he, like so many others, had to yield to what he could not escape. Redlich's diary is unique in the extensive literature we already have about Theresienstadt, not only because of his crucial position in the ghetto, but because it unfolds the day-by-day impressions of an acute observer quite fully aware of the historical significance of events he was witnessing and recording. For the victims, including ultimately Redlich himself, as they were pulled into the maelstrom of doubt, despair, and the terror of deportation, the perspective of an objective spectator became impossible, except at brief, irregular intervals.

We are familiar with the physical images of Theresienstadt: a grim fortress town with high scarps, deep moats, and huge, moss-covered walls through which streams of Jews poured into the ugly brick barracks. We know that aged invalids and war veterans had signed fraudulent contracts and paid thousands of marks for the right to go to the "privileged resettlement" in Theresienstadt, that old German Jews brought with them their top hats, tails, lace dresses, and parasols, only to be quickly diminished in dirty attics and underground cells where they died of shock, pneumonia, diarrhea, and hunger. We recall our first horror in looking at the stark drawings of Leo Haas, Bedrich Fritta, and Dr. Karl Fleischmann; the inexpressible pain of the children's drawings and poetry; the astonishing musical and dramatic productions created in the anterooms of hell; the tortures and killings in the *Kleine Festung*; Rabbi Leo Baeck's reassuring ministrations to the prisoners and stoical self-discipline that won praise even from the stern, uncompromising Adler; the sadistic ruse of the "family camp" in Auschwitz and the *Verschönerungsaktion* in preparation for the visit of the International Red Cross in June 1944. Redlich writes of all of these. But with the impressionistic detail and selectivity that only someone plunged into such surreal events, uneasily aware of an undefined menace, and racing up and down the slope from hope to dread, can describe.

He is acutely sensitive to the unrelieved suffering, to individual and social breakdowns, to class and cultural conflicts, miserable rations, fear of epidemics, the strains of a huge population mixture with its national and ideological tensions, the injustice of privileges he and other Jewish officials enjoyed. Yet Redlich is, after all, a young vigorous man with a sweetheart, Gerta Beck, still in Prague, to whom he could write only intermittently. And so, his diary is written for her until she, too, comes to Theresienstadt September 12, 1942. In the meantime, he writes ardently in his notes about a romance and sexual liaison with a youth counselor, Kamila Rosenbaum, but feels guilty about it. Others in the ghetto steal, bribe, collaborate, and lie in order to avoid the transports and to snatch a morsel of relief. Clutching the precipice, many Jews flung away the moral baggage that balked their survival. But many others, like Redlich himself, struggled with their conscience and recoiled with remorse over what they saw and what they did.

For us who were not there, who can only fleetingly glimpse the Holocaust universe we now speak of as Planet Auschwitz, it is useless as well as presumptuous to be judgmental. No one who was not there has any right to judge, for all taboos, moral guideposts, and familiar baselines crumbled. Redlich shrank from making such decisions, yet he had to. The Nazi officials passed down quotas for the transports to the Transport and Appeals Committee, and Redlich was on both. He and all of the others knew that the destination of the transports was fraught with danger, an unknowable menace, which one must try to avoid. Yet, except for Rabbi Baeck and perhaps a few others, no one knew the exact nature of the destination. We cannot plumb all of the intensities or torments of Redlich's life in Theresienstadt, but in the very questions he asks himself, in the dilemmas he cannot resolve, in the swift pitch from hopelessness to hope, and, at the very last, in the flickering thought that he, his wife, and his son may meet the rest of the family somewhere after the deportation from Theresienstadt—possibly in another camp—we have a man touching bottom, reaching into his deepest self, straining for bonds of human solidarity, inexplicably denying and defying the final defeat.

NORA LEVIN

Introduction

Egon "Gonda" Redlich was born in Olmütz, the onetime capital of Moravia, on October 18, 1916. The youngest of five children born to a lower-middle-class Jewish family, he grew up in the tumultuous interwar years when Tomas Masaryk and Eduard Benes tried, in vain, to steer an independent, democratic course for Czechoslovakia. Gonda's father operated a candy store and offered the family a modern, non-orthodox view of Judaism. His brother Robert (fifteen years his senior) and three older sisters all gravitated toward community or socialist ideologies. For the most part, the youngest Redlich had little time for religion or politics. Bar Mitzvahed in 1929, his main interests were swimming, skiing, tennis, and Ping-Pong.

After four years of what onetime companion Willy Groag called "tennis madness," Redlich, angered by anti-Semitic incidents in school, joined Maccabi Hatzair, a Zionist youth movement. Gonda also attended the group's summer camp at Bezpravi, and it was there, perhaps as a result of an infatuation with one Stella Berger, that he became fully committed to the leftist Zionist movement. Like most young people, his gymnasium days were filled with parties, movies, dances, hikes in the country, traditional coursework, and dreams of a profession (law).

When the Nazis occupied Czechoslovakia in March 1939, Gonda gave up his legal studies and began working with other youngsters, preparing them to make Aliyah (emigration) to Palestine. Many of his closest friends already had fled the country—Hanus Sylvester, a refugee from Galicia, had gone to Palestine; Stella and her sister Dita both were married and managed to get to America; his new girlfriend Nimka Federer was sent to Denmark to work with Jewish children. At this time, Gonda met Willy Groag, who remembers a special quality to Redlich's character: "his gray eyes, almost transparent, gazing from old-fashioned glasses, his high brow, the clarity of his thinking. At times he was like a sweet little prince from a story. At times he resembled a sleeping, little girl with a red face and smile. At times he seemed like an infant had disguised himself as a professor. Always, however, the contrasts worked: the cool look and the warm hand; his casual dress and his careful movements; his delicate body and great strength; his shy character and his sharp wit, all combined to give force to his teaching" (Hebrew edition, p. 9).

Over the next two years, Redlich also impressed Zionist leaders with his work in a school in Prague. Soccer coach, counselor to boy scouts, he taught Hebrew and Jewish history, eventually becoming assistant director of the school. When he was deported to the Terezin transit ghetto in December 1941, his reputation as an educator was established. He was the clear choice of ghetto elders to head up the *Jugendfürsorge* (the Youth Welfare Department, which would be responsible for housing, care, and education of fifteen thousand children who passed through the ghetto).

From the start, Redlich was aware of the historical significance of events unfolding about him. His journal was a conscious effort to record as much as possible for posterity. As he wrote (August 8, 1942): "Life in Terezin offers many interesting insights. To the historian, to the sociologist, it is a limitless well of experiences and achievements." At times, he became morose, possessed of doubts, especially after transports of friends and children departed for unknown parts. As a member of the ghetto leadership that decided who was to go and who would stay, he felt guilt and shame. On other occasions, he clutched at rumors, hoping that the Germans were telling the truth about Nisko, Madagascar, a second better ghetto in Czechoslovakia, or improved conditions with a Red Cross visit in June 1944. The diary reveals how Terezin's residents reacted to major events, like the assassination of Reinhard Heydrich or the German defeat at Stalingrad. It criticizes divisive Jewish leaders in the *Ältestenrat* and Zionist movement (December 1942) who seemed unwilling to set aside national or ideological differences in the face of overwhelming disaster. It offers poignant images of children defending their right to steal in a world gone mad, of confessing Christians suddenly thrust into a concentration camp because a parent was Jewish, of the old and sick being given less food so the healthy might have a better chance at survival. In what may be the most timeless question of all, Redlich asks (November 3, 1943): "Is a man who is given two portions of food fit to judge a thief who is given only one portion, when he tries to take another out of the kitchen?"

With all the anxiety and sadness, the diary is still the chronicle of a man, a husband, a father. Given sometimes to poetry (see June 13, 1942, and October 13, 1943), sometimes to prophecy (he accurately pinpointed the mass migration of survivors to Israel with American assistance on November 6–8, 1942), Redlich was no saint. Early entries in the diary exude devotion to his fiance "Beczulkah," Gerta Beck. Yet such love did not preclude a dalliance with coworker Kamila Rosenbaum. At the birth of his son Dan (for whom he began a second diary in March 1944), Redlich, whose marriage was not officially ratified, uses what normally is a distasteful term, *mamzer* (bastard), in the journal.

It is unfair, however, to moralize about Redlich's behavior in that terrible era. His love for the Jewish people, for Israel, for his family, Gerta, Dan, and the children, is unquestioned. When Gonda, his wife, and his child were about to be sent out of Terezin shortly before his twenty-eighth birthday in October 1944, he still expressed optimism about the future. Of Willy Groag he asked, "Why else would they permit us to take a baby carriage with us?" (Hebrew edition, p. 18). Their destination—Auschwitz/Birkenau.

Before he was deported, Redlich concealed both his longer diary (written on sheets of office calendars) and that which he dedicated to his son (in a notebook) in a woman's purse. They remained undetected until 1967 when Czech workers discovered the documents in the attic of one of the houses and turned them over to the State Museum in Prague. Before survivors at Beit Theresienstadt in Israel, working from copies, published a Hebrew edition in 1982, only a few excerpts, deliberately selected to embarrass the Zionist movement and the state of Israel, were published by the Czech communist government.

This edition is the product of collaboration among a number of individuals, each of whom played an indispensable role in the project. I wish to thank Chana Abells of Yad Vashem, who first brought the diaries to my attention; project coordinator Dr. Herbert Hochhauser of Kent State University; a longtime friend and scholar Dr. Shlomo Moskovits of Chicago; Eti Gal, Esther Shudmak, and John Redlich in Youngstown, all of whom proofed translations; Mary Beloto, Paula Burke, Janet McLain, and Denise Mangine of the Youngstown History Department; Ruth Bondy, author of the separate Israeli edition with its own annotations, who, with Alisa Shek, offered invaluable corrections and insights; and my colleague Dr. Laurence Kutler, a Semitics scholar with whom I labored untold hours, determining precise dates of entries, clarifying glosses and nuances, and converting the Hebrew/Czech text on microfilm into readable prose.

SAUL S. FRIEDMAN

Translator's Note

The principles that guided the translation of Gonda's diary require only a few words of elaboration. I have endeavored to exercise a detached judgment when choices among a variety of translations arose. Modern American idioms have been employed whenever possible in order to convey a sense of Gonda's perceived intent.

The translation attempts to remain generally faithful to the original Hebrew-Czech. The reader is asked to be attentive to the fact that Hebrew was Gonda's acquired language and is occasionally interspersed with glosses.

I acknowledge my indebtedness to Dr. Shlomo Moskovits, Sydney Pazol, and Ms. Eti Gal for their advice and corrections in the preparation of the diary. A special word of gratitude to Dr. Saul Friedman whose guidance and encouragement enabled this translation to reach conclusion. Needless to say, all errors are my own.

LAURENCE KUTLER

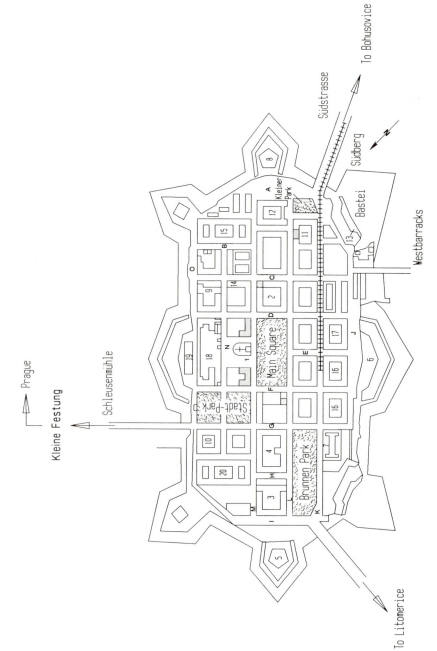

THERESIENSTADT

Prague

Kleine Festung

Schleusenmühle

Stadt-Park

Kleiner Park

Main Square

Brunnen Park

Südstrasse

Südberg

Bastei

Westbarracks

To Bohusovice

To Litomerice

N

Terezin

Theresienstadt (Terezin in Czech) is a star-shaped fortress city located forty miles northwest of Prague. Built by Joseph II in honor of his mother, Maria Theresa, in the eighteenth century, Terezin was a classic example of Hapsburg *Schlamperei* (disorder). Its "impregnable" ramparts were never assaulted, never defended. In 1888 some of the walls were pulled down, and civilians were permitted to take up residence in the defunct fortress. During World War I, the nearby *Kleine Festung* (small fort) served as a prison for Gavrilo Princip, assassin of the Archduke Ferdinand; army mutineers; and other opponents of the regime. When the Nazis annexed Bohemia-Moravia in March 1939, they needed additional prison space. On June 10, 1940, the Prague Gestapo converted the *Kleine Festung* into a main concentration camp for Czechs. A year later, on November 24, 1941, Terezin itself became a major transit camp for Jews being deported to their deaths in the East. Although some survivors claim the population reached 75,000, official records place the highest figure on September 18, 1942, at 58,491 in *Kasernes* (barracks) designed to accommodate 7,000 combat troops.

Legend for map opposite

Streets
A   Bäckergasse
B   Jägergasse
C   Badhausgasse
D   Neue Gasse
E   Turmgasse
F   Rathausgasse
G   Berggasse
H   Postgasse
I   Egergasse
J   Seestrasse
K   Bahnhofstrasse
L   Langestrasse
M   Haupstrasse
N   Parkstrasse
O   Wallstrasse

Buildings
1   Terezin Church
2   SS Headquarters
3   Podmokly Kaserne (German Quarters)
4   German Quarters
5   Ustecky Kaserne (Storehouse/hangings)
6   Sudeten Kaserne (Jewish men/later SS records)
7   Officers Casino (Gendarmes' Quarters)
8   Central Bakery (Stores/food)
9   Brauhaus (Delousing station)
10 Zentralbücherej (Library)
11 Hamburg Kaserne (Schleuse)
12 Hanover Kaserne (Men)
13 Jäeger Kaserne (Men)
14 Blindenhem
15 Magdeburg Kaserne (Ältestenrat/Prominents)
16 Prominents (Later)
17 Geniekaserne (Hospital/Aged)
18 Central Hospital
19 Kavalierkaserne (Aged)
20 Dresden Kaserne (Women/ Jail of Jewish Police)
▧   Children's Homes

1942

January

Redlich's choice of Hebrew for his diary was deliberate, offering him practice with the language he hoped to use in a Jewish homeland after the war and also serving as a barrier to translation should the Germans discover his notes. Some of his entries make for rather stiff or formal reading, and he later confesses to difficulties with the language (see entry June 25–26, 1942). These first entries in January are illuminating because they reveal the terrible burden of responsibility instinctively felt by Jewish officials in Terezin charged with selecting persons for transport to the East.

January 1, 1942. Last night the craftsmen celebrated New Year's and became completely drunk.[1] I had an interesting argument with Pl[2] regarding our work here. I found out that they are still talking about yesterday's incident in all the barracks.[3] The men's behavior is very bad.

---

1. Redlich employs the term "engineers" to include 342 Jewish artisans and carpenters who were sent to Terezin from Prague on November 24, 1941, to prepare the ghetto for later arrivals. By January, nearly 10,000 Jews were dispatched to what was supposed to be Reinhard Heydrich's "paradise ghetto." The original workmen from *Aufbaukommando I* lived relatively free from the threat of deportation until September 1944 when they too were sent to Auschwitz. See testimonies of Ruth Bondy Bashan, #47, and Avraham Ophir, #224, Hebrew University Oral History Project, 1965, and Shlomo Schmiedt, "Hechalutz in Theresienstadt—Its Influence and Educational Activities," *Yad Vashem Studies* 7 (Jerusalem, 1968), 108-9.

2. Friedrich Placzek was the head of administrative personnel.

3. There were eleven military barracks plus 219 housing complexes for 3,700 Czech civilians who lived in Terezin until the summer of 1942. To accommodate the Jews, the Nazis pulled the majority of their 3,000 garrison troops in 1941–42. The deportees were first housed in two *Kasernes*—the Sudeten barracks for men and Dresden for women. Girls and children under twelve stayed with the women.

In the morning, I accompanied a woman who was visiting her very sick husband. I showed her permission slip.[4] The policeman said that her husband passed away during the night.[5] I trembled with fear, but fortunately the policeman erred, mistaking the woman's husband for another dead man.

The children received their regular portions of milk.[6]

January 2, 1942. A woman in the barracks died of blood poisoning.[7] There is no other news. I refuse to write in Hebrew on *Shabbat*, preferring Czech instead.[8] Everything I write is dedicated to B.[9] I am not permitted to write her, apart from this book, lest she know what I have seen, felt, or learned.[10]

January 3, 1942. Shabbat. The Sabbath is set aside for a weekly review. Perhaps one day everything that I write here will be meaningful. For all of this there is but one goal: some day to inform Beczulkah

4. Initially, no one was allowed out of the barracks without escort or a signed pass. Husbands and wives were not permitted contact with each other. Jews were also to avoid streets where Nazi soldiers or Czechs resided. Violation of this rule resulted in flogging or imprisonment in the ghetto jail. Major offenders might be transferred to the *Kleine Festung*, an auxiliary fort that served as the central prison for the Gestapo in Bohemia.

5. The SS employed more than one hundred Czech gendarmes in the winter of 1941–42. According to Zdenek Lederer, one of the most reliable sources of what transpired in Terezin, their attitudes ranged from sympathetic to vicious (Lederer, *Ghetto Theresienstadt* [New York: Fertig, 1983], 35, 78). For others, any sign of neutrality was regarded as a positive sign (testimony of Hanka Fishel, Hebrew University Oral History Project, #94). The SS also created a Jewish security service, or *Ghettowache*, with a normal complement of two hundred men. Identified by special hats, jackboots, and the batons they carried, these men were responsible for maintaining order in the ghetto and assisting with deportations. See entries May 15 and November 3, 1942.

6. Ruth Bondy estimates the weekly ration at one-fourth liter.

7. The Dresden barracks was located near the northernmost rampart in Terezin. All girls and children under the age of twelve were sent here with their mothers. By August, the ghetto's housing office reported more than 4,400 persons registered in the barracks.

8. Redlich's upbringing was not Orthodox. From the moment he was sent to Terezin, however, he attempted to strengthen his Jewish identity. Writing in Hebrew on all days but the Sabbath was a peculiar example of this commitment.

9. Gerta Beck (b.1916) was a sewing teacher from Bohemia who became Redlich's sweetheart when the two worked in Maccabi Hatzair in the prewar days. Affectionately referred to throughout the diary as "Beczulkah" (a diminuitive of Gerta's family name), she arrived in the ghetto on September 14 and married Gonda a week later. In March 1944, their son Dan was born.

10. Under rules of martial law, the SS decreed that it was illegal for anyone to communicate with the outside world from December 1941 until February 1942. When the ban was lifted, Jews in Terezin could send one postcard per month, provided the messages were printed in block letters and consisted of no more than thirty words in German. At the end of September, the rule was relaxed still further and Jews could send five cards per month.

what I am unable to write her, how I have lived and what has happened to me here.

January 1st.: the New Year! a woman with a sick husband. Hebrew.

January 2nd: everything is the same. A woman died of blood poisoning. We became indifferent—"nothing is new."

January 4, 1942. I had to stop the children's visits to the women's house because of a new outbreak of scarlet fever.[11] A funny occurence: a man died of *Sepsis* [blood poison]. The members of the Khevre Kadisha burial society wrote as the reason for death "skepticism."[12]

Somebody placed a garland of flowers on the grave of a dead Jew.

A child asked for permission to visit his father. I asked him: "Where is your father?" He answered: "In jail."

Two women disappeared and returned today.[13]

In the evening, I heard a terrible piece of news. A transport will go from Terezin to Riga.[14] We argued for a long while if the time had not yet come to say "enough."

January 5–6, 1942. Our mood is very bad. We prepared for the transport. We worked practically all night.[15] With Fredy's help,[16] we managed to spare the children from the transport.

11. An exception to the rule about visits were children between the ages of twelve and sixteen who were housed in ground-floor stables of the Sudeten barracks. An order issued December 27, 1941, permitted them to see their parents once weekly. Because of the outbreak of scarlet fever, which resulted in eight deaths early in 1942, the visits were suspended.

12. A pun on the German "Sepsis" versus "Skepsis."

13. When Christians still lived in Terezin, escape was possible. Zdenek Lederer tells how some Jews simply removed the Star of David and took a bus or train from the Bohusovice station. Freedom carried with it little security. Escapees were quickly apprehended when they tried to return to Prague or cross the border. In all, only 33 persons out of more than 140,000 interned at Terezin succeeded in running away (Lederer, 61).

14. This would be the first of sixty-three trains bound for the East from Terezin and the only one where the SS specified a destination: the ghetto in Riga, Latvia, already overcrowded with German Jews and survivors of Latvian atrocities. From the very beginning, Redlich is haunted by what these deportations might mean. Of 1,000 persons sent out on what was labeled Transport O, only 102 survived the ordeals of Kaiserwald and Stutthof.

15. When the Nazis created the transit ghetto, they also set in place an *Ältestenrat* (a thirteen-man Council of Jewish Elders), whose task it was to maintain order among the Jews. Among the least desirable assignments in this shadow government were the transport and appeals committees, whose task it was to designate individuals for deportation. Redlich worked with both committees, and his diary is permeated with doubts and guilt.

16. Another prewar colleague of Redlich's, Fredy Hirsch (1911– 1944) had been a member of Maccabi Hatzair. Assigned to the ghetto's housing office, he worked closely

The mother of one child did not want to get out of the transport because her sister who was quite sick was traveling.[17] I do not have permission to visit the women's house.

I had to speak with this woman next to the gate. A policeman stood near us and finally, losing patience, ordered us to finish the conversation, which was unimportant to him. The decision to go with a child into the unknown, in the winter, all of this was "not so important." We took with us permits to leave the barracks.

January 7, 1942. We were not able to work because we were locked in the barracks. I asked the authorities to remove children from the transport and was told the children will not be traveling. In my opinion, however, it was impossible to try to extricate two grown-up female *chaverot* (female members of Hechalutz).[18]

Our work is like that of the Youth Aliyah [to Eretz Yisrael.[19]] There we brought children to freedom. Here we attempt to save the children from the face of death.

January 8, 1942. The Germans ordered the construction of gallows. All the people that sent letters are expected to be in grave danger.[20]

with Gonda, trying to find quarters for children and spare them the agony of the transports. Despite their efforts, more than 99 percent of the children who came to Terezin were deported. Survivors recall Fredy Hirsch as a man of extraordinary courage ("sehr mutig") who was "for the children a God." See testimonies of Peter Lang, #181; Hanka Fishel #94; and Eli Bacher, #19, Hebrew University Oral History Project.

17. Until 1944, unaccompanied children under the age of twelve might be granted an exemption. The same was true of individuals certified by physicians as too sick to travel. The key word is "might." The SS capriciously altered the population mix of the ghetto to meet its needs, first favoring the elderly who had rendered military service to the German or Austrian state, then switching suddenly to exemptions for the robust to impress a Red Cross delegation that visited the ghetto in 1944.

18. Redlich's *Jugendfürsorge* (Youth Services Department) required the services of a number of specialists: pediatricians, psychologists, teachers, day nurses. The children's houses also employed recreation leaders, and counselors (*madrichim*) who lived with the youngsters, supervising them and calming their fears. Among the latter were a number of teenagers of both sexes, members of Zionist organizations. Apparently, Redlich was unable to secure exemptions for two young girls. The work of the Youth Services Department is described by Schmiedt, 114; and in the testimonies of Peter Lang, #181; Dov Barnea, #25; and Esther Milo, #212, Hebrew University Oral History Project.

19. During the 1930s, the Youth Aliyah movement, chiefly inspired by Henrietta Szold, managed to shuttle several thousand Jewish children from Germany and central Europe to settlements in Mandatory Palestine. For information on the Auslands-Hachsharah of Hechalutz, see Reminiscenes of Shalom Adler-Rudel, #3, Hebrew University Oral History Project. Gonda worked at the Youth Aliyah school in Prague.

20. Because the Nazis had intercepted illegal communications, they constructed two platforms for hangings in the courtyard of the Ustecky barracks, which served as a supply depot. See entry January 10.

Haven't we reached the limit? Yet we still argue among ourselves concerning our living quarters. When I think about it, all of this is insignificant compared to the fact that it is possible some Jews may die whose only crime has been the writing of a letter to their relatives.

January 9, 1942. Eng. Z.[21] wants to decide every matter in an "authoritarian way." But we should not be made objects of hatred by our fellow Jews because we took responsibility. We are nothing but puppets that listen to each order. Already opposition is crystallizing between the executive and subordinate officials. If the person who is sending letters is not caught, the regulation on sending and receiving mail will be canceled.

The transport to Poland left Terezin with the elderly, the sick, the crippled, the imprisoned, etc. The arrangements in the children's rooms continue to improve.

Incidents of contagious disease, especially scarlet fever, are spreading. We received the news on Friday night when I was attending a Bar Mitzvah celebration.

January 10, 1942. Yesterday we read in the Orders of the Day that another ten transports will go. There is reason to believe that an additional four will also depart.

An order of the day: nine men were hanged. The reason for the order: they insulted German honor.[22]

A sick woman (epilepsy) who is seven months pregnant will travel on the next transport. E.[23] called together a gloomy *Appel* (roll

21. Otto Zucker (1892–1944) was the chief deputy in the *Ältestenrat*. Onetime leader of the Zionist emigration office in Prague, he had a reputation for being a tough, stubborn man. On several occasions, he stared down SS officers who were trying to force him to make selections from craftsmen. On September 28, 1944, when the Nazis made a sweep of long-lived ghetto personnel, Zucker was handcuffed and taken away.

22. Practically any act (failing to tip a hat, not moving out of the path of an SS man, attempting to deflect a blow) was interpreted as an insult to German honor. These nine men, and seven more hanged on February 26, were executed primarily for violations of the rules dealing with mail and packages.

23. Jacob Edelstein (1903–1944), a Socialist Zionist, was designated as the first Elder of the Jews when the *Ältestenrat* was organized. Redlich employs the abbreviation "Aleph," which was the first letter in Edelstein's name in Hebrew. A committed Zionist, Edelstein was the leader of the Czech Jews who dominated political life in the Terezin ghetto until he was replaced by a German Jew, Dr. Paul Eppstein, on January 31, 1943. For some, Edelstein was "the spirit of everything that's lost," a tireless worker who had time for everyone, a realist who sensed the meaning of the transports to Poland but who told others, "We have to develop a delaying tactic, gaining time is our motto. And we have to preserve human dignity." See the twelve-page report of Dr.

call or assembly) of heads of rooms and proclaimed the rules of Dr. Siegfried Seidl.[24]

January 11, 1942. Shabbat. This week: a transport, executions. Beczulkah, I cannot stop thinking about you. I want to write to you. Perhaps in spite of it all they will allow mail. Of course, you worry about me. But look what I have discovered in this difficult period: it's often easier for a man to cope with what is happening to him than it is for the onlooker. It is obvious that we are going about quietly like corpses. Many people work day and night, sometimes continually.[25]

In spite of it all, Beczulkah, we're not the only ones suffering in this terrible century. Maybe later we will appreciate more how nice it is to be alive. After the days of suffering, everyone will feel the meaning of freedom. How good it is to live.

January 12, 1942. After days of suffering, everyone feels what freedom is, what happiness is, to live, when many acquaintances are boarding the transports. Every one of us doubts whether we could exempt one friend, even if that friend might be a famous person. All this effort is like *Protekzia.*[26]

During the children's inspection, a policeman drove a child to the women's house where there is an epidemic. The doctors picked out the sick that were not able to travel. They were joking—this was real gallows humor.[27]

Edith Ornstein, Prague, 1945, Microfilm Roll III, Beit Terezin Archives, p. 10. H.G. Adler was less charitable, referring to Edelstein as "dishonest," "dogmatic" and "third-rate" (*Theresienstadt, 1941– 1945: Das Antlitz Einer Zwangsgemeinschaft* [Tubingen: J.C.B. Mohr, 1960]). See Schmiedt, 116.

24. Like his two successors as camp commandant (Anton Burger and Karl Rahm) Seidl was a young Austrian. Born in Vienna in 1911, he joined the Nazi party three years before Hitler came to power and moved upward through the Death's Head units of the SS. Remembered as a strutting brutal man, he was hanged by a postwar tribunal in Vienna in July 1945.

25. Everyone in the ghetto between the ages of sixteen and sixty- five worked nine to ten hours per day. Women peeled potatoes, cleaned soup vats, swept courtyards, washed stairs and latrines, and served in the *Krankenstube* (sickrooms) or gardens outside the walls. Men were assigned to carpentry, leather, tailor, and machine shops. Some slave laborers went to the mines of Kladno, construction sites in Purglietz or in Budweis. For some, the worst job was that of splitting mica ("Glimmer") needed for German military devices. If the work, done under the close scrutiny of the SS, was flawed, an inmate might be summoned back to his bench at 4 A.M., four hours before his companions reported to work.

26. Coined during the decline of the Hapsburg Empire, the word implied undue influence, favoritism. It was later adopted by desperate people in the ghettos and concentration camps.

27. An example of the critically ill being spared, while the healthy were deported to their deaths.

My mood was pretty bad today. To select [rather than] rely on luck to decide the fate of others is a difficult task. It is difficult because everything depends on chance. Late afternoon, good news causes joy—only one transport will go.

January 13, 1942. Another five transports will arrive this month.[28] To begin with, they ordered the wife of one of the men who was hanged to leave Terezin. Today, they canceled this order and permitted her to stay here.

I have been very tired. I am not able to exempt children. Perhaps I'm more afraid of people than I need be because I see everything from too many perspectives.

Yesterday, there was some strange news. People said the army had triumphed over the might of the state.[29]

We live in a depressed mood and each piece of news is received with great faith. Frequently great disappointment comes upon us. But we always hope anew.

January 14, 1942. Margarine has disappeared in one of the children's homes.[30] The counselors suggested that portions be reduced, giving the children bread alone without any of the other food. I did not agree. Tomorrow, I'll speak harshly to them concerning this matter. I was forced to hand over a list of the children in the children's house. I fear that this is related to the restriction on sending letters.[31]

28. Redlich was correct. Between January 18 and 30, five transports, ranging in size from six hundred to one thousand persons, most of them from Pilsen, did arrive in Terezin. The Nazis were proceeding with the clearing of all Jews from the Protectorate of Bohemia-Moravia.

29. A puzzling entry, but typical of the many rumors Redlich cites in the diary. Perhaps there was discussion of a possible military coup in Germany. Any such optimism would have been misplaced. One week later, on January 20, 1942, Heydrich presided over a conference of Nazi leaders, Am Grossen Wannsee 50-58, where "the Final Solution" of the Jewish Question was discussed and where Terezin was earmarked as a way station in the murder process. See Protocol of Grossen Wannsee Conference, in John Mendelsohn, ed. *The Holocaust: Selected Documents in Eighteen Volumes* (New York: Garland, 1982), vol. 6, 1-33.

30. The disappearance or theft of margarine was no small matter. In Terezin, normal rations consisted of black coffee for breakfast, a watery vegetable soup for lunch, and potatoes or noodles for supper, no more than eight hundred calories per day. People risked jail or deportation for shabby, black market cigarettes that cost as much as 150 *Krone* apiece. According to one survivor, "Cigarettes were as good as gold in the camp." People's eyes "lit up," chess tournaments ceased, when people learned cigarettes were available (B. Curda-Lipovsky, *Terezinske Katakomby* [Prague: Delnicke Nakladatelstvi, 1946], 139, 186-87). Ersatz beer was obtained by fermenting yeast in the coffee. Every barracks struggled to secure adequate rations. For differential rations, see entry June 7, 1942.

31. A reference to the men who were hanged.

January 15, 1942. It's a very small world. While visiting the women's house, I spoke with Robert's ex-wife.[32] When I was about to leave, a child approached me and asked if I would take him out.

A year ago, my dear mother passed away and I prayed in *minyan*. "May her memory be a blessing."

The head of the house reproached me that the children are not busy. It is difficult [this sentence is repeated several times] to teach without any supplies. I suffer from the fact that there is no satisfaction with my work.[33]

A counselor's father died in Prague. I am very depressed. I called the counselors and spoke to them concerning ways of improving the situation.

January 16, 1942. The carpentry shop must fill the orders it receives from every quarter. The Germans order them to finish all kinds of work for the camp commandant and chief inspector.[34] The carpenters polish furniture, and we desperately need equipment for the sick, etc., to live from day to day.[35]

The name of a child on the list led to the discovery of a woman who sent a letter. To her luck, she was registered on a transport. They

32. Robert Redlich (1901–1945), Gonda's brother and a community leader in Ol-mutz. See entry September 3, 1942.

33. Officially the Nazis forbade teaching Jewish youth. See entry July 26, 1942. Nevertheless, the *Ältestenrat* kept the fifteen thousand children that passed through the gates of Terezin busy with classes in art (utilizing every conceivable scrap of paper, including discarded bureaucratic forms and wrapping paper for painting and montages), dramatic performances, journalism (the boys of building L417 typed out more than eight hundred pages of *Vedem*), religion, history, geography, and language instruction. Pencils and crayons were so precious, several students would share one to the nub. See Dr. Oliva Pechova, et al., eds., *Arts in Terezin, 1941–1945* (Prague: Terezin Memorial, 1973), and the testimonials of Eli Bachner, #19, and Ruth Bondy, #47, Hebrew University Oral History Project.

34. For note on Commandant Seidl, see entry January 10, 1942. His chief assistant, Camp Inspector Karl Bergel, was a short, stocky man in his forties. Bergel came from Dortmund where he had been a hairdresser. Infamous for his drunkenness and cruelty, he controlled the ghetto police and reportedly broke the ribs and skulls of Terezin inmates (Lederer, 76-79).

35. When the Germans evacuated a barrack, they literally took everything with them, leaving the Jews the bare stone floors for beds. On August 22, 1942, the ghetto's *Raumwirtschaft* (housing office) devised plans to construct multi-tiered wooden bunks that could service between five and ten persons. The housing office authorized specific amounts of space between beds--2.4 meters for sick persons, 0.9 for the healthy—living space (two square yards) less than one-fourth the standard set by Czech law ("Probleme der Raumwirtschaft an die Leitung," August 23, 1942). See also plans for bed types, January 6, 1943, Raumwirtschaft File, Microfilm II, Beit Terezin Archive.

called her from the train. In the end, they left her on the transport. My task was to speak to the child. But when I was about to, the child had departed.[36]

They are shifting quarters in the women's house. It's impossible to describe the confusion there now. How rumors spread. The bus [to Prague] did not arrive. Instantaneously, there were rumors that the borders [of Germany] are closed for a revolution is coming, etc.

January 17, 1942. Shabbat. I am sitting in the empty room. Tomorrow, we move to another room. It saddens me, Beczulkah. I miss you. I do not forget.

This week: the second transport left.[37] In the women's barracks, there is shifting about. Do you know, Beczulkah: good moods change rapidly to bad, then back again.

Who knows how you are? When a man has a free moment, only then is he conscious of his situation. Believe me, it would be easier if I were with you.

January 18, 1942. A transport with many acquaintances from Pilsen has arrived. Elderly people (one woman ninety years old), the sick, and only a few can work.

We have shifted living quarters. If additional transports arrive in the coming month, we will be forced to shelter people in the walls that surround the city. The rooms there are filthy and wet and cold, with stone floors.[38]

Those on the transports told me that in Prague I am considered dead. They told me that in Prague a story is told that I was shot.

36. For deportation eastward.

37. Transport P left for Riga on the 15th. Most of the one thousand Jews were shot in the Pikwicka forest. Only fifteen survived.

38. In the best of *Kasernes*, the Magdeburg barracks, where the ghetto administration was housed, office space was limited and inventory (desks, tables, benches, etc.) at a premium. Crowding and filth in the Dresden barracks were overwhelming. Eli Bachner was eleven years old when he entered Terezin early in 1942. His worst impression was of sleeping on a floor in a great hall filled with shouting women (Bachner testimony, #19, Hebrew University Oral History Project). Resi Weglein, a nurse who came from Stuttgart in August 1942, recalled the stench on the ground floor of the women's barracks. "The first impression as we came in from the loft," she wrote, "was now you are for certain in the Inferno. It (the room) buzzed and growled, there was shouting and screaming, a strange twilight given off by a small incandescent lamp hanging on the beams. People lay in dirt" (August 21, 1945, Microfilm III, p. 11, Beit Terezin Archives).

I am writing at noon, when everything is okay. They promised me that the order banning letters will be rescinded. We may be able to write once a month.

January 19, 1942. Hope and depression alternate with one another every day. Yesterday, a rumor was hatched that Turkey declared war. A serious man told me he read this in the paper. Each of us hopes the situation will change. Instead, evil rumors.

January 20, 1942. Today it became clear that yesterday's rumor was false. A great disappointment. I fought to obtain a children's room in the army barracks where I live. At first, I thought I would have to give up the room. Meanwhile, I realized that many children will stay here. They want to squeeze them into a small room with more children than the number of adults who lived in the room previously.

I will have to take out the sixteen-year-olds and put them in adult quarters. I have searched my soul to see whether I was not acting too vigorously.

January 21, 1942. Moments of satisfaction. The woman director of the youth office conducted me to a room where they were celebrating the birthday of a small child. The other children sang songs. The sun came out and warmed the room, and I almost forgot all the difficulties of our situation.

The counselors have searched for a room to live in. I am ashamed that there is too much space in our room. I tried to convince the others, but to no avail. To my mind, two comrades would not be a bother. Quite the contrary, they would be helpful in our work.

The second transport from Pilsen arrived. They say the soldiers who accompanied them abused the Jews and called them shameful names. They whipped and tortured them.

January 22, 1942. I saw the hospital[39] and the house for the elderly.[40] A very terrible sight. Two of the counselors found a small room and

39. At first, both the Sudeten and Dresden barracks had their own surgical centers and sick wards. As the ghetto population grew and epidemics broke out, the Vrchlabi barracks became the central hospital, with twelve hundred more beds in the Engineers and Frontier barracks (Lederer, 135-36). For Resi Weglein, all of Terezin was "a great Lazarett." For her, the indelible, frightful sight was of "millions of agonizing spirits," covered with insects, lying in the sick rooms, dying, as "we nurses knew we could not help them" (Weglein memorandum, 14).

40. Many of the aged, feeble-minded, and mentally deranged were dumped into the *Kavalierkaserne* behind the central hospital. They lay there naked on stone floors or primitive palliasses in "ice cold and total darkness" until the SS whisked them away in September 1942 (Weglein memorandum, 21). See also the drawings of Leo Haas and

decorated it nicely and handily. We are permitted to write letters. It isn't clear yet if we will be able to write once a month or more. I am very happy. I will write to my beloved and she will send the letter home. It still isn't clear if they will permit the sending of packages.

January 23, 1942. Today I passed by the rooms. There is still much work. Last night was pleasant. We spoke with Yaakov[41] about many things.

January 24, 1942. Shabbat. New transports from Pilsen. A woman of ninety. We may have to accommodate the people with shelter in the walls of the basement. The frightened impression of the new-comers.[42] A dispute with Fredy in the children's house. Beczulkah, the work is becoming more ordered. But in spite of this, it is difficult. Man truly is a terrible egoist. If the room is not warm, instantaneously he acts dreadfully. At such times, I am very sad.

January 25, 1942. My work continues to progress in an orderly fashion. All the children's rooms make a good impression. Today, I also arranged the organization of a bureau in the women's house. The directors work very hard and even want to be involved in all the details of the work, but this is impossible because there is too much work. In Prague, people think I have been imprisoned.

January 26, 1942. Fr. [Fredy Hirsch] announced some competitions for neatness in the children's rooms. He also asked for prizes from the economic department. Today, I took the prizes and distributed them myself. He was very angry, but I spoke with him and managed to make up with him. He was sorry that he couldn't work with me.

Bedrich "Fritta" Taussig in Gerald Green's *The Artists of Terezin* (New York: Hawthorn, 1969), 103-7.

41. Jacob Edelstein, *Judenältester* of Terezin.

42. Rena Rosenberger was "horrified" when she and her daughter arrived from Wasterbork in January 1944. "Out of windows, we saw spiratic [sic], livid faces full of curiosity. These people had an easy expression on their faces and their complexion had a colour I have never seen before. . . . It was a shame to see the inmates of the ghetto sitting there starving, discolouring faces" (thirty-two-page Rosenbergerger memoir, summer 1945 and summer 1963, Beit Terezin Archive, pp. 2, 10). Apparently the newcomers did not look better to the veterans of Terezin. A forty-six-page yearbook composed by Fred Kramer and Leo Haas in 1942 offers sketches of frightened, submissive people clutching luggage, coming "one transport after another" from the Reich—"the old, infirm, those in need," then the tearful separation of husbands and wives, fathers and children, as guards stood by with rifles ("Heutestehen 24,000 Menschen in Arbeitseinsatz," report dated December 4, 1942, drawings by Leo Haas, written by Fred Kramer, pp. 5, 40, Beit Terezin Archive).

I promised him that I was prepared to resign my position if he would take it. He is getting tired of his job. It isn't very nice.

The third transport arrived with 617 people.[43] I argued with the head of the barrack. I am not satisfied with him.

I was told there were quarrels between Dov and Honza.[44] According to hearsay, Honza did not act in a fair manner toward our friends.

January 27, 1942. When it is cold outside, everything seems bad. The happy mood passes and everyone feels the difficulty of the situation. In these moments, I miss my girlfriend.

I will be forced to enlarge my department because lately there are nine hundred children under sixteen years.

Perhaps, next month, my mother-in-law and brother-in-law might come.[45] I will try to help them as much as possible.

I heard that they are already making up a list of Christians who will leave Terezin.[46] Today I want to write the first letter. The dead have not all been of the Jewish religion. But, of course, the burial ceremony was always Jewish.[47]

January 28, 1942. Today the transport will arrive from Brno. We are awaiting our acquaintances.[48]

I did not work the entire day. I arose late, and in the afternoon, I worked intermittently. I had my first lesson with Rav. Unger.[49]

Vinczi's parents arrived with my cousin Neugueb.[50] His son died in a concentration camp last December.

43. The third transport from Pilsen in January.

44. Two youth leaders. It is unclear from the entry who these men were. Honza apparently was not a member of the Maccabi Hatzair movement. He may have been Honza Brammer, head of the Youth Labor Service.

45. Redlich already refers to Gerta Beck's mother and brother Vitek as in-laws even though his marriage won't take place for months.

46. Reference to the several thousand Czechs living in and near Terezin.

47. Ruth Bondy estimates that perhaps as many as 10 percent of the deportees in Terezin were not Jews by religion but only under definition of the Nuremberg Laws, Israeli edition, p. 48.

48. The third transport bringing friends of Redlich to Terezin.

49. Dr. Zikmund Unger was chief rabbi in Terezin until his deportation in 1944. Redlich studied Hebrew and Talmud with him.

50. "Vinczi" was Dr. Robert Weinberger (1914–1977), another member of Maccabi Hatzair from Brno. An attorney, Weinberger lived with Redlich for a time, working with the Transport Committee. After the war, he emigrated to Israel and lived his last years in Netanya.

January 29–30, 1942. A transport arrived from Prague. Tela[51] came and offered news from our apartment. The situation there is not pleasant. The number of comrades in the movement is shrinking. The economic situation is getting worse because salaries aren't sufficient. Zeev is seriously ill.[52] They operated on him twice without anesthesia.[53] He wrote me a letter in Hebrew.

In Prague, people tell themselves that the living conditions here are worse than they really are. My work increases and expands at a great rate.

My beloved sent me a nice photograph. My joy exceeded all bounds.

January 31, 1942. Shabbat. Beczulkah sent me nice photos. If only she knew my happiness. She apparently suspects that she will remain alone and will not be able to reach her mother or me. We hope that she and her mother will arrive here. I miss her so much, she doesn't know how much. Beczulkah, my dearest, is it possible that I live better than you with your constant fear in Prague? Let us hope that I can write to you soon.

February

As resentment toward the ghetto administration over space, bedding, heat, and food mounted, Redlich immersed himself in study with rabbinic scholars. None of the Jewish inmates of Terezin knew that a meeting had been held among high-ranking Nazi officials at the Berlin suburb of Wannsee on January 20, 1942. There Reichsprotektor Reinhard Heydrich outlined "the definitive solution of the Jewish problem." Among his proposals: labor utilization of Jews in the East

51. Ela Polak was a music teacher from Maccabi Hatzair. She made Aliyah to Israel after the war.
52. Zeev Shek (1920–1978) was also a Maccabi Hatzair counselor from Olmutz. He later became Israel's Ambassador to Vienna and Romania and was instrumental in building Beit Terezin.
53. Redlich transliterates the Czech "narkose" into Hebrew.

that would lead to their withering away and the maintenance of a
Reichsaltersheim, *a kind of "paradise ghetto" for aged and privileged
Jews in Terezin.*

February 1, 1942. I have already been studying with Rabbi Unger a
number of days. It's quite interesting. We learn Rashi, portions of the
Mishna and Gemara, etc.[1] All this is very interesting for me because
I can see the learning process of Eastern Europe and I get to know the
Talmud.

They have arrested one of our assistants. According to the ghetto
police, he was stealing baggage.[2]

February 2–4, 1942.[3] The women counselors want to quit their work.
I tried to obtain better food and one free day for them. I hope that
their work will be better now.

There is an engineer named Trud. who was called here because
he is an expert in heating. He has a wife and two small children. One
of them is a year old. I asked them to move their quarters, because we
have an obligation to them. There are several levels and rights in the
administration, and this is a situation which is not proper.

We are beginning to organize our work in the women's houses
where there are 420 children. One man complained that there are
plenty of idle youths who lie on their beds or bunks all day. I called
him to my chambers and spoke to him.[4]

Today I am sending my first letter to my beloved. Sometimes
there is much work while our strength is lacking. We will have to replace the women counselors who work with the boys with male
counselors.

1. For Dr. Unger, see January 28, 1942. Rashi (Rav Shlomo ben Yitzhok) was an
eleventh-century sage from Alsace whose writings are considered to be seminal inter-
pretations of Judaism.

2. Suitcases and other personal belongings were confiscated from deportees upon
their arrival in Terezin and deposited in the Ustecky barracks.

3. There is no clear break between entries February 2 and 4.

4. Eventually, Redlich's *Jugenfürsorge* would be responsible for a number of children's barracks—*Kinderheim* (ages four to ten), *Knaben* and *Mädchenheim* (ages ten to
sixteen), and *Jungarbeiterheim* (ages sixteen to twenty). The youth services department
apprenticed youngsters in electrical, carpentry, and machine shop work, preparing
them for postwar settlement in Palestine. Another important activity was tilling vegetable gardens where beets, cabbage, celery, rutabagas, onions, and potatoes were
grown for the SS. See Adler, 547–73. See also "Ablieferungsbuchführung für Müd-
chen," a thirty-page delivery book of girls ages twelve to seventeen, Microfilm II, Beit
Terezin Archives, and Bondy testimony, #47, Hebrew University Oral History
Program.

February 5–6, 1942. I wrote a letter and suddenly heard that it was forbidden to send long letters of more than thirty words. I am greatly disappointed. My relationship with the counselors is complicated. I know that the work of both male and female leaders is becoming too difficult. I am also aware that my living standard is easier and more comfortable than that of the male counselors. But in spite of this, I must require a day's work from the *madrichim* for I know very well that their situation is much better than that of other Jews.

The transport which is to come from Prague will be housed in rooms with a stone floor and no stove. There is still hope that we will be able to construct some stoves.

February 7, 1942. Shabbat. God! May the letter be sent in order that Beczulkah may know how and where I live.

Sometimes a transport arrives, and when it does they unload, in the fullest sense of the word, old women from the coaches. I thank God that my mother has already passed on.[5] My dearest beloved, today, my thoughts again are about you. I am sad. How happy I would be if I could be with you. But when I see the transport, I hope in my heart that you will not come, at least not yet. Perhaps it will be better in the spring.

February 8, 1942. The transport from Prague arrived. At the fair, they found five thousand crowns on one person.[6] They wanted to punish the entire transport by depriving them of food for twenty-four hours. Of course, the entire transport is composed of elderly and sick people.

February 9, 1942. They returned my letter to my beloved. I have to write a letter of only thirty words. If only I were able to describe this humiliation—writing and counting each word. I cannot write what I feel, while always considering the length of the letter.

Among us are "sinners of Israel."[7]

5. For one impression of the arrival at Bohusovice, see B. Curda-Lipovsky, 36-37. She talks of "new victims of the Gestapo" disappearing from life to catacombs where they were buried alive." As they marched five abreast into Terezin, it was as if they were entering Dante's Inferno with the inscription "VSICHNI, KDOZ, SEM VSTUPU-JETE, ZANECHTE VSI NADEJE!" (Abandon hope, all ye who enter . . .) See also entry March 11, 1942.

6. The fairground in Prague where the transports were collected. In the original diary, Redlich inscribed the words "yarid hamizrach" (oriental fair), then crossed them out. In such circumstances, it was only to be expected that deportees would try to smuggle money with them. An amount this large, however, was deemed a major offense.

7. Presumably collaborators.

February 10, 1942. There still is no new barrack for women. There-fore, they are placing women one by one in rooms of two other bar-racks. Space for women who come later will surely be the worst of all.

The situation in the sick house is very bad. Men and women sit, for example, at the same time in one latrine.[8] Dirt can be seen in all rooms. At the women's house, I took a youth into a children's room. He used such foul language that all the women in the room asked me to take him away. His mother was sick. During one of her fits, the youth said: "I wish you were dead."

I have a retarded child in the children's room. I hope all goes well with him. One child was in the fair building in Prague for weeks. They took him from a transport and left him there till the next one. I have been remembering all that has occurred these last few months since the transports began.

February 11, 1942. We wanted to prepare a large hall in the women's house for the children. At present, they are settling additional women from the new transport in this hall.[9]

Today I handed in a request for permission to marry *per procuram.*[10] I am curious as to what will be.

Yaakov complained that the children's room is filthy. It is difficult to keep clean if brooms and other cleaning materials are missing. Yes-terday, we made up a list of members of the movement to protect them against possible deportation to Poland.[11]

February 12–13, 1942. Who will arrive on the transport today? When will the troubles end?

A woman traveled to Riga because she thought that her husband, who was in Nisko,[12] went to Riga. Now her husband is here. He re-

8. Terezin's sanitation was deplorable. For more than 150 years, the residents of the fortress drew their water from wells. Primitive cisterns and mains were upgraded in the summer of 1942 after it was discovered the wells were polluted. The lines that formed before the few communal toilets that functioned were an agony for the sick or handicapped. What little cold water there was for washing was gone after the early riser used the showers. Till the day of liberation, each inmate was allotted four gallons of water daily, one-fifth the basic requirement for a normal Czech town. People could wash three kilograms of their belongings every six weeks. See Lederer, 51; Adler, 331; Karel Fischer File, Microfilm III, Beit Terezin Archives; and *The Book of Alfred Kantor* (New York: McGraw Hill, 1971), 19.

9. Another three thousand persons arrived from Prague between January 30 and February 12.

10. Literally through an emissary or in absentia.

11. Members of the Hechalutz youth movement.

12. Nisko was supposed to be the Jewish Reservation near Lublin after the Nazis conquered Poland. Thousands of Jews were sent to this region in 1939–40, where they perished from exposure and starvation. According to Livia Rothkirchen, Edelstein vis-ited Nisko in the fall of 1939 when thirteen hundred men were sent there from Mora

turned from Poland and volunteered to register for a transport because he had heard in Prague that his wife was here in Terezin. This is typical of our lot—"continually to wander in the earth."

The rabbi told me a nice Midrash: among Jews it is said there is an advantage to being the majority, for the majority rules. A Jew asked if that is so, why not convert to Christianity? The rabbi answered: if we believe with a perfect heart, then the majority does not rule.

The first child has been born in Terezin. His name is Tomas.[13] The *chaverim* that serve as Zionist youth leaders have disappointed our expectations. They are indifferent and do not take care of incoming members.

February 14, 1942. Shabbat. They returned my letter. I wrote thirty words. The first child in Terezin. Everyone calls him A.K.1.[14]

The lines of people are like deaf mutes during the time when coffins are taken out of the barracks. It really is one of the strongest impressions in Terezin.[15]

Hatred for the leadership remains strong. How are such things possible? Obviously we have here two dubious types. Sometimes they can make a man sick. But on the whole—even if people are egoistic—they do not go over corpses.[16]

February 15, 1942. Hatred against us has not ceased. Yesterday, people insulted me because I spoke German.[17] Perhaps they are right. But all this fuss if we speak this or that—a trivial thing.

via. The illusion of Nisko served the Nazis' purpose, as Jews who were deported later wanted to believe that somewhere in the East there actually existed a quarantine land ("The Role of the Czech and Slovak Jewish Leadership in the Field of Rescue Work," *Rescue Attempts during the Holocaust: Proceedings of the Second Yad Vashem International Historical Conference, April 8–11, 1974* [Jerusalem: Yad Vashem, and New York: Ktav], 429).

13. Tomy Fritta was the son of talented artist Bedrich "Fritta" Taussig. After the war, he was adopted by Leo Haas. A total of 207 children were born in Terezin, under the most frightful circumstances.

14. Symbolic of the first transport that reached the ghetto in the *Aufbaukommando*.

15. Estimates vary on the number of daily fatalities in Terezin. Klara Caro, whose husband was once a rabbi in Cologne, put the death toll at 140 per day during an epidemic in 1942 ("Starker als das Schwert" [Stronger than the sword], twenty-seven-page report, September 1946, Microfilm III, p. 4, Beit Terezin Archives). Dr. Edith Ornstein reckoned 200-250 dead each day (Ornstein report, 6). Lederer's figures for 1942 are 15,981, approximately 1,300 each month (1423).

16. Redlich's idiom probably means the unwritten rule was that people were not supposed to capitalize on misfortunes of others.

17. Those resentful of *Ältestenrat* officials seized upon any pretext to further dissension in Terezin. Like many residents of Bohemia, Redlich felt comfortable speaking German. During the interwar period, however, when Czechoslovakia was attempting to manifest its own identity in central Europe, ultra-nationalists deemed anything German as disloyal. Members of the Hlinka Guard, an anti-Semitic Slovak movement,

Last night, a funeral made a great impression upon me. The lines of men in the darkness, the yard, the field, the coffin raised in silence, the lanterns flickering—I will never forget this sight.

We want to arrange an exhibition of the children's handicrafts. We have already gathered many interesting things made by children. For example, a child drew in the hall of the fair.

They will not give us coal as of tomorrow. Only if the temperature goes below zero.

February 16, 1942. If I were to insist upon permission for couples to be married *per procuram*, the Germans might send my beloved with the next transport. It is better for me to wait for the situation to develop here.

It's difficult to be at peace with the women. They are always fighting. It's sometimes hard to speak with people who live under worse conditions than I. The *madrichot* (female counselors) requested that I find them a room to live in. How many women leaders live in the children's ward. A cumbersome situation, but I found a room for twenty-five women. When I suggested this room, the women did not receive it kindly. But there are no smaller rooms. It's a difficult situation since I live in a small room and it's hard to ask my assistants to do things that I do not.[18]

February 17, 1942. Eichmann came.[19] We are awaiting important decisions. I am curious to see what will happen if the Christians leave Terezin. The Jews are crowded together and space in the rooms, especially in the women's quarters, is very limited.

Sick women lie among the healthy. One mother, sick with measles, lies with her child who is also sick. The women who go to the sick houses with their children return without finding their old places. A youth of fourteen died. Not too long ago, we wanted to

attacked German-speaking Jews. It is understandable how the use of German might be regarded as unsuitable in the ghetto.

18. Redlich's colleagues recall that he shared a small room with two others in the Magdeburg barracks, which doubled as administrative headquarters for the *Ältestenrat*. Normally, unmarried residents had to share the small, dark rooms. High-ranking ghetto personnel, their families, or luminaries had the luxury of a single room to themselves.

19. Literally "ish-alon," Hebrew translation for SS Obersturmbannführer Adolf Eichmann, head of Bureau IV-B-4 (the Jewish Question) of the Reich Main Security Office. A close associate of Reinhard Heydrich, Eichmann came to Terezin shortly after the Wannsee Conference to see how matters were proceeding with the creation of the sham "Reichsaltersheim." According to Hannah Arendt, Eichmann was severely disappointed, realizing immediately that because of size, Terezin could only be a transit camp (Arendt, *Eichmann in Jerusalem* [New York: Viking Oress, 1964], 81).

move his lodgings to another barrack. His father did not agree, and we did not move him. What would have happened if we moved him against his father's wishes? Responsibility here is sometimes too much to bear.

February 18–19, 1942. We started up studies in the women's quarters. The young people do not know the basics of arithmetic, fractions, etc.

There is much work, but the different administrative sections support us now with all their power. There are problems with the boys in the children's ward located in the women's quarters. The boys are educated only by women counselors, and discipline is lacking. The youth masturbate, and the counselors find it difficult to control them.

There is a Professor Schwefel here with the personality of the character from the novel *Der Schuler Gerber hat Absolviert.*[20] He proposed that he teach in the youth wards. I will give a sample of his writing to a graphologist so he can do a character analysis.[21]

February 20, 1942. People are criticizing the distribution of food. Today I reported about an unpleasant matter. They put a crazy woman into the children's ward. When I left, I asked myself will my efforts have any meaning or purpose? A procession of women passed on the street. Two Christian children were riding on a sleigh. On seeing them sliding in the snow, one of the Jewish women in the procession said that Christian children were better off than their children. She was right, and I felt her complaint was justified, even though I was not to blame for this situation.

One hundred men will travel to Kladno, supposedly to work in a quarry.[22] They may also prepare quarters for the Germans who would then leave Terezin and go to Kladno.

February 21, 1942. Shabbat. Last night "a living newspaper."[23] I lectured on Trumpeldor.[24] Truly a delightful function. In the afternoon,

20. *The Student Gerber Has Finished His Studies* was a popular novel published by Friedrich Torberg in Berlin in 1930. A major figure, Professor Kupfer, was a know-it-all. During the war, Torberg later joined the Czech Brigade of the French army and escaped to the U.S.
21. Willy Shoenfeld was the handwriting expert who made character analyses to see if people were suited for their work. Redlich was following a standard practice.
22. A mining town several hours away from Terezin. The men returned in June 1943. Simultaneously, the Nazis removed sixteen hundred Jews, including some families, from Kladno to Terezin. See February 22, 1942 entry.
23. A program of spoken articles.
24. Russian-born Joseph Trumpeldor (1880–1920) was an inspirational hero to Zionists. One of the few Jews decorated by the czar for service in the Russo-Japanese War

there was a Sabbath party. In the evening, a children's play. The children's program this time was very good from the standpoint of acting. (A parody of the plays of Voskovec and Werich.)[25] Toward the end, they sang popular songs, and the audience reproached them, much to my happiness. We are beginning to express a cultural life. Although there is not much free time, I still would like to be culturally active for the others, too.

February 22, 1942. Yesterday there was a children's play. The children are great actors, and I liked their songs. Toward the end, they sang "explosive" songs—but to my joy a fellow started to sing "Hatikvah."[26] Others joined in, and it was a good lesson for the children. I was pleased that there are still good Jews here.

There's no easy solution to a question concerning one of our young *chaverim*. If we put our friends in the youth wards, isn't it the same as giving preferential treatment?

A transport will arrive today from Kladno. Depressing. Yaakov criticized my work. I don't know what he said, but I am depressed. The women counselors have not gotten their living quarters.

February 23, 1942. Sometimes we're reminded of all the things that depress us. It is forbidden to go out without permission. It is forbidden to go into a shop,[27] forbidden, forbidden, forbidden. The worst thing is the fact that each of us is getting used to it.

We received a letter which a friend brought in the transport. People are complaining that we are not writing.

February 24, 1942. A conversation with Yaakov. He began with a question: "What are we doing?" He doesn't see everything we have done here. Perhaps it's not so easy to see. I was explaining to him

---

(he lost an arm in combat), Trumpeldor helped create the so-called Zion Mule Corps which distinguished itself at Gallipoli in 1915. He and Zeev Jabotinsky were responsible for creating the Jewish Legion, which fought alongside Allenby in the Middle East. After World War I, Trumpeldor emigrated to Palestine. His death came at Tel Hai, a remote settlement in the Galilee that came under assault by Arabs.

25. Two actor-playwrights who operated a satirical theater in Prague before fleeing to the U.S.

26. The singing of the Zionist anthem headed off problems over popular hits in the ghetto.

27. There had been a number of small shops once operated by Christians along Main Street, from the square to the Magdeburg barracks. After January 1943, Jews could buy clothing, shoes, toys, food, even perfume with ghetto *Krone*. The shops were inventoried with merchandise that had been rejected by the SS (Lederer, 52).

what we are doing, what was happening. But in the middle of my words, he said: "I am tired and must get some sleep." I knew he didn't hear one word I said. Perhaps it's cowardice, but I am not prepared to assume responsibility for thirteen hundred children.

In the evening, we made up the program for Purim. It will be a satire on the ghetto situation.

February 25, 1942. The mother of one of the youths was a clerk in the office. Despite this, she constantly interferes in affairs of youth services. For example, she has sent women inspectors to the children's rooms, without permission. Now her son is sick and she talks against us and causes harm to our work.

I spoke with L.[28] I told him that I cannot be burdened with sole responsibility, that I want Fr. [Fredy Hirsch] to come and help administer my office. I said that tomorrow the insane will arrive from Veleslavin.

February 26–27, 1942. Haragim. Killings. Seven young men died as heroes. One died because he bought candy. According to one who heard them, he cried, "May my mother be blessed." L. [Leo Janowitz] told me some interesting things about the jail. The Germans inspected the women's ward today. They laughed, called out, and joked. . . .

The chief warden of the jail is a Jew.[29] While he was with other Jews, people who were about to die, he stole a sausage, meat that had been passed in secret and in danger into jail.

I received a letter with thirty words from Prague. An aunt is requesting help for her sister. They wrote me from home:

"My dearest, write what you are doing. Are you healthy? We miss you. We are healthy. Do not worry."

February 28, 1942. Shabbat. Beczulkah, I received a letter from you: "Gondulka, dearest. I am happy to be able to write. I am working steadily. I hope that your work gives you satisfaction. I miss you terribly. I am waiting for news from you. Your dear ones are healthy and all right. Yours, Gerti."[30]

You don't know the feeling—to receive a letter from a loved one. A letter at once good and sad. They also wrote me from home.

28. Dr. Leo Janowitz was secretary for the central administration, hence Jacob Edelstein's closest associate. He was deported in September 1943.
29. For more on the "jail" in Terezin, see entry June 5, 1943.
30. The original is in German.

March

Terezin was abustle with rumors that several thousand Christian residents would be moved out and the entire fortress community made into a Jewish city. This would certainly alleviate the problem of bedding that intruded into Redlich's diary for more than two weeks (see March 14–15). There were also rumors of Jewish settlement on the island of Madagascar. In reality, the Nazis were already sending people to their deaths at Izbice in eastern Poland and the country estate of Maly Trostinec near Minsk.

March 1, 1942. My beloved wrote: "My dear, I am happy to be able to write. I am working steadily. I miss you greatly. I am pleased with all the news. Your friends are healthy." There is a fragrance in the air.[1]

I miss you. I know how hard life can be. How many men live in worse conditions than I? Some people's future is more difficult and darker than mine.

March 2, 1942. The hangman also works in the health department. He is a small man with broad shoulders like "the bellringer of Notre Dame."[2] He performs autopsies and, in general, takes care of corpses.

We received news from Prague. Strife between the parties has not ceased.[3] Our opponents take advantage of the fact that our leaders are not in Prague. In the newspaper, they write that the Jews will be going to one city.[4] The meaning of the matter is clear.

1. The approach of spring gave Redlich optimism, even though overcrowding already was causing problems. Adler estimates there were twelve to fifteen thousand Jews in Terezin by the end of March, a figure twice the normal population of the fortress. They were allotted only 58 percent of the available space (Adler, 691).

2. Literally the Hunchback of Notre Dame. When Edelstein was ordered to find someone to perform autopsies, Ada Fischer volunteered. A brutish sort of man ("like a gorilla," recalled Eli Bachner), Fischer previously had worked in the pathological institute in Brno. Later, in Birkenau, he was the *Oberkapo* of the crematorium. Despite his soft speech and friendly manner (he patted children on the head and gave them food), children were afraid of him and adults shunned him. See testimony of Eli Bachner, #19, Hebrew University Oral History Project.

3. As elsewhere in Europe, Prague Jewry was divided among the religious and non-orthodox, assimilationists and Zionists, socialists and a smattering of Jabotinsky revisionists. Redlich's diary rebounds with his impatience with leaders who would not forgo their own egos for the sake of the common good. See entry May 13, 1942.

4. Ironically sensitive to what history might say, the Nazis prohibited calling any "Judenwohnbezirk" a ghetto. On February 28, *Reichsprotektor* Heydrich announced that

March 3, 1942. Parachutists came down upon northern France.[5] An interesting conversation with Yaakov. He told us of certain negotiations between Jews and Germans in the spring of 1940. The Germans demanded that Jews mediate with the aim of preventing America's entry into the war on Britain's side. The negotiations ceased in the summer of 1940 after the great German victories in France. When a great movement to prevent America's entrance into the war was born, the Germans thought there was no need anymore to seek Jewish mediation.[6]

In a conference, the Germans proposed a Jewish state in Alaska, Rhodesia, or Madagascar.[7] Among the Germans, there was no agreement whether this state would be based on agriculture or industry. Also the degree of Jew hatred among the various German groups differed.[8]

all Gentiles would have to be out of Terezin by May 30, at which time the fortress officially would become a Jewish city.

5. A minor commando raid since Dieppe did not occur till August.

6. During the Great Depression, a number of self-proclaimed American führers (William Dudley Pelley, Fritz Kuhn, Joe McWilliams, George Deatherage, Father Charles Coughlin) tried, unsuccessfully, to channel latent rage and frustrations into national movements. With the outbreak of the war, these elements bonded with pacifist groups (university students and professors, conservative business interests, the Quakers, even the Communist party) to form the America First movement. Fifteen million strong by 1941, an isolationist tide that included senators like Robert Taft and Arthur Vandenberg, celebrities like the Gish sisters and Eddie Rickenbacker, Henry Ford and Charles Lindbergh could not be ignored by Washington policy makers. See Gustavus Myers, *History of Bigotry in the United States* (New York: Capricorn, 1960); John Roy Carlson, *Under Cover: My Four Years in the Nazi Underworld in America* (New York: Dutton, 1943); Leo Lowenthal and Norbert Guterman, *Prophets of Deceit: A Study of the Techniques of the American Agitator* (New York: Harper and Bros., 1949); Ralph Lord Roy, *Apostles of Discord* (Boston: Beacon, 1953); and George Seldes, *You Can't Do That* (New York: Modern Age Books, 1938).

7. In July 1940, Edelstein was summoned to Berlin where he and Jewish leaders from Austria and Germany listened as Eichmann outlined a plan to relocate Europe's Jews on the island of Madagascar. While some scholars, notably Lucy Dawidowicz, discount the seriousness of SS leaders, documents indicate that Himmler, Hans Frank, Heydrich, even Hitler himself favored the scheme. Later that summer Dr. Franz Rademacher of the Foreign Office was assigned the task of looking into shipping possibilities. The plan became academic when England failed to sue for an armistice and Germany invaded Russia in June 1941. Still, desperate Jews grabbed at the illusion of a reservation in Madagascar, much the same as Nisko.

8. To the very end, there were Nazi leaders, Albert Speer and Hans Frank among them, who argued against wholesale genocide, not so much out of humanitarian reasons but for needed wartime manpower. For a discussion of Oswald Pohl and the SS Economic-Administrative Main Office (WHVA or *Wirtschafts-Verwaltungshauptamt*), see Raul Hilberg, *The Destruction of the European Jews* (Chicago: Quadrangle, 1967), 557-60.

March 4, 1942. Friedl, a traitor from Mandler's group,[9] is imprisoned here. They suspected that he received a bribe. Purim was celebrated in the children's ward. There was some confusion because all the people could not push into the room. The women who could not get in objected. We promised that the children would perform a second time.

Yesterday, there was a big disturbance in one room. A friend of Mr. Weinberger took sick.[10] They moved his lodgings to a barracks which has no toilet. He asked Mr. Weinberger to get involved. Previously, Mr. Weinberger spoke up about the matter with Mr. L. Mr. Löwinger refused to do anything about it. He's right—you cannot make special exceptions when it comes to people you know. The old man was very angry with us.

Life is difficult here. Young and old are irritated. At least the young have the strength to endure suffering. The elderly are afraid, weak, and lonely.

March 5, 1942. There is a possibility that the Germans may establish another ghetto in Moravia.[11] The children rebelled against Sigi Kwasniewski.[12] They are led by two youthful demagogues.

I did not agree to let the children play theatre every night in their rooms. I knew it would make them arrogant and they would think they wouldn't have to listen to anyone. The counselor made a mistake by giving them too much freedom. Now they are asking that I assign another counselor to the room.

March 6, 1942. A new transport list was issued today.[13]

My beloved wrote: "I want to be with you." I would also like to be with you, my lovely, would that I could. I long for you. But it would be better if you come in the spring when they will open the gates of the barracks.[14]

9. Robert Mandler organized a group that worked with the SS in various cities of the Protectorate, selecting Jews for transports to Terezin. Hated by the deportees, he and his comrades were called "the Circus."

10. Weinberger was the father of Vinczi, one of Gonda's comrades. See January 28, 1942.

11. After Eichmann's visit, the SS did give thought to creating a second ghetto in another small town in Moravia. The scheme never got beyond the planning stage.

12. Sigi Kwasniewski (1921–1944) was a member of Hechalutz who became director of the German-speaking youth in barracks L414.

13. Transport As to Izbice near Lublin departed Terezin on March 11. Of 1,001 deportees who thought they were going to Nisko, 6 survived.

14. If and when the ghetto was cleared of its Gentile population, Jews would be allowed out of their units without permits. Despite Heydrich's February 28 decree, Terezin was not a "Jewish city" until July 2.

The transport to the East will depart at 11 o'clock. In one room on the bottom floor of the women's house, they discovered smuggled packages.[15]

March 7, 1942. Shabbat. What a subject for a drama. Room 34 in the Dresden barracks was slated for deportation. E. [Edelstein] received permission to spare two families. He declined. The women should agree among themselves who should stay. In the end, the Council of Elders should decide. The transports to Poland and exemptions are a terrible job, full of responsibility. Who has the right, based on appeal, to be exempted from the transport? The young people? The elderly? There is no answer. And it seems you always miss something.

March 8, 1942. Somebody smuggled several parcels into one room of the women's barracks. All the women in the room will be punished by being sent on a transport. Yaakov was given the right to exempt only two women with their families. Yaakov refused to do it. He proposed that the women themselves choose who would stay. Now the matter is being left to the Council of Elders to decide.

The first wedding took place here today.[16] I was heartened, because I too might possibly take a wife here.

Every day we try by administrative means to exempt children from the transport by appealing to the administration. We worked till midnight.

March 9, 1942. We worked all day, making up lists for the transport.[17] In the evening, I wanted to go to the women's house. Even though I have permission to enter the house after seven, the policeman would not let me.

15. Soap, cigarettes, jewelry, food, all were considered contraband, and from the start the SS enlisted the support of Czech gendarmes and German women from Litomerice in searching the barracks. See entries of March 7 through 14, 1942, for punishment of women in Room 34 of the Dresden barracks.

16. Lederer reports there were 463 religious and 96 civil marriages in Terezin. Despite the lack of privacy and severe stress to which these people were subjected, there were only 9 divorces (Lederer, 67).

17. Certain persons in Terezin held privileged status when it came to transports. These included ghetto administrative personnel and their families, persons married to Aryans, foreign nationals, war invalids or those holding military decorations, and persons over sixty-five. Under such discriminations, orphaned children above the age of twelve or fourteen could always be snatched to fill out the quota of one thousand deportees. The Youth Services staff had the onerous task of wrestling with which of these healthy children to sacrifice. Like Redlich, others sensed that *Ostentransport* was something to be avoided. Before each transport, says Edith Ornstein, there was chaos, fear, depression, relief that one was spared. Then as the unfortunates departed, "You watch with tear-filled eyes, with clenched fists and say: forget never, never" (Ornstein memo, 5-6).

We enlarged our department today.

March 10, 1942. In the evening, I was summoned to Yaakov. Seidl was there. I was frightened, because it isn't a good sign when the German commandant comes to visit the Jews. He demanded that 250 women be removed from the transport and that they be replaced with 250 men.

This whole operation was to take place during the night, in the dark. They announced to people sleeping securely that they have to leave with the transport within a few hours. And this is the picture of people and the place: mud, refuse, and rows of Jews who are waiting in front of a kitchen, for a bathroom, before a water drawer.

March 11, 1942. A mother volunteered for the transport, thinking that her son was in it. In the morning, at the station, she realized that her son was not in the transport. It was impossible for the transport to leave within a few hours as demanded by the Germans. It was suggested that an engineer could not be ready in the station.[18] S. [Seidl] said if the engine was not in its place on time, not to blame him. They [Jewish representatives] went to the station and asked the railroad workers not to supply a locomative at the appointed time. Seidl knew this, but his friends searched for an engine. Consequently, we had more time to prepare the transport.[19]

March 12, 1942. Seidl's staff hasn't ordered the killing of Jews. His superior[20] spoke privately with some high-ranking Czech officers. They asked him, "What will become of us? It seems our fate will be the same as the Jews. What is going to happen?" The Nazi said that

18. Until the spring of 1943, deportees had to march two kilometers to and from Bohusovice (Bauschowitz). At that time, a more convenient terminal was built on Bahnhofstrasse (a euphemism, since there was no real railway station) near the southeast rampart of Terezin.

19. A confusing entry. Apparently Seidl and the SS failed to order the transport in time and deliberately delayed the arrival of the engine. Their anger, expressed toward the Jewish leadership, was a screen for their own inefficiency.

20. If, as seems likely, Redlich is referring to Reinhard Heydrich, Protector of Bohemia and Moravia, we may have our first reference to the Nazis' commitment to genocide. Heydrich had hinted at this in Prague in October 1941, when he informed a number of colleagues that as they were moved to the East, "Die Juden haben sich die Wohnungen in die Erde hinab zu schaffen" (Jews will have to build their dwellings under the ground). In the same meeting, Heydrich let it be known that Czechs who interfered with the deportations would share the fate of the Jews (Minutes of the Prague Conference on the the Solution of the Jewish Problem, October 17, 1941). Three months later Heydrich chaired the Wannsee Conference in Berlin that formally embraced the concept of the Final Solution.

for Jews any little transgression will be punished by death. And in order to demonstrate that they really meant it, those poor souls were hanged.

March 13, 1942. We have been working daily on the matter of appeals (*reklamatzia*). It's hard to decide because the appeals vary so much.

I had a conversation with doctors who were to advise us which of the sick were to be exempted. I was very surprised to learn that the doctors did not think this was a difficult problem. They confront it very lightheartedly. Favoritism is rampant. Every official, even if he is only an attendant in an office, tries to exempt his acquaintances— and for the most part he has succeeded.

March 14, 1942. Shabbat. Protekzia. Protekzia. In serious matters like exemptions from the transports, it shouldn't happen. There are things that weigh heavily upon us and I don't know how we will be able to justify them in the future. Old men and boys are sent and *Protekzia* was rampant. We had to make up each list several times.

The appeals of our *chaverim* are also a difficult matter. Do we have the right to do it or not? The difference [between exempting members of the Hechalutz movement and *Protekzia*] is small. Only here we don't speak of personal acquaintances. In spite of it, do we really have the right to appeal? Young men . . .

Hatred toward the staff regarding the beds continues. A solution to the drama; in the end, none of the women left Room 34.

March 15, 1942. Hatred toward us because of the beds has become deeper. Do we have the right to appeal for members of the movement? They are young and in their place come the old, the sick, children. Four transports are coming from Brno.

The distance between the administration and the others has become greater. They rebuke us because we favor the Zionists.

I participate on the committee making up the program for the city's transfer.[21] We argued over each detail of life here in the first Jewish city. A child gathered what he found in a room of the barrack. We are preparing an exhibition of children's work.

March 16, 1942. There isn't any news. It seems to me that the work of the council regulating life in the ghetto is, for the most part, theoretical. Most of the things that the council does is determined by the Germans. People hope that the tearing apart of families will stop.

21. The *Ältestenrat* erroneously assumed Terezin would become an all Jewish town by the end of May.

March 17, 1942. The second transport left for the East.[22] The people traveled in cattle cars. My relationship with the counselors is still good. In the evening, a talk with the women counselors. I lectured for almost a full hour, but the counselors were so tired they did not pay attention to the lecture. Not the same attention I usually require. I wanted to kindle a debate on Jewish education[23] but failed. I hope I will succeed next time.

What do you tell a child that steals coal? The child sees everyone stealing and loses all sense of morality.

March 19, 1942. Today the first transport from Brno is arriving.[24] They say that all the orphans are coming. This month another three transports from Brno will arrive. One assimilated counselor said he heard that I wanted to put him on the transport list to the East. I explained to him that I don't use my position to advantage by exploiting people who have a different viewpoint from mine.

March 20, 1942. There is a female counselor who is working with me. She is very bright and decent. She was a dance instructor in Prague and also a dance soloist in the theater. We argue about Zionist issues. If we want to make propaganda for the Zionist cause, we can only do it through personal contact.

March 21, 1942. The female counselor who towers over everyone else is K. Rosenbaum,[25] a teacher of rhythmics and dance. Her son is in a childrens' home, sick. Despite that, she is taking care of so many things in a self-confident way that I admire her. I have talked with her about Zionism.

We opened a successful exhibition.[26] Perhaps S. and B.[27] will come and see it. After four transports from Brno, we expect one going out to Poland. Beczulkah, I miss you. Know that outside it is spring. The mountains glisten with a very brilliant blue.

22. Transport Ab to Izbice, of whose one thousand deportees three survived.

23. Czech Jews were similar in many ways to their brethren in America. For the most part clustered in urban centers, fairly well-educated, with an intermarriage rate close to 30 percent in Bohemia, because of their orientation toward Reform Judaism, few were familiar with traditional Hebrew books beyond the Siddur or Haggadah.

24. Incoming Transports Ac (March 19) and Ad (March 23) each brought one thousand persons, making a trade-off for those Jews deported to Izbice. Actually, they were the third and fourth trains from Brno, the others having arrived in December 1941.

25. Kamila Rosenbaum. In the absence of Gonda's fiance, their relationship developed into a bittersweet romance.

26. Of children's arts and crafts.

27. These references are to Commandant Seidl and Camp Inspector Karl Bergel. See entry January 10, 1942.

March 22–23, 1942. A transport will arrive from Prague in the first days of next month. Before that, another transport will depart for the East.

Today they issued an order of the day requiring that Jews form each of the [incoming] transports write out all their reasons for being exempted from the [outgoing] transports. A fear has been instilled throughout the camp. Today a second transport from Brno arrived. During the transport, two people died. Permission was denied to remove them from the railroad cars. Instead, they brought them here.

Vinczi's sister, a physician, told of the large amount of work en route.[28]

March 24–25, 1942. Today has been a beautiful spring day. The weather is warm, and through my body I feel the sluggishness of spring. The mood is also better. We want to build beds for the small children.

A thousand women will travel to Krivoklat to plant trees. We negotiated with the administration concerning the concentration of youths in one of the army barracks. Maybe this program will succeed. At first, I was against the concentration. But now I see that if we put the children together many good things will occur: large, airy rooms, the possibilty of getting rooms for classes, etc. Teachers from Brno will be coming now, and they don't want to work in the same line as counselor and teacher. It's difficult to fulfill their requests. I believe they must work at any job, just like the others.

March 26, 1942. Today, women from the *Ältestenrat* will arrive.[29] Much preparation for their reception. There is a lot of nervousness because of the lack of women for the tree planting. The question always exists if I should call my beloved and write her to come here. I'm very tired now.

March 27, 1942. One child remains on the appeal list.[30] They wanted a doctor to check him out, but the boy died. The old men and women in the army barracks were without a washroom or toilet—a dreadful sight.

A number of counselors also have arrived. One evening, they discussed news with Fr. Zucker.[31] She wants to work with us. I am yearning for my beloved.

28. Dr. Robert Weinberger's sister. See entry January 28, 1942.

29. Transport St from Prague carried twelve women, spouses of Jewish council members who resided in the Magdeburg barracks.

30. Outgoing Transport Ag, which left for Piaski in Central Poland April 1, numbered one thousand persons. Four survived.

31. Fritzi Zucker was the wife of Deputy *Ältestenrat* leader Otto Zucker. See entry January 9, 1942. She worked with German-speaking children.

March 28, 1942. Shabbat. One thousand women to Krivoklat, a transport to Poland. One hundred men to Oslavany.[32] Commotion, tension, responsibilty. Objections from every side. For example, Mrs. Saxl is angry with me because I won't submit an appeal on behalf of Dita.[33] *Protekzia.* . . . Of course it exists everywhere. I still don't need it for anyone, because I am alone here. It's hard to remain decent, a friend. It's hard not to become covetous, envious of everyone and everything. Fr. Z. [Fritzi Zucker] wants to work with us. Fredy reminds me of a soap which gets bubbly but does not clean.

March 29, 1942. All day there is work related to appeals from the transports. On Passover, we want to organize a conference of the members of the movements.[34]

The German supervisor (*mashgiach*)[35] loves to inspect procedures involving autopsies and surgery on the sick. There are many weddings here now. The number of dead grows constantly each day in the spring. One day thirteen people died. The rooms in the barracks where the new transports have arrived are awful.[36]

Women will not accompany their husbands to the station in the next transport. During the journey on the train they will share the same compartments.

March 30, 1942. Work, much work . . . everyone is too nervous. Outside the weather is nice. Even though the cold persists, the sun is shining from afar. It's possible to see the blue mountains.[37]

32. A mining town in Bohemia

33. The daughter, Dita Saxl, was a member of the Netzach movement. She later committed suicide in Israel.

34. Reference is to Hechalutz.

35. A pun on SS Camp Inspector Karl Bergel, who is likened to an inspector of kosher meat.

36. By August, there were 4,400 women in the Dresden barracks, originally projected to hold 3,500. The Hamburg barracks was 800 over its limit of 2,900. There were 4,050 in the Sudeten barracks (supposedly fit for 3,800), 1,581 in the Podmokly barracks (capacity 700), 1,150 in Vrchlabi (capacity 900), and 3,250 in the Hanover (capacity 1,900). As the weather grew warmer, everything in Terezin was covered with dust. The foul-smelling rooms grew rich in flies, lice, and bedbugs. The yearbook of Leo Haas and Fred Kramer shows hundreds of women in bare rooms, their minds on one thought: "We are prisoners. Nothing is there. Room, corridors, the dirty stairs, latrines and washrooms overflow. The sick without care" (Haas and Kramer *Yearbook,* Beit Terezin Archive, p. 7). The night gave no rest, for as Rena Rosenberger states, "You were bothered by bugs. It was a hobby to count the bugs you killed during the night. There was another accounting in the morning, the dead covered with a rug, waiting to be picked up" (Rosenberger report, 18).

37. Terezin is located in scenic country with cherry trees blooming on Bohemian hills and river barges sailing along the nearby Ohre River.

When my beloved arrives, will I have the right to live with her?[38] I think that I do not. But will I withstand the test?

March 31, 1942. Today the fourth transport from Brno arrived. From one of the windows of a room, you could see the procession. Women quarreled with each other by the window because there was not enough for everyone.[39]

April

With the arrival of spring, there was some hope that conditions in the ghetto might moderate. A survivor, Eli Bachner, recalled how the SS permitted Jewish youth to play soccer on the Bastei, earthen ramparts near watchtowers. The spring also saw the outbreak of a number of epidemics, including measles, scarlet fever, and tuberculosis. As death became more common, Redlich, who confused some of the diseases, laments a shortage of wood for coffins.

April 1, 1942. Seder, the evening of Passover. I wasn't at home because I was speaking with *chaverot* in the women's house. I am responsible for the entire movement [Maccabi Hatzair], and I don't know if I can remain in my position to the end, for it's a question of nerves. I always have to admire K. Ros. [Kamila Rosenbaum]. She is the perfect model for women in the Kvutza [collective settlements], even if she isn't a Zionist.

April 2, 1942. An interesting debate on political issues. I wanted to visit our comrades in the evening, but I didn't have the time. There

38. In contrast with the overcrowding in other barracks, residents of the Magdeburg barracks were very fortunate. Council members, staff and families, notables like Rabbi Leo Baeck, even some informers numbered 1,031 persons in August 1942, in a facility projected to hold 2,130 (Housing Office Report, Beit Terezin Archives, August 22, p. 1).

39. When transports were coming or going, a curfew was in effect for the ghetto and windows were to be sealed. Nevertheless, Gonda and other Jews peeked through the windows for glimpses of the sad convoys.

was a discussion with the work office concerning the appeal of the women's counselors from the transport to Krivoklat.

I spoke with K. Ros. on Zionism. She wrote me a note complaining about the head of the house, Brauner,[1] who was a sycophant. Parts of the letter: it's impossible to obtain mattresses.[2] However, as soon as his cousin arrives a bed is set up in the children's house with the appropriate number of mattresses. Now Mr. Brauner comes to the house daily, speaking nonsense. The letter ends with the words: if one only says "shalom" it's enough.[3]

April 3–5, 1942. In another women's house, a *madrichah* [counselor] stopped me and gave me her diary. In this diary, I read of an interesting Zionist debate. She asks herself: why do Jews cling to life here? What is so valuable about life? The entire diary is written in a nice style.

The woman counselor doesn't understand the meaning or purpose, the destiny of our people, because she is an assimilated Jewess.

What should I answer the women counselor?[4] I have become a real Zionist here. Nevertheless, I understand the doubts of others and I don't have the will to argue with them. I think that every man must struggle till he finds the meaning and purpose in the work that a Jew is born to. Nevertheless, I want to answer the two letters.

April 4, 1942. Shabbat. Four months of Terezin. On the whole: I have turned into a Jew in the fullest sense of the word. Czech songs and culture have lost all their meaning. I am reaching a goal which I have longed for: to be a Jew, with all that the word means. I have much work and am working with renewed vigor.

A prolonged argument about a suitcase. Igo[5] and Erich[6] want to keep a parcel that allegedly was sent for them. (Vintzi, as usual,

1. The name is unclear in script but appears to be Brauner.
2. All forms of bedding were at a premium. In the Hamburg barracks at Langstrasse 5 the fortunate ones shared wooden bunks. Others simply tossed palliases, if they had them, on the floor. People improvised by constructing tiered bunks with plywood partitions for limited privacy.
3. Kamila Rosenbaum was upset because all it took to gain preferential treatment was to represent oneself as a Zionist.
4. This entire paragraph is listed under April 5 but obviously is related to the entry of April 3.
5. Igo Rosenfeld was a member of Edelstein's staff.
6. Born in Znaim, Czechoslovakia, in September 1910, Dr. Erich Oesterreicher was a lawyer who became a leader in the prewar Hechalutz movement. In December 1941, members of that movement made a decision to split their numbers between individuals who would accompany Edelstein into Terezin and others who were to maintain contact with the outside world (Hungary, Palestine). In October 1944, Oesterreicher, who headed up the Labor Department in the ghetto, attempted to smuggle

didn't express an opinion.) I don't know who has the proper claim. Meanwhile, gardeners stole the parcel. The big argument wound up with the "working people" getting the parcel.[7]

April 6, 1942. Parcels full of food have arrived. Igo and Erich said that friends in Prague sent them this food and that in their opinion this was the deciding factor. I said that if the food was bought with the money of the Hechalutz, we have to distribute it among the working Hechalutz. How much the more since they received one parcel and did not share any food with the others. In the end gardeners took the parcel and didn't want to share its contents. Now they have settled the matter and members of Hechalutz, gardeners from Room 8, have received the food.

Today, a young, foolish German came[8] to inspect my department. I told him, "Five clerks," and he was satisfied.

April 7, 1942. I reviewed the tests in the work office.[9] The students work on interesting lessons. I myself tried to work at the lessons and saw that they are too hard. I see that most male counselors lack initiative—they do their work mechanically. It's my opinion that a few new counselors would bring an important new force to our work.

April 8, 1942. An uncle of my beloved traveled on one of the early transports to the East. I didn't know that he was here. I found out only recently—when his son came to the ghetto and told me.

There is no room. We do not know where to put people. The Germans suggested that we build beds in the entranceways and corridors.[10]

April 9, 1942. The crowding of people into the rooms is terrible. There isn't enough room. Ing. [Zucker] angered people because he

a letter bearing his signature to the free world. When it was intercepted, he was deported to Auschwitz where he was tortured till his death in the gas chambers (Oesterreicher File, Beit Terezin Archives, pp. 1-2).

7. The Jewish Council in Prague attempted to send supplies to their brethren in the ghetto, and some of these (bedding, furniture, food, medicine) were passed by the SS to the hospitals. Incoming members of Hechalutz risked their lives, smuggling food, money, and medicine to the *Fraueneinsatz* of Grete Wiener and Edith Ornstein or Redlich's *Jugendfürsorge* (Oesterreicher File, p. 1).

8. A junior grade SS officer who, because of his youth, was called "Kindergartner" in the slang of the ghetto.

9. To determine suitability for work assignment, the *Ältestenrat*, like its counterpart in Prague, administered a battery of psychological, verbal, and quantitative tests in the ghetto.

10. At this point, the ghetto's population was thirteen thousand.

took community officials who arrived and settled them in better rooms than the others. I received a postcard from my brother. He writes that my beloved might travel from Olmutz.

April 10, 1942. I received a package of food from my dearest. It was all wrapped with such fine taste that it is impossible to describe my joy. I am only sorry that my beloved did not reply to my postcard. I was so happy all afternoon. I also received some nice Hebrew books from Engineer Zucker.

April 11, 1942. Shabbat. Beczulkah, it's dark, Saturday night. Tomorrow a new week begins. I think of you. Today I was out walking about the walls. We will be getting playgrounds for the children there. The area is very wide and has many possibilities.[11] I saw the gallows from above. Everything makes a surrealistic impression—the caves in the wall, the quantity of tiered planks, the graves where so many feet have trod, flattening the earth. After a while, I played soccer again and got tired. Yesterday, an interesting evening in the Podmokly barracks.[12]

April 12, 1942. I toured the walls of the city. They will be giving us large areas full of grass for the children's play area. I also saw the gallows. Its appearance was very eerie. There is great anticipation about the future children's play area.

After a while, I also played soccer. On Friday evening, there was an interesting conversation in the women's Bodenbach [Podmokly] barrack. In a few days, two transports will travel east. It's difficult to choose the people who will travel because many community officials arrive on the last [incoming] transports.

The question is further complicated whether they have the right to exempt people from the [outgoing] transport. In any event, it will not be easy to compile the list of transports.

April 13, 1942. An argument with Fredy. If they ask me who to exempt from the transport—healthy Zionists or the sick, children, orphans—I will answer that the harm is not so great if healthy Zionists travel. On the other hand, I asked myself: and you, what would happen if you were to come here? Would I not require that you receive compensation for your labor?

The whole problem here is very difficult. For here there is no

11. The thirty-foot-high walls and ramparts of Terezin were covered with vegetation. In some places, the ramparts were broad enough for soccer fields. Redlich received extraordinary permission to have sick children take walks there.

12. Located near the Dresden barracks in the north, Podmokly or Bodenbach once housed the arsenal, later German billets.

problem that goes according to fixed law. For every problem touches upon actual questions of life and death.

April 14, 1942. An argument about [marriage] relationships. I don't know, but it seems to me that when a man finds a woman he should live with her all his life.

At night, I have disturbing dreams, but I don't want to believe in dreams because all dreams are a mist of lies.

Perhaps the arguments of the day continue to influence my dreams at night.

April 15, 1942. My aunt is very sick. My cousin has already suffered too much this year. His father died. His youngest son died. And now his mother is sick, and according to him, there is little chance of recovery.

In the afternoon, I also felt bad. I threw up, and in the evening I took fever. It's not so pleasant to be sick.[13]

April 16, 1942. I lay down all day. I wanted a little time to rest. But now I am longing to be healthy. Yesterday I thought over many things, for I haven't studied or done anything. I remembered many things that I hadn't thought about for a while. Twenty-six individuals (who were being punished) arrived from Prague.[14]

April 17, 1942. There is a man working with me who is sick with consumption.[15] They want to transfer him to a hospital, a special ward for people with tuberculosis.[16] He is clinging to life and refuses to go. It's hard for me to speak to him, and I am unable to reach a decision, to say to him to go. It's all difficult. Every day, there are work appeals.

April 18, 1942. Shabbat. There isn't any salt.[17] The quality of the food again has gone down. In the evening, they took Löwinger out of here because he took sick with scarlet fever. I wouldn't want to be sick here. At 4 A.M. my aunt Carolina passed away.

Last night, there was a Shabbat party in the Dresden barracks. It

13. The first of several illnesses for Redlich.

14. Normally, transports consisted of one thousand persons. This small transport was made up of Jews who had violated segregation laws.

15. An unnamed clerk living with Redlich.

16. By the summer of 1942, an estimated 30 percent of Terezin's population was ill with some malady. Wrote nurse Resi Weglein: "of tuberculosis, which has become our chief concern, I knew almost nothing." In all, 1,375 persons died of tuberculosis in Terezin.

17. Sometimes in 1942, there was no salt for a week or longer.

was nice, reminiscent of the days of summer camp. Walter Freud was truly effective and diligent.[18]

A question was asked by the German command: can we bury without coffins?[19] Already two wagons of wood have been used for coffins. Even after death one needs *Protekzia* in Terezin: for the sake of a dry place in the cemetery.[20]

April 19, 1942. There isn't any salt for the food. Friday, they brought a sick person that lived with me to the hospital. Measles.

I attended my aunt's funeral in the evening. She died of pneumonia. Even after death you need influence. The earth is wet and moist. Caskets stand in water. Only if you know the grave-diggers will they choose a rare dry place for the dead.

It's also forbidden to accompany the dead to the cemetery. They carry the casket on a simple cart. Nevertheless, a sense of splendor hovers over—the splendor of the kingdom of the dead.

April 20, 1942. My brother-in-law's sister arrived. I wrestled with myself: is it my duty to appeal or not? In the end, I chose compromise. I sent a note to Z. [Zucker]. I told Y. [Yaakov] that the sister of my brother-in-law was on the list. I did nothing else. We shall see.

April 21, 1942. The young girls go to work in the gardens. There are many sick with scarlet fever in the children's wards and elsewhere. The number of dead grows larger each day. Sometimes, the number climbs to more than twenty.

April 22, 1942. Another two transports will go east this month. Still, there is hope they will postpone the departure. Fr. [Fredy] said that we are obligated to volunteer. I told him that if someone must vol-

18. Walter Freud was a member of Young Maccabi. He directed the puppet theater and served as chief counselor in L410.

19. At first, death had some dignity in Terezin. Individual caskets were marked with the deceased's name and draped with a black flag bearing a Jewish star. They were carried to the cemetery on hearses, which doubled as transportation for the incoming elderly or children taking a ride. As the death toll mounted and caskets were stacked in the mortuary and on the wagons, Leo Haas and Fred Kramer claim that "*hunderte von Mannern*" were drafted to dig graves (*Yearbook*, 45). Eventually supplies of wood became so limited that some dead, particularly those labeled "unbekannter Mann" were buried simply in shrouds. The cemetery was located near the river. Poorly placed graves might be flooded out when the river overflowed its banks. In September 1942, the SS resolved many of the problems by opening a crematorium outside the walls, which, according to Vaclav Novak, disposed of the remains of thirty thousand victims, Jews and non-Jews, from the ghetto, Little Fortress, and the Litomerice concentration camp (*Terezin: Dokumenty* [Prague, 1975], 72).

20. It is surprising that Redlich makes no reference to one thousand Jews shipped out to Refowiece on Transport Ap this date. Four survived.

unteer, he is the most likely since he is a bachelor. He doesn't have any relatives in Europe.[21] Among those who have arrived are German Jews who won medals in the war.[22]

April 23, 1942. We worked all night. We selected the people for the transports.[23]

April 24, 1942. Another four transports will go east this month.[24] A debate has developed whether a ghetto or settlement under German control will be set up here or if it will be a way station for people who must travel further to the East. I was very sad, for many children will go.[25] But it's our fate: always to build anew.

April 25, 1942. Shabbat. Chaos that didn't exist till now. To choose four thousand people for transports inside of one week.

Lottka K. wrote from Poland to Prague that we behave in an unbelievable manner here, that we could have exempted her from the transport, if only we wanted to, etc. According to her, all she would have had to do was offer us bread and a sausage. It hurts, but I don't carry a grudge about it. People in the age bracket sixty-five to seventy-five are traveling. Yesterday, they decided that parents of workers will go. On Sunday, people over sixty-five first entered the transport but were later returned.

The chaos was caused by the rumor that E. [Eichmann] arrived at L. [Litomerice][26] and S. [Seidl] is afraid of a mess.[27]

21. The Beit Terezin Archives contain letters from Alfred Hirsch dating between 1940 and 1943, expressing concern for the morale of the children and thanking correspondents for packages.

22. Reference probably is to Jews who fled to Czechoslovakia before March 1939.

23. Transport Al went to Lublin where 350 men between the ages of eighteen and fifty-five were separated from the other 650 aboard the train and sent to a makeshift camp near Piaski. The rest were gassed in Maidanek. Of the original group of men, only one survived.

24. Of four thousand Jews sent east, thirty-three survived. Some were housed temporarily in synagogues in Warsaw. At least one work crew was selected to help with the expansion of the Treblinka death camp.

25. Redlich was unable to spare the children from deportation. Despite his depression, he is still not fully aware of their fate. Others like Peter Lang shared this feeling (Testimony #181, Hebrew University Oral History Department Project). Especially poignant, however, were the reactions of the children who were not deported. Said Eli Bachner, "From the moment one knew that a child of my class or the next class was assigned to a transport, the others were sorry and a lot of people were upset about that."

26. In 1944, a subsidiary of the Flossenburg concentration camp would be set up at Litomerice. Fourteen thousand Poles, Yugoslavs and Russians would work in a factory ("Richard") hidden underground in a limestone mine.

April 26, 1942. Today there was an accounting of male and female counselors. I am depressed because I lost my best aides the day before yesterday. They have allowed people over sixty-five to be sent. Now they forbid it. A grandmother of two young girls wanted to go with her granddaughters. I feared the family might travel without her. Today, I was pleased to hear that she will travel with her family. And now—she will remain here and the family will travel.

A comrade wrote from the East that we don't care enough about our [movement's] members. She wrote: "If I had given a sausage and bread to Vinczi or Gonda, I wouldn't have gone on a transport." I was very depressed when people related the matter to me.

April 27, 1942. The last transport did not arrive with all its luggage. It happened that some people came with twelve suitcases, while others had none.[28]

We worked all evening, for in six days four transports will depart. The time is short, but the work is great.

At the last minute it was discovered that many of those who boarded the transport were sick. It was difficult to solve all the problems and sometimes we were compelled to cause great suffering to many people.[29]

Last night, there was an argument between Fredy and Popper.[30] Fredy reviled Popper and said to him that he is another Mandler. Sometimes it seems to me we truly are like Mandler.[31]

April 28, 1942. I let two sisters who were listed as clerks with me go east. They left their old mother here. I don't know if the mother-in-law of E.[32] will travel.

Everything that has been done till now is just too horrible. I see that a man grows accustomed to many things: no sleep, no rest, to

27. Not only were the SS anticipating the arrival of German Jews, transports of Czech Jews continued to arrive—nearly twelve thousand between March 29 and July 22. To alleviate crowding, some Jews had to go.

28. One of the many incoming transports from Prague that swelled the ghetto population to more than twenty thousand. Leo Haas and Fred Kramer described the incessant transports bringing the sick, those in need of help, and how their baggage disappeared on carts at the railroad depot (*Yearbook*, 40).

29. Outgoing Transport Aq carried one thousand persons, families and children, to Izbice. One woman survived.

30. Dr. Egon Popper headed the Administrative Department of the *Ältestenrat* transports of 1944.

31. See entry March 4, 1942.

32. Edelstein and his wife Miriam had a son Arieh who was ten years old when they went into the ghetto. They, along with Edelstein's mother-in-law Mrs. Olliner, were sent to Auschwitz in December 1943.

work at a job that throws his nerves into disarray and that brings only damage and death to others. All my friends help me with my work in an exceptional manner.

April 29, 1942 Fr. [Fredy] wanted to write a letter to Prague describing the relationship here. I saw that the note was influenced by his anger against Pop. and Berg.[33] Fredy doesn't realize that he endangers the entire community with these letters. I went to Zucker and asked him to prevent the letter from being sent to Prague.

May

Redlich notes, in passing, violations of rules against smoking and smuggling foodstuffs. There is also a cryptic entry (May 28) referring to the assassination of Reinhard Heydrich by Czech partisans in Prague. Redlich's principal angst this month, however, centered upon his developing relationship with Kamila Rosenbaum and the guilt he felt toward Gerta Beck who had not yet arrived in the ghetto.

May 1, 1942. We have heard that Jews who received battle citations were coming. Transports from Jihlava and Olmutz will arrive this month. I am very nervous all of the time.

One of my clerks carried a lettuce[1] to a barrack. A [Jewish] policeman stopped him and started taking bits of it from the basket. The clerk slapped him on his wrist. Now the policeman believes the clerk should be punished. My position isn't easy. I'm not satisfied with the aide, but I won't be able to deal with him in a proper manner. If only I could fire him.

My relationship with C.K. [Kamila Rosenbaum] is quite strange.[2] Today I decided to write my beloved to come here.

33. Dr. Rudolph Bergman was a Czech representative on the *Ältestenrat* where he served as head of the financial department.

1. Redlich uses the term "salat" instead of "chasah," but lettuce is clearly intended. Fruits and vegetables generally were unavailable to any of the ghetto's residents. Those who worked in the gardens for the SS attempted to smuggle something back to be exchanged for bread and other articles.

2. In the absence of Gerta Beck, this relationship developed into a full-blown

May 2, 1942. Shabbat. My dearest, I want you to come here. I do not know, I am not sure, if this decision is correct, but I cannot do otherwise. I am frequently tired. Even so, I will try to make you happy. I won't be angry if you don't come, if you decide otherwise.

It must be clear to you that you will become the wife of a complicated man, a busy one. Despite the facade, he suffers from some severe problems and complexes. Indeed, you know me, and you know my difficulties. But I think I love you.

May 3, 1942. I did not like our council.[3] It appears that our comrades are waiting for us to take care of their material needs for them. At present, I am trying to find out about letters coming from the East which are full of anger against us because comrades who travel there think that we seek only our own leisure and comfort. I am very nervous and have decided to write to my beloved telling her to come here.

May 4, 1942. Several *chaverot* [female comrades] live together with their mothers in one room. Today one of these mothers asked that I chastise those girls who are behaving badly toward their mothers.

A strange life. A married woman announced to me today that she loves me.[4] And I respect her husband, who knows about it, and I do not know what to do.

May 5, 1942. Edelstein "the Little"[5] won't go to school willingly because his friends ask him if the floor of his apartment truly is covered with carpets, if the food for his family is different from the food of other ghetto people. When he tells the truth, the other children do not believe him.

May 6, 1942. I was looking forward to visiting K.R. [Kamila Rosenbaum] this evening. Unfortunately, I had to remain in the barracks[6] because they need people for the transport which is leaving the ghetto on the ninth of this month.[7]

I am waiting to find out if my beloved will be coming. Generally, my mood is a little better. In spite of all this, I cannot work with sufficient energy.

sexual liaison. Redlich was troubled by the possible consequences. See entries May 9–11, 1942.

3. A meeting of members of Maccabi Hatzair.

4. Kamila Rosenbaum?

5. Arieh Edelstein lived with his parents in the Magdeburg barrack. He was shot in Birkenau in June 1944. See also entry April 28, 1942.

6. Redlich was working up lists with the Transport Committee.

7. Transport Ax to Sobibor left on the 9th with one thousand persons. None survived.

May 7, 1942. I was very depressed in the evening, for my beloved did not say whether she was coming or not. After a little while, though, I recovered, for I remembered that it still was possible for her to get my letter. Right now, I love her truly and deeply. I find happiness in the knowledge that she will come to me in a short time.

May 8, 1942. Our mood is better now that the sun is shining and sending its warmth and brilliance to us. The old men sit happily in front of the barracks and take in the warm rays of the spring sun. The day is longer and maybe we will overcome our difficulties. In spite of this, transports are leaving.[8] The danger is not past.

May 9, 1942. My dearest, maybe on this Shabbat, I will be recording my thoughts for the last time without you. Perhaps you will not come. Of course, you cannot know how much I need you here. I only know that I must overcome an internal crisis if you do not come now. You certainly must know that for a man like me temptations here are great. Temptations that are forbidden, not merely because one must uphold certain moral principles. No, it is forbidden to yield to them because of selfish reasons, because surrender like this will not bring satisfaction and only cause or lead to new troubles. I love you more that I ever knew when I left Prague, dear. . . .

May 10, 1942. An interesting Hebrew circle: a lecture on Agnon[9] and his writings. Contents of his book: *Maalot v'yeridot.* It's like the basic theme in the book of Job. It's the fate of man alternately to suffer and to be happy. Man's lot is like a ladder: he rises to the highest level and then falls to the bottom. There, he has to get back on his feet in order to climb again.

This lonely existence is not without its perils. People frequently come to the women's house. Converse with them. Start a dangerous game.[10] It's not hard to conquer and break a woman's heart. The women feel more than I what it's like to be cooped up in prison.

8. Another two thousand Jews were sent to Lublin on the 17th and 25th. Of these three thousand deportees, one survived.

9. Shmuel Yosef Agnon (1888–1970) was a master of Hebrew novels and short stories and the first Israeli to win the Nobel Prize (for literature in 1966).

10. Only a few men were permitted visits to the women's barracks. Still fewer were allowed to have their wives stay with them in a private room. Despite the problems of accessibility and lack of privacy, people risked these encounters. As one youth wrote, "stuffed into the common Jewish flats, lying down on wrapping paper spread on the floor, we saw the fall of all conventions, the warmness and fragility and passing of human relationships, true unselfishness as well as naked egoism. We heard the gasping of dying persons as well as the breathing of couples making love" (Marie Rut Krizkova, "Literature: One of the Faces," *Arts in Terezin*, 25).

Everyone feels abandoned and despondent. In this mood, it isn't very difficult to awaken love—how much the more so with young girls. It's also hard for a man to resist the evil inclination and not play this dangerous game. For hidden in each man is the desire to be liked by a woman, even if she is indifferent to him.

May 11, 1942. One father visited his sick son. The camp commandant came and arrested him since he wasn't working during working time.

It's easy to sense great tension in the women's house. Maybe the mood is related to the weather. Spring is the time of love. The women are shut up within four walls.

May 12, 1942. Great disappointment. My beloved hasn't arrived. She did not come in on this transport. She will not be coming on the next one. I decided to write her again in a postcard that she should come here because I feel abandoned and lonely. Sometimes I feel she doesn't love me anymore. Perhaps I'm wrong.

May 13, 1942. A major discussion among high-level officials. A debate between Zionists and assimilationists.[11] In my opinion, it's all useless. Every man with a set of fundamental principles will defend his own viewpoint. For the Zionists, twenty students who learn Hebrew are better than two hundred people who have been influenced to become Zionists with one conversation.

May 14, 1942. I took part in a legal proceeding.[12] The judgment made a very strange impression upon me. The plaintiff was a young man

11. Dr. Chaim Yahil notes that the Zionist movement in Republican Czechoslovakia had been advanced by Joseph Rufeisen, Franz Kahn, Hannah Steiner, Edelstein, and Zucker. During the interwar period, the Zionists had the greatest influence in Slovakia and Sub-Carpathia where hostility to Jews ran highest. In Bohemia, they encountered opposition from the Orthodox, socialists, communists, and assimilationists. These groups carried their ideologies with them into the ghetto (*Zionism* [Jerusalem: Keter Publishing, 1973], 158-59).

12. The *Ältestenrat* was ordered to establish its own courts to deal with matters of arbitration, labor disputes, and juvenile problems. Punishments might consist of a token fine, forfeit of a meal or free time, or imprisonment in the ghetto jail. Staffed by professionals, the courts were listed under the Department of Internal Administration. Some were regarded with loathing by ghetto residents who caricatured the judges as fat men with false angel's wings. With good reason: in a May 1945 memorandum dealing with deportees, chief jurist Dr. Heinrich Klang dismissed starving people who had stolen food as "gemeine Verbrecher" (common criminals). See Adler, 452-72.

who stole some candy. He defended himself and said an older man enticed him into stealing the things. The judgment: a serious rebuke.

May 15, 1942. Today they banned the ghetto police force. They caught a policeman who was carrying several letters written by Jewish policemen. During a roll call, the head of the camp dismissed the Jewish police.[13]

Great tension. The Germans designated a final date for handing over contraband. They threatened to stop child welfare programs if Jews continue to smoke and engage in forbidden activities.[14]

May 16, 1942. Shabbat. A great "calamity." Meanwhile, the 25th has been designated as the last day to hand over contraband.

Arguments again between us and the supply department.

Order of the day: if the contraband traffic continues, child welfare activity will cease. According to rumor, four levels of punishment will be initiated: (a) youth service activities will cease; (b) teaching will be forbidden; (c) workers' aid will be forbidden; (d) food rations will be reduced.

Serious arguments about issues in the ghetto. Some say we are forcing Jewishness on the children. We are a minority against the majority here. We are strong, but we do not take advantage of it. We are forbidden to take advantage. Nevertheless, the time will come when our opponents will blame us for everything, even what we did not do.

May 17–18, 1942. It's possible that tomorrow my mother-in-law will arrive.[15] The conflicts between the Zionists and the assimilationists sadden me. I think it's ridiculous when they complain about us that we are forcing the children to become Zionists. Nevertheless, I am

13. Members of the Jewish police repeatedly flouted rules by smuggling letters and packages in and out of the ghetto. They and their families were shipped to Lublin on May 17. None of the one thousand passengers aboard Transport Ay survived. In place of the Jewish police the SS designated fifty men over the age of forty-five as *Ordnungswache* (maintenance guards). This group was reorganized in the fall of 1942 when Dr. Karl Löwenstein arrived. Onetime aide-de-camp to the German Crown Prince and commander of the ghetto police in Minsk, Löwenstein would be jailed temporarily in the ghetto until the Nazis decided how best to use him. See entries September 23, November 3–7, 1942, and January 1, 1943.

14. Smoking was deemed one of the worst offenses by the Nazis. The police scandal held serious repercussions for Redlich's program.

15. Redlich is not yet married but already refers to Gerta's mother as his mother-in-law.

angry because after the war[16] our detractors will surely say that the Zionists were enemies of Czech culture and all progress. In reality, most of the counselors are assimilationists. I have to admit that there aren't enough male and female Zionist counselors. In my eyes, it is better to organize a good non-Zionist education than a poor Zionist one. We lack initiative in work. All my assistants are tired and sometimes irresponsible in educating our youth.

May 19, 1942. I want to write a play on the following subject: the problems of a man who is nominated, against his will, for a particular task. He reaches a point where he is forced to do something against his basic principles, in order to be able to save some people. Others think he has abandoned his conscience, and they speak harshly against him, and his only son opposes him. Nevertheless, the man remains resolute.

May 20–21, 1942. One of the doctors met a [German] soldier who said to him: "*Saujud* [Jew-pig], in a while the war will be over and we will return home." I am very nervous now. I feel the big prison [Terezin] with its policemen. If you go out of the house, you must show your exit permit. If you want to enter a barrack, you must show your permit. If the policeman is in a bad mood, you cannot go in. There is a lack of faith in the administration. The problem of the Zionist aides is not so simple. How do you get used to physical work? How do you survive in collective life?

May 22, 1942. My mother-in-law has arrived.[17] I like her because she is so much like my beloved. She is very decent. It was the first time I was at the station and saw a transport arriving. I didn't see it, but I heard that the Germans struck the elderly and the sick who wanted to travel by auto.

May 23, 1942. Shabbat. Mother arrived. I call her that because, in a certain way, she resembles my mother. I think I'll reach an understanding with her. Gerty is a lot like her. I don't know, but I think she may not be coming. I was informed that she has much work, but she

16. According to Ruth Bondy, the entry of the United States into the war gave European Jews reason to hope the end of the conflict was at hand. Now, at every major social function, Christian holiday or Jewish, the question discussed was not if people would survive, but what they would do once the war was over. See also entry July 25, 1942.

17. The woman arrived with 650 persons on Transport Aw.

appears fine. Even so, perhaps her situation would be better here. Vitek and Medah[18] are also fine. Medah doesn't make the same impression that I recalled. There is something "Japanese" about her.[19]

May 24, 1942. We worked all night on matters of appeal. I am very happy because I managed to exempt my mother-in-law and brother-in-law. I am afraid that my mother-in-law is such a good-hearted woman that these details would anger her.

In the evening, the women counselors shouted at me. Soon we will have been here a half year. Tomorrow, a transport goes east.

May 25, 1942. No special news.[20] Much work. I have to visit my mother-in-law each day, at least for the time being. It isn't easy to work in the women's houses. It's also not easy to work with the women counselors, with women in general. It's always impossible for me to express an opinion since straightforward opinions don't work.

May 26, 1942. Jews from Germany, medal winners from the war, may be arriving in a couple of days. Their relations with Czech Jews will not be friendly.[21] The situation now is very strange, for we don't know when the next transports will arrive.[22]

May 27, 1942. They have jailed one of my best assistants. According to rumor, a policeman saw her speaking with a German. It isn't clear yet what will happen. A hundred officials from the Brno community have arrived. I was sick today and lay down in bed all day. A severe running nose. In another week, we will have been here a half year. A hard time, but very interesting. If only the Holy One, blessed be He, were to redeem us this year.

18. Brother and sister of Gerta Beck, Gonda's fiance.

19. Perhaps "Mongoloid." The girl may have suffered from Down's Syndrome.

20. After making several references to Transport Ax, which left for Lublin with one thousand people, Redlich makes no entry on the 25th, the date of departure. One man, a watchmaker, survived the ordeals of Belzec, Maidanek, and Sobibor.

21. German Jews, traditionally regarded kinsmen who lived to the East with disdain. Czech Jews reciprocated toward the Germans, whom they regarded as foreigners in their land, interlopers in the ghetto community who had forced the expulsion of friends and family. As the German populace swelled, half the seats of the *Ältestenrat* were ceded to them, and eventually in January 1943, Dr. Paul Eppstein replaced Edelstein as *Judenältester.*

22. June saw twenty-six transports bringing 4,200 Jews from Austria and Germany. The greatest press of Germans came, however, in July (14,400), August (11,000), and September (12,100).

May 28, 1942. Assassination of the governor.[23] The situation is very tense and upsetting. My relationship with my mother-in-law remains very good. I visit her each day and I like her. I like my sister-in-law more and more. Today, we spoke a great deal about my dearest. I insulted my mother-in-law, for I said she loves my sister-in-law more than my dearest.

May 29, 1942. In the newspaper today: anyone who gives sanctuary to persons not registered with the police is guilty of hostile acts against the state and, together with his family, will be shot.[24]

The camp commandant [Seidl] asked the jailed clerk if she were sick. She answered that her eyes hurt. The commander asked: "Do you also want your mouth (*deine Fresse*) to hurt?"

May 30, 1942. Shabbat. So life goes on here. Next week we will have fulfilled half a year of our stay here. You must come, love. Even if I am a little delicate and tired now as a result of this cold and possibly because of the food we've been eating. I know that I need you. The thing that bothers us lately is an everyday fact in marriage here.[25] People get used to it. Apparently it's nervousness caused by circumstances. And what circumstances we are in. Hasn't my nervousness won out these past months?

May 31, 1942. There is no news. We received permission to take children sick with whooping cough to the field. We had an interesting Hebrew seminar today. Rabbi Weiss told us of life in the cheder and yeshiva. He had a quick-tempered, aggressive teacher in the cheder,

23. On the morning of May 27, 1942, Reinhard Heydrich, Protector of Bohemia and Moravia, suffered a broken spine when his automobile crossing the Moldau bridge into Prague was attacked by Czech partisans. The man responsible for creating the Terezin ghetto lingered in pain until his death on June 3. Immediately after, the village of Lidice, held responsible for the act, was obliterated and two transports of Jews (AAk and AAi) left Terezin for the East. There were no survivors. One of the most critical events affecting the ghetto, the assassination, seems almost lost on Redlich's concern over his relationship with his mother-in-law. See also entries May 29, June 1, 4, and 12, 1942.

24. Residents of the ghetto were kept apprised of news that the Nazis wanted to give them through the official paper *Neuer Tag* until the Stalingrad debacle in 1943. Actually, Terezin knew of Heydrich's murder almost immediately, when flags at the SS headquarters building were lowered to half-mast. Later, on Tuesday, June 16, all twenty thousand residents, including children, were marched out of the barracks and lined up before a set of tables—one containing photographs of "evidence" (a suitcase, bicycle, coat) from the scene of the crime, the other with prepared statements that the Jews were to sign testifying to their innocence (Adler, 101, and Bachner Testimony, #19, Hebrew University Oral History Project).

25. Survivors identify the marital dilemma as impotence.

who struck the children. He told us of the remorse he felt while he was reading the "ethical literature." In these books, the boy recognized all the punishments of Hell and learned fear, a great fear.

June

The conclusion of the first six months in the ghetto comes, and Redlich wonders how the people have managed to endure for this long. His entries detail punitive action taken by the Nazis against the Czech village of Lidice and other communities for the assassination of Heydrich. In a rare moment of contemplation and hope, after jotting his first poetic entry (June 13), Redlich talks about going on to Artza, the Hebrew term for Eretz Yisrael or Palestine.

June 1, 1942. Killings, persecution—terrible, terrible. They shot a famous author. How many famous professors have been shot? The situation is like life in the Middle Ages. Then, the king inherited possessions of those killed, and now the Führer inherits. A person may receive the death sentence just by approving the assassination of the governor [Heydrich]. It's enough if an informer says this person expressed approval.[1]

June 2, 1942. They brought new prisoners to the concentration camp.[2] They forced them to run through the city. An old man wasn't able to run. He was carried by two Jews. Among the slain today was a Jewish man, seventy-three years old.

June 3, 1942. I have been sick. I'm still not healthy. Today, my mother-in-law visited me. I like her more and more.

1. Ruth Bondy estimates that twenty-three thousand persons paid with their lives for the assassination. The Nazis were aided in their investigations by a swarm of informers. In reality, there is no real way of reckoning the dead. When the Warsaw Ghetto was cleared of more than five hundred thousand Jews in the summer of 1942, the SS dubbed the action "Einsatz Reinhard" in honor of Heydrich.

2. Workers in gardens outside the city walls watched as Nazi guards abused prisoners from the Little Fortress. Some were forced to push wheelbarrows loaded with stones. The first transport from Berlin arrived in Terezin this day, carrying fifty deportees.

June 4, 1942. The governor[3] [Heydrich] died. It's enough for me to lie in bed, but I'm still not healthy. I feel a great weakness. My body is very thin. Generally, my health isn't good. Today marks a half year of our stay in the ghetto. Time has passed quickly. Life is hard but very interesting.

June 5, 1942. Tomorrow, the women will return from Krivoklat.[4] Young women are arriving from Germany. Their husbands were jailed and they were sent here.[5] My mother-in-law visits me each day. I am still sick. I have no appetite. The situation, in general, is very disturbing. At the end of the month, transports will arrive from Austria. I wonder if my relatives will come from Olmutz.

June 6, 1942. Shabbat. I am still sick. My mother-in-law comes every day, and I get along with her fine. Apart from this, there are too many visitors, even if some of them are close friends (Kamila, Otik,[6] etc.).

Today the women from Krivoklat will return. Women and children have arrived from Berlin. A terrible *Appel* was held with them. The entrance to the yard was closed off to us on threat of execution by shooting.

Will my family come or not? Either way, my situation will not be easy. On the other hand, worry and responsibility. On the other hand, the feeling of a certain moral shame.

June 7, 1942. In my opinion, many Jews currently thought to be dead will return after the war. It seems to me that the Germans are overly nervous now.

Lately, the bread has been mouldy.[7] People get accustomed to everything: to refuse and loathesome things.

3. Redlich uses the code word "Pasha" for governor.

4. See entry March 24–25, 1942.

5. Approximately three hundred persons arrived from Berlin and Munich on the 4th and 5th of June. They included spouses of members of the Herbert Baum group, which in May had set afire Goebbels's propaganda exhibition "The Soviet Garden of Eden." Many of these young people were shot without trial. In her celebrated study of Nazism, historian Hannah Vogt devotes more than twenty-five pages to German resistance to Hitler (*The Burden of Guilt* [New York: Oxford Univ. Press, 1964], 235-61). There is no mention of the Jewish-communist Baum group.

6. Ota Klein (1921–1968) was head of L417, the children's ward. He was also a leader of Netzach, an acronym frequently employed in Redlich's diary, which stood for Noar Tzofi Chalutz Shel Hashomer Hatzair (Pioneer Scout Movement)—connected with the kibbutz movement in Palestine. See Bondy testimony, #47, Hebrew University Oral History Project.

7. Jews received approximately ten ounces (three hundred grams) of bread daily. Bread and cigarettes served as an unofficial exchange in Terezin. A loaf of unspoiled bread that brought eighty *Krone* early in 1942 might be worth fifteen hundred ghetto

June 8, 1942. They brought a cabinet to our room.[8] I remember the words of the commandant when we came here: "Don't be afraid. Your situation is good. You will live like human beings. Everyone will receive a bed and a closet." Now we have a closet. Is this enough for a proper existence?

June 9, 1942. Tomorrow, I want to go out. I have been sick for ten days. There is much work to do now. Transports will be coming and going. I am so tired. But what can you do? Life here in Terezin isn't easy. Just don't get sick. Stay healthy till the end comes. We hope that happens soon.

June 10, 1942. I went out for the first time. Life is very interesting. Each day passes quickly. Every day—our stay in the ghetto continues for many days.

People say a transport went straight from Prague today to the East.[9] My brother-in-law's sister arrived. I hadn't seen her for a long time.

June 11, 1942. Yesterday, the train passed with the transport directly to the East. The train stood at the station for nine minutes. The people didn't know that it was traveling directly to the East. They traveled in cattle cars. When they were in the station, the Germans did not permit them to leave the compartments. The women who had relatives here—perhaps parents or husbands—began to cry.

June 12, 1942. In the paper yesterday: they punished a village terribly. They shot the men and sent the women to concentration camps. The children were handed over for a "decent" education. They destroyed the village, in the fullest sense of the word. They sent thirty Jews from the ghetto to work in the village. They traveled with rakes. They also sent the sheep and cattle here.[10]

marks later on. In May, the *Ältestenrat* introduced "differential rationing." Heavy duty workers were granted more bread, margarine, sugar, at the expense of the aged, infirm, even children. "Schwerarbeiter" received 342 grams of meat weekly as opposed to 243 for children and 225 for "Nichtarbeiter." Inexplicably, members of the Ältestenrat received 465 grams, cooks and butchers anywhere from 600 to 800 (Adler, 344–47).

8. With fifty or more strangers sleeping in the corridors and overcrowded halls of the barracks, people kept their possessions on or under their "beds."

9. The only survivor of one thousand deportees was a woman who leaped from the train.

10. As a reprisal for the assassination of Heydrich, the Nazis destroyed the village of Lidice on June 9, ostensibly because Czech partisans had been helped by the villagers. Of the villagers, 1,999 men and boys were shot, 195 women were sent to the Ravensbruck concentration camp, and 90 children with Aryan features were given over

All day there is work with the transport. Exemptions get harder and harder. If the ratio between the workers and the ill gets to nine thousand to thirty thousand the situation will be terrible.[11]

June 13, 1942. Shabbat. My love, these are days full of blood and sorrow.

When man is alone and yearning for a kiss, like a child.

My love, these are days when man escapes into the night.

To dreams and pictures that are guarded in the recesses of this heart.

To memories, questionings, the desires of a better tomorrow. For the tranquility of God, to which he is also entitled.

When life will be better, happier, and more serene.

June 14–15, 1942. I fear that the transports will not stay in one place in the East. What will happen when we go to our land after the war? What will our position be toward the others? I already feel that for me Aliyah[12] will be an escape, an escape from people here in Europe, an escape because of life here in the *Galut,*[13] an escape when you compare the old life to the new. I will go to the land [Israel] without any vain hopes. I know that there are only people there, weak men, with all the frailties of humanity. But I also know that a righteous idea lives and thrives there. Perhaps in Eretz Yisrael we will get close to realizing our soul's desire. I emphasize close because man never is a clear and perfect creature.

June 16, 1942. Today we were awakened at five in the morning. Every one of the residents of the settlement was forced to swear by his signature that he did not see the backpack, the bicycle, or gun of the

to German families in Poland. Animals, excepting sheep and cattle, were shot. All houses were blown up and salt sown into the fields symbolic of the total destruction of the Christian community. Seidl personally supervised the work detachment from Terezin, which worked for thrity-six straight hours, digging trenches for the dead. Similar treatment was meted out to villagers of Lezaky on June 24 (Gerhard Jacoby, *Racial State: The German Nationalists Policy in the Protectorate of Bohemia Moravia* [New York: Institute of Jewish Affairs of American Jewish Congress and World Jewish Congress, 1944], 253-57).

11. From the summer of 1942, the percentage of seriously ill remained fairly constant at about 30 percent because of scarlet fever, erysipelas, septicemia, typhoid, typhus, diphtheria, polio, cerebrospinal fever, gastroenteritis, pnuemonia, and tuberculosis, all of which were endemic to the ghetto. Zdenek Lederer estimates that at times the death rate due to disease alone was anywhere from eight to thirty times the norm (143-44).

12. Hebrew term for emigration to the land of Israel.

13. Hebrew term for the Diaspora or forced dispersion of Jews.

assassin.[14] In this way, the Germans hope to frighten the Czechs. Whether they will succeed still isn't clear.

June 17, 1942. Jews have arrived from Cologne on Rhine.[15] They said the whole city was destroyed by English bombs. The world is so small. In our store,[16] we sell sweets produced by "Elona." Yesterday, I spoke with a small girl who told me that her father had a factory for sweets. The girl's name was Elona, and so they called the candy by her name.

June 18, 1942. I continue to study with Rabbi Weiss. He is an expert in Hebrew, and I can learn much from him.

They continue to send the Germans [Jews] on, apart from the women whose husbands were shot in Berlin.

A few days ago, I was in the infants' room. I was happy to see the great work being done in this area.[17]

June 19, 1942. I met with a group of children who are sick with whooping cough. The Germans permitted us to lead the sick children to one grassy area. I asked a child: "Are you sick?" He answered, "No." I said: "But if Germans ask you, you have to answer that you are sick." The child said: "I am not a liar."

June 20, 1942. Shabbat. Seventeen hundred Jews from Germany are here now. The problem of coexistence with the Czech Jews isn't simple at all. I spoke with the German youth that arrived with the transport of widows today. They are very good-looking and appear very intelligent.

Tomorrow, Viennese Jews are expected to arrive. There isn't much news from Prague. What there is, isn't good. Some of their women and children traveled directly to Poland. I know of at least one incident like this. According to other information I have received, the situation in Prague is very tense. There is shooting in the streets, and the people are very nervous.

14. Reference to items found at the scene of Heydrich's assassination.

15. Nearly two thousand persons poured into Terezin on the 16th from Bonn, Coblenz, Kiel, Hamburg, Luebeck, Treves, Wilhelmshaven, Ludwigshaven, and Cologne.

16. Gonda Redlich's father Max had a candy confectionery store in Olmutz.

17. Periodically, in July 1942 and again in April 1943, Terezin's commandant would issue a directive instructing Jewish physicians to report and/or terminate pregnancies. The *Ältestenrat* would be responsible for implementing these decrees. Abortions were encouraged to the seventh month. Despite the threat of deportation eastward for violators, people continued to risk bearing children secretly in the ghetto. See entries for July 7, 1942, and July 7, 1943.

June 21, 1942. I spoke with an old man from Germany. I asked him how old he was. He answered: "Eighty-two." His children are in England and America. This is the fate of the Jew. Children and parents of some people in the ghetto are sent on transports which go directly to the East, to Poland.

June 22, 1942. They have operated on my beloved.[18] I have wronged her with my anger, because she didn't write to me and didn't send me anything to eat. My lovely and petite dearest, why did you work so hard? Did you want to block out the suffering? I miss you very much.

June 23, 1942. We have the right to request that our relatives be here. I wrote out a request for my beloved. It is difficult and unpleasant, but alas, a fact that my beloved is sick. Why don't they permit the elderly to die in peace? The elderly come here without any belongings.

June 24, 1942. There is no news. My life is tranquil now. I don't have much work. In the afternoon, I can lie down, sunbathe in the garden.[19]

The kindergartens are expanding. There is more than enough work among the children.

June 25–26, 1942. I have already been studying Hebrew for three years. In spite of this, there are always new words whose meaning I don't understand. The Hebrew language is really difficult. I am very diligent, but I cannot say that I know the language. What will people do who have only begun to study in Eretz Yisrael? They will never learn the language. Indeed, it is incumbent upon all Jews in Eretz Yisrael to learn Arabic too. What will they do? They don't know Hebrew or Arabic. I am very conscientious.

June 27, 1942. Shabbat. People from Olmutz have arrived.[20] They slander my brother.[21] I am sad. An aunt and cousin arrived. I must

18. Gerta Beck was working as a clerk in Olmutz and suffered appendicitis. See entry in diary for their son, June 11, 1944.

19. Administrators were permitted to rest on the barrack ramparts only with special permission.

20. The first 900 came on this date. Another 900 arrived on the 30th, 900 on the 4th of July, and 745 on the 8th.

21. Apparently unhappiness was directed to Gonda's brother Robert, who was accused of favoritism. As noted above, eventually all of the Jews of Olmutz were transferred to the fortress city.

help them. Can I? Beczulkah, it is now five days after your operation. If only you would take care of yourself.

In June: twenty-four transports arrived and four left. Of those entering, fifteen thousand came from Germany proper (*Altreich*), most of them very old. Opening of the ghetto. New problems with the dwellings of the young. We need a lot of energy and great consistency. God, help me.

June 28, 1942. The Führer said: "The coming war will eradicate the Jews of Europe."[22] I know it won't happen, but the supply barracks are a small example of the meaning of "the destruction of European Jewry."[23] How many times have we thought there can be no worse place than where we are living. But always the Germans find a worse place for us.

June 29, 1942. My cousin and her husband are waiting for my help. The situation is not a pleasant one for me. My brother and brother-in-law [Robert Redlich and Bohusch Goldstein] promised that I would help anyone who has a letter of recommendation in his possession. I took part in a discussion with the housing committee today.[24] In my opinion, a lot of chaos can be expected in the coming months because many transports will be arriving.

June 30, 1942. I helped Viennese Jews yesterday.[25] They are old, lice-ridden, and they have a few insane people among them. Despite this, I was surprised the reception committee operated in an excellent fashion.[26] Everywhere the Jews' life is like the play [by Bertold Brecht] *The Three Penny Opera.*

22. From Hitler's Reichstag speech of January 30, 1939.

23. All accounts testify to the special agony of the aged, who continued to arrive in Terezin in 1945. A sad litany (Jewish middle names thrust upon them by the Nazis)—Charlotte Sara Schneller, born in Vienna April 16, 1857, died July 6, 1942; Dr. Paul Israel Weiss, born in Vienna August 15, 1883, died February 4, 1943; Willy Israel Eisenbach, born in Leipzig in 1871, deported to Terezin February 1945; Fanna Sara Rohrig from Leipzig; Isidor Israel Seeling, 62, from East Prussia. See Transportliste and Matrik Files, Beit Terezin Archives, Microfilm II. Abandoned to the worst housing facilities and given reduced rations, they suffered from sickness and the pain of memories. A poem symbolized their lot:

> Spieglein. Spieglein in der Hand,
> Wer ist die Schönste in diesem Land?
> Rita, du weist's, bist die Schönste hier,
> und keine wagt sich in dein Revier.

24. An administrative committee whose job it was to dispose of housing taken over when Christians left Terezin.

25. One thousand Jews came on June 21 and 29 from the Vienna district.

26. The Zionist student Egon Loebner worked as a *Koffertrager* helping the incoming deportees. Among a group of fifteen sharing a hearse in September he observed an

July

While one group of Nazis were busy in Warsaw deporting thousands of Jews to their deaths, others completed the transformation of Terezin into an all Jewish town. The forty thousand people who crowded the fortress city overtaxed the antiquated sewage system, which broke down on July 20.

July 1, 1942. My relationship with K.R. [Kamila Rosenbaum] is very strange. She fancies me as the pure youth who has never known a woman. It's not easy to explain my mood. I love my dearest, but nevertheless I lust after K.R. I am doing something against my principles, but I do not feel as if I have sinned.

July 2, 1942. We want to change our living quarters. I requested a small room. I want to live there with my beloved. There will be a great deal of confusion this month. The number of transports coming in will be larger, and it's not clear how the work force now here will manage.[1]

July 3, 1942. [While] under anesthesia, my dearest called for me.[2] Rumor has it that they imprisoned and shot three *chaverim*.[3] Some of our comrades denied this.

One girl, who is a member of the movement, gave me information about my beloved. She wanted to volunteer [to come], but the

older woman shouting, "Do you know who I am? I am the daughter of Herzl!" Trude Herzl-Neumann, the fifty-five-year-old daughter of the founder of modern political Zionism, was being shifted from a mental home where she had resided for eleven years. Her husband Richard, a wealthy clothing manufacturer, would arrive later. See article by Loebner, "The Prophet's Daughter," typed manuscript by Anita Engel, "Herzl's Youngest Child," and ten-page diary of Trude Herzl-Neumann (where she complains of everything from the loss of her personal baggage to the fact the ghetto leadership is ignoring her), Herzl File, Beit Terezin Archives. For a note on her death, see also Redlich diary entry March 17, 1942.

1. Redlich was correct. July proved to be the busiest month for Terezin. Fifty-eight incoming transports brought 10,645 Czech, 10,433 German, and 4,000 Austrian Jews. By the end of the month, the ghetto's population had swelled to more than 43,000.

2. During an operation on Gerta Beck.

3. Three members of Hechalutz who had tried to live with false papers among Gentiles were arrested and shot after the murder of Heydrich.

doctors wouldn't permit her because she is still weak. My sister's sister-in-law arrived, and Naomi's parents.[4]

July 4, 1942. Shabbat. My dear, a week ago today you underwent an operation. How are you feeling? When will you come? I have learned much here. It seems to me that I have become a more experienced, mature man. When I think of you, I always have such good feelings, that I must protect you. I love you so much, I am very sad.

Granted I am self-centered. Father is about to arrive. You surely would handle everything for him better than I. Love, dear. . . .

July 5, 1942. Much work. Next week, we will be shifting quarters of the children and youth from the barracks to the school. The rooms there are nicer. But it is impossible not to see the difficulties with an operation like this. It's still not possible to leave the barracks without permits. The mothers, what will they say? They want to see their children, and in this regard they are correct.[5]

July 6, 1942. Preparations for the shift of living quarters. A transport with aged persons has arrived from Prague.[6] The [Czech] police have left their assigned positions, and in their place are Jews.[7]

July 7, 1942. Today we went outside for the first time without a police escort. The arrangements at the gate were quite good.[8] They permitted men to visit with women. The doctors must report each birth, how much time the men and women, parents of children, have already been in the ghetto. In the camp commandant's notes, it was written: doctors must be reminded not to shirk their responsibilities.

July 8, 1942. My father has arrived.[9] His mood is good enough. The sickness of age has not taken hold of him. He is healthy, thank God.

4. July 2, one thousand Jews came from Prague, 150 others from Berlin, Munich, and Dresden.

5. Children who were living with mothers were going to central dormitories.

6. Transport AAn with one thousand people.

7. Consistent with the transfer of the fortress town to the Jews.

8. This was the day when Terezin truly became a ghetto for Jews only. For the first time in months, people were able to visit one another freely. There was a feeling of relief, much the same as when the Nazis sealed the Jews of Warsaw in with a wall in November 1941, a sense of false security that at least people were now among their own.

9. Seven hundred forty-five people arrived from Olmutz this day. Max Redlich survived the Holocaust. Most of his family perished in Auschwitz.

The new situation interests him greatly. He is interested in every-thing. People from Olmutz revile my brother.[10] I don't know, but it seems to me that it would be better if he were here.

July 9, 1942. The work of the counselors in the new school is very nice. The rooms are airy and pleasant. According to the counselors, the children are very happy. All the people greet me and hope I will help them. And what are my prospects? What to do? I see that I have become hard.

July 10, 1942. The ghetto continues to grow apace. People walk in the streets.[11] Traffic is especially heavy between the hours of six and eight in the evening.[12] One of my friends' father is seriously ill and lies in the sick room. He told me that he invented a great thing—how to nickel-coat things that are not made of metal.

July 11, 1942. Shabbat. Father has arrived. I do not behave properly with him. I should be more patient. I know this, but I am very tense and egotistic. I need you here very much, Beczulkah. Apart from this, the whole month of July has been total chaos. Every day another transport. One is to leave on the 11th of the month.[13] It's been de-creed that we must squeeze more people into a place fit for forty thousand.[14] In short, more problems for this community.

The school has been designated to be a showcase of Terezin.

Willy and Manya:[15] I still like them. All of Olmutz can be found here. Because of this, I was afraid to look at the transport of people for I recognize almost everyone.

July 12, 1942. New problems with our work. This week we gathered together all the youth ten years old and over. After we received a new house,[16] we gathered the girls together. I do not have enough help-

10. Probably a reference to Gonda's brother Robert.

11. Edith Ornstein recalled that it was so crowded people literally had to walk sideways. "In the summer the thickest dust, full of germs covered the streets. You see only old people, their white heads, slowly slinking through the city, symptoms of death about them" (Ornstein memo, Beit Terezin Archives).

12. Curfew was at sunset.

13. Outgoing transport AAx did not leave until the 14th, with one thousand per-sons bound for Minsk. Some men were sent to work in the fields and roads at Maly Trostinec. Ultimately, two survived by fleeing to Russian partisans.

14. The figure is ten times the garrison planned for Terezin.

15. Willy Groag and his wife Manya, close comrades in Maccabi Hatzair. Their stories are recorded in the Hebrew University Oral History Project.

16. Building L410.

ers. The work now is very great. My father complains about me. He is right. I am not always at home and he feels lonely.

July 13, 1942. All the Jewish residents of Olmutz have now come to Terezin. Life here continues to evolve. One of my acquaintances escaped from the Germans by going to an insane asylum.[17]

July 14–15, 1942. They ordered us to bring the German Jews to the transport. Three people committed suicide.[18] After a few hours, the Germans canceled the order. An insane man was put into the transport. He was a privileged person who escaped to an asylum. Now he has been placed in a transport, and all the insane people are in great jeopardy. A German policeman shot at a Jew. The bullet struck him in the lungs. The wound was operated on and he is in mortal danger. Tomorrow, two transports from Prague and Hamburg will arrive with other small German groups.

July 16, 1942. At the railway station, a Jew heard a conversation between a Czech policeman and the camp commandant [Seidl]. The camp commander said to the German who shot a Jew yesterday: "You are a hero." The commander added: "A true hero does not aim a bullet at the nearest man at only two paces."[19]

July 17, 1942. Interesting discussions in the Reception Committee of the city.[20] The technical problems are so great that we can never succeed under these conditions.[21] Questions of space are so difficult to solve that finding a place for the new arrivals is like a game of chess.
The problem of preventing epidemics in the city is very serious.[22]

17. Some Jews tried to evade deportation by entering mental asylums. The ruse failed, when the Nazis inevitably cleared such institutions.
18. There were 273 suicide victims, another 211 attempts in Terezin. Some hanged themselves. Others leaped from windows or slashed their wrists. The majority, however, tried poison (Veronal). Suicide was more likely when there were more deportations and when the end of the war seemed remote (264 attempts in 1942 as opposed to 50 in 1944) [Adler, 316].
19. An SS man, nicknamed as "Kinderheim" because of his youthful looks, shot and killed a Jew for alleged disobedience. On another occasion, he murdered ten Jews by throwing them from a cattle car.
20. Reference to the group, noted March 2 and 15, responsible for overseeing the conversion of the fortress into a Jewish town.
21. Apart from being responsible for supplying Terezin with heat, water, and electricity, cutting the railroad spur into the ghetto and maintaining repairs of buildings, the Technical Department also had to collect garbage and rubbish and keep the streets clean.
22. Apart from scarlet fever, epidemics of typhoid, jaundice, and conjuctivitis flared in the summer of 1942. The Health Department under Dr. Erich Munk labored valiantly, innoculating people against disease.

July 18, 1942. Shabbat. God, what a life! Multifaceted, threats, full of contrasts that race by quickly, terribly fast. The presentation of a cabaret on the one hand, and on the other, old people dying.[23] Transports arrive daily in this city which can normally absorb three thousand people. A chess game! Today there are thirty thousand people here. There are days when two thousand people arrive at once. Problems of disinfection, eradication of pediculosis [lice infestation], space, kitchen, mattresses, creating beds, a colorful mosaic of life and death. They imprisoned the leader of the transport department. They arrested S. for stealing.

July 19, 1942. In Prague they imprisoned a teacher who taught Hebrew in a school for youth who were about to make Aliyah. He stole property from suitcases and embezzled a lot of money. They also imprisoned almost all the transport administrators here.

So many contrasts in life here. In the yard, a cabaret with singers, and in the house the old and sick are dying. Great contrasts. The young are full of desire to have a full life and the old [are left] without a place and without rest.

July 20–21, 1942. It will not be possible to use the toilets, for the sewers are stopped up. Life races by at such a rapid pace that one does not feel the length of time he has been here.

I am devastated, but the large amount of work enables me to forget my sorrow. Who knows? Perhaps with the change in my living condition[24] my luck will change. Today, during the evening hours, we will move the central storage unit. Almost all of the workers

23. Terezin's *Kaffeehaus* is generally portrayed by artists Bedrich Fritta and Alfred Kantor as a desolate place where people sat wanly, sipping ersatz tea and listening to jazz combos like the Ghetto Swingers. Some artists like Karel Svenk (1907–1944), who wrote the so-called anthem of the ghetto ("Where There's a Will, There's a Way"), composed their own music. Sometimes bands played on outdoor stages that were used for puppet shows and dramas. Attics and other large halls also served as sites of major cultural events. Tickets were required for these performances, which included Klavier recitals, "Bunte Musikstunde" (polkas, soprano arias, violin caprices, and a rendition of "Chiribiri Bin"), Passover programs, and the operas *Carmen* and *The Bartered Bride*, the latter performed no less than thirty-five times. The cultural life of Terezin was memorialized in Josef Bor's novel *Terezin Requiem* (Prague: Cekoslovenskby Spisovatel, 1964), and in Joiza Karas, *Music in Terezin, 1941–1945* (New York: Beaufort, 1985.) See also Wirt Abt-Musik File, Beit Terezin Archives; Tana Kulisova, et al., *Mala pevnost Terezin* (Prague: Naise vojsko, 1957), 75–76; and entries October 26, 1942, and March 29, 1943.

24. Redlich probably is referring to his upcoming marriage.

worked at night, even those who worked all day. We will take charge of the Christian kindergarten.[25]

July 22, 1942. When will my beloved arrive? I don't think it will be easy to save her belongings. The Germans decreed that all suitcases be turned in, in order to share belongings.[26] The true explanation of the order is something else: to steal the best belongings for themselves. They will leave each person only essential clothes and linen. All of this is bringing great confusion to the camp.

July 23, 1942. They are preparing another ghetto.[27] Israel David's brother has arrived.[28] He told us that there is great disagreement between the Zionists and the assimilationists. The Zionists want to stay in Prague. The assimilationists recognize the importance of sending their faithful to the ghetto. In my opinion, the policies of our friends in Prague are not correct.

July 24, 1942. We will take upon ourselves the care of orphans who live in the wards. There is a certain fatherless orphan whose mother lived in another city—the boy came here a few months ago from Brno. Now the mother has arrived. But she was placed in a transport and hesitated to take the boy with her. It was a difficult problem. In the end, she decided to travel with the boy.[29]

July 25, 1942. Shabbat. Till when, my love? I again submitted a request for you to come. Meanwhile, life here goes on, crazily, with twists and turns, and no relaxation.

What will eventually happen? And when will it all end? None of us will leave this turmoil without being affected. Will deliverance ever become a reality? Will we ever turn into pioneers? Will we ever

25. Once the ghetto was cleared of its Christian populace, institutions came under *Ältestenrat* control.

26. People were permitted to bring with them to the ghetto fifty kilograms of personal belongings in one handbag and a backpack. The Nazis confiscated what appealed to them and turned the rest over to storehouses in the Hamburg and Usti barracks and the bakery. See also entry August 7.

27. The delusion of another ghetto, mentioned in the entry of March 5, 1942, persisted through the fall of 1943.

28. A teacher from a Zionist school in Prague where Gonda also worked.

29. Transport AAy left Terezin bound for unknown parts on July 28. None of its one thousand passengers survived.

become workers? How many "true" Zionists are there here who will not desert us? I read Achad ha-Am[30] daily. It truly is brilliant writing.

July 26, 1942. Instead of forty thousand, forty-five thousand people will arrive. The situation at the place where they distribute the suitcases is horrendous. They steal all of the belongings there. The Germans steal. The Czech police steal. And a great shame, Jews also steal. They are going to forbid teaching children to read or write.[31]

July 27, 1942. The daughter of a doctor killed by the Germans complains to her mother: "Last year, news came on my birthday that my father had died. This year, they put my grandmother on a transport, also on my birthday. What will happen next year? What kind of disaster will take place?" A question, the question of a Jewish child.

July 28, 1942. A teacher who taught with me at the school for Youth Aliyah has been imprisoned in the *Kleine Festung*. They took him during the days of persecution after the assassination [of Heydrich] because a man who lived with him was, by mistake, not registered with the police. Some friends saw him walking with the other prisoners.

July 29, 1942. We were called upon to work all night as a group of clerks. We carried a corpse from the house to the barrack. The house administrator did not know where to put the corpse. Now the dead lie among the living. During the day, we also worked at the station.[32]

July 30, 1942. We unloaded coal from a train to a truck. The Germans transported the coal in trucks. One of them cursed and slapped us. Rain poured down and we were all thirsty, tired, and sleepy. In order to protect ourselves against the rain, we sat under the cattle cars that stood on the tracks. It was nearly dawn when we came back [to the ghetto].

30. Achad ha-Am (1856–1927) was a Zionist leader who preached the necessity of reviving Jewish cultural identity in the Galut through education. Israel would serve as the hub of a proud Jewish people.

31. Officially, only songs and games were permitted. As in other ghettos, teachers offered formal instruction in a numer of areas. Lookouts were posted at the entrances of the children's schools. Whenever the SS came by, all books and study materials were stashed out of sight. Later, the Nazis did organize a sham school to impress a Red Cross commission. See entry June 23, 1944.

32. By the end of July, there were twenty-five thousand persons over the age of sixty-one in Terezin. More than half were women. Because of the lack of manpower, administrative personnel were pressed into service, digging graves and unloading trains. See also following entry July 30, 1942.

July 31, 1942. Frequently, the old men and women leave their barracks, and upon returning, they do not find their living quarters.[33] My dearest is trying to come on a transport, but it is not a simple matter to get into one. I asked again that she come.

August

For the first time, the monthly deaths in Terezin passed one thousand. As the end of summer presaged a flurry of additional transports to Treblinka, Auschwitz, and Maly Trostinec, on August 8, Redlich concluded that the purpose of the ghetto was to sap and ennervate the young and kill the aged.

August 1, 1942. Shabbat. And so this was the month of July. . . . Nerves tense as a chord. People arrive by the thousands, the aged that do not have the strength to get the food.[1] Fifty die daily.

I wait for you, my dearest, however small my hope may be that you will come. Amid the whirlpool of life: a mixture of the fate of man, chaos, tumult. I am very nervous. I have much work, and my moods aren't especially good. On the 4th of the month a transport will leave.

August 2, 1942. Two children who came from Berlin have been stealing. They were members of the widows' transport (transports of women whose husbands had been shot).[2] It is forbidden to bring

33. Such confusion was not untoward, considering the crowding and contests for space. Eventually, some youth groups would organize themselves to assist the elderly in going to the latrines or securing food. See entry April 14, 1943.

1. Meals consisting of thin coffee, gray lentil soup, or rotting vegetables were distributed from communal vats or troughs set up three times daily in courtyards. Resi Weglein remembers standing in line for more than an hour and then getting something cold to eat. The process was especially difficult upon the aged, many of whom were sequestered away on the third floor of barracks. Their quarters were sometimes described in quaint terms as "lofts" or "cubby-holes." In reality, they were, as Bedrich Fritta sketched, overcrowded attics. Open to the rafters, the rooms were stifling in the summer, freezing in the winter, and exposed to the dripping rain.

2. Members of the Baum group. See entry June 5, 1942.

these two children over to the other children. For this reason, the children live among the old, and become more and more mischievous, in the worst sense of the word.

August 3, 1942. There is a man without the Jewish badge.[3] He is a Christian, and his sons are fighting as German soldiers in the war. Also a woman whose husband fell in this war as a German soldier was sent here with her three children.

It's raining outside. The old men and women wait outside, and the rainwater falls upon the food.

August 4, 1942. Rumor has it that a high-ranking officer will be arriving.[4] The camp commander [Seidl] decreed that the old and maimed must walk back and forth outdoors. He wants the city to appear overflowing to the eyes of the officer. In my opinion, the camp commander does not want more transports of the elderly and sick to come [here].[5]

August 5, 1942. Four hundred fifty youngsters live together in the new school under the supervision of a young director.[6] Normally, the development of the group like this would seem ideal. But conditions of hard life, lack of food, and enslavement cause their development to be not as good as one imagined.

August 6, 1942. One of a group of workers outside the ghetto was killed during working hours. He lay on the ground, badly wounded, while the German officer refused to call for first aid. A German gardener saw it and called for help. The wounded man died after a few hours in the hospital.

August 7, 1942. I read a Jewish man's will. He is asking to be buried at home, in "the land of his birth," and not in the ghetto. According to the will, this Jew was converted and was a Christian believer.

3. A black Star of David on a patch of yellow. Required of Jews.
4. Probably a reference to SS Sturmbannführer Ernst Möhs, one of Eichmann's chief aides. Möhs served as liaison between Berlin and Terezin, and his visits signaled policy changes in the ghetto.
5. Transport AAz left this day for White Russia. Most of the one thousand persons aboard were taken to a onetime Jewish country estate near Maly Trostinec where they were either gassed or shot.
6. L417 and its director, Ota Klein. See June 6, 1942. There was a method to the numbering of the various houses. From July 1942 to July 1943, the ghetto was laid out in a pattern where the longer streets running north-south were labeled L1, L2, etc., and those intersecting were labeled Q1 through 9. These were later given regular street names. L4 became Haupstrasse, L5 Parkstrasse, etc. L417 meant that Klein's new dormitory was situated at #17 of L4 right next to the central plaza.

The *Judenältester* [Edelstein] requested permission from the camp administration to take linen from the storage unit.[7] They permitted it, but the camp commander wrote that he himself changes underwear only once a week.

August 8, 1942. Shabbat. Life in Terezin offers many interesting insights. To the historian, to the sociologist, it is a limitless well of experiences and achievements.[8] Soon it will be nearly eight and one-half months of our stay here. This passed quickly, astonishingly so. It seems to me we will never have any peace. This apparently is the purpose of the ghetto: to sap the powers of the youth, to kill the aged. Perhaps there won't be the great pressure as in July, but pressure will always exist.

August 9, 1942. Transports will continue eastward. Tomorrow, eight hundred men and two hundred women will arrive. The work isn't as heavy now as it was last month.[9] Despite this, we will have no rest. They don't want to let us rest. The young lose their nerve and the old. . . .

August 10, 1942. If you wander throughout the streets of the ghetto, you encounter old men and women. They go to receive food, and frequently they get lost on the way. A transport has arrived with 1,450 people from Prague. They sent sixteen-year-old youths as "laborers." The ghetto is too full.

August 11, 1942. Negotiations with one of the elders of the district. The rooms are full. The people roll about on the floor. They lack utensils. The dead lie among the living for an entire day, the sick on floors of stone. The walls drip with moisture. At noon, people that

7. For ghetto inmates, from goods requisitioned by the Germans.

8. Precisely the reason that H.G. Adler subtitled his monumental study of Terezin *Geschichte, Sociologie, Psychologie.* In the preface to this eight-hundred-page book, Rabbi Leo Baeck referred to Terezin as an "experiment in the power of evil," one that had relevance for common morality and psychology, but a test especially significant to Jewish psychology. Victor Frankl, a physician, who spent three years in Nazi prisons, offered similar thoughts in *Man's Search for Meaning* (Boston: Beacon, 1959). Redlich played the role of psychologist in a report issued in December 1942. The greatest task facing his department was that of neglect, a feeling of despair that afflicted 8-10 percent of the children and that was brought on by the destruction of family life, poor nutrition, inadequate sanitation, "the crushing of all ideals" (Adler, 551).

9. The next outgoing transport would leave on August 20. September and October proved to be the busiest months with fourteen departing transports carrying twenty-three thousand persons to Maly Trostinec, Treblinka, and Auschwitz.

live in these houses stand in the courtyards. The food gets cold. Sometimes it rains.

August 12, 1942. We are receiving moldy bread now. My thoughts wandered to friends who are not here with us. Their view of the world must certainly be different from ours. What will happen to my beloved? Will she come here? Many friends have arrived. I am curious to know what they say.

August 13, 1942. The city is too full.[10] Despite this, a transport with one thousand people is expected tomorrow. No one knows if there will be places for these people, where they will put them. A difficult problem. Difficult also is the question of transportation. There aren't enough horses to pull the wagons.[11] There aren't enough men for work.

August 14, 1942. The food is tasting better now because new potatoes have arrived.[12] There isn't enough space for the people who are already here. No one knows what will be done for the people who come tomorrow. They want to settle them in attics. Three transports will go eastward.

August 15, 1942. Shabbat. There wasn't room for thirty-seven thousand. There wasn't room for forty-thousand. There wasn't room for forty-five thousand . . . and tomorrow another one thousand will arrive from Vienna. Where will we put them? Into the attics. A dangerous precedent. The houses and barracks are full beyond their capacity. And what will happen with the thousands that are in *Zeughaus*,[13] the *Jaegerkaserne*, and in the other places that are not heated? Little room, no room—and in spite of this if three transports go, among them will be many workers needed for the building of the ghetto.

10. More than fifty thousand Jews. Adler estimates that by mid-summer 1943, Terezin's population density was 130,270 per square kilometer, a figure equaled only by the Warsaw Ghetto. The figures for Berlin and Prague were 4,751 and 5,820 repectively (Adler, 327).

11. Draft animals were brought from towns cleared of Jews to assist with the transport of the elderly, supplies, etc.

12. Potatoes were usually of an inferior quality and, because of the time lag between harvesting and delivery in Terezin, rotten.

13. Several barracks housed outgoing deportees before their departures. Most prominent of these was the Hanover barracks, situated a few yards form the railway depot. Originally designed to serve as stables, the Hanover's stalls came to be identified as the *Schleuse*, the floodgates. According to Adler, *Schleuse* came to be one of the most commonly used terms in the ghetto. As a verb, *schleusen*, it meant unauthorized taking; as a noun, *Schleusung*, it referred to contraband (Adler, L).

August 16–17, 1942. There is no room—but what to do? If the Jews demand space, perhaps the Germans will send more transports eastward. Aside from this, orders come from the capital [Berlin], and the capital is far from the ghetto. We had only a short respite after last month.

Yesterday, a German policeman was walking in the streets and smoking. He wasn't dressed in uniform, and one of the Jews did not recognize him.[14] The Jew admonished him, and the German slapped him. They began to quarrel. Another Jew came and another German policeman who fired into the air. Luckily for the Jews, the Germans were drunk and settled the matter, for they did not want to bring it to the attention of the camp commander.

August 18–19, 1942. One of the young girls has been having [sexual] relations with a married man. They wanted me to take her to the girls' residence. I took her there, but the girl was more mature than the others. The relationship between her and the rest of the girls was not good.

On the way, I met an old lady who was unable to find her way home. I encountered her, and she told me that she used to be an actress for many years. In the Great War, she used to visit the front and perform before the German soldiers. Her son was cremated along with fifty to sixty dead persons who are cremated daily. As of today the number has grown to seventy people.

August 20, 1942. Very hot. Yesterday, they stripped the clothes from women that came from Germany and checked them naked. Maybe they wanted to find gold or silver.[15] They thoroughly checked the transport which will leave the ghetto, until few retained anything but the clothes on their backs.[16]

August 21, 1942. Rumor has it that they want to send seventy thousand people to Terezin. Yesterday ninety-six died in one day.[17] Three

14. The Jew thought that another Jew was smoking publicly, which was strictly forbidden.

15. Searches were frequently conducted in all ghettos to obtain money and/or jewelry, which was deposited with the *Reichsbank* in Berlin or in Swiss bank accounts. Clothing, especially heavy coats that could be used by combat troops or civilians, was also sent back for "Winter Relief." In Prague, the Nazis confiscated 603 pianos, 71,000 carpets, 778,000 books. Many of these were stored in synagogues intended to serve as museums for vanished Jewish culture when the war was over. See David Altshuler, ed., *The Precious Legacy*, (New York: Summit, 1983), 19–29.

16. Transport Bb left for the stables of Maly Trostinec with one thousand passengers. None returned.

17. With 2,327 fatalities, August marked the first of nine consecutive months when the monthly death toll in Terezin passed 1,000. Between July 1942 and June 1943,

transports will go at the end of this month. It's hard to make up a list for the transports because everyone is trying to stay in Terezin, trying to find any assignment or work that will fend off the transports.[18]

August 22, 1942. Shabbat. Ruth Gaertner[19] wants to volunteer for the transport because her fiancé is included in it. A strange life here. . . . It reminds me of Czermna, when no one wanted to register for a "stormy" transport.[20] Ruth will travel to the unknown with a man and everything between them is unclear.[21] Strange, but understandable.

Aside from this, the next [incoming] transport will be catastrophic for me if nobody comes from Prague. Beczulkah, I want you here.

August 23, 1942. A new woman in the ghetto was unable to find her way back home. She cannot speak or understand anything. Lucky for her, she was carrying linen stamped with the number IV 786.[22] I was happy to find her address. But to my sorrow, I discovered the number IV 786 belonged to eight transports from Vienna. Everyone with this number except one, was a woman. I handed the woman over to a policeman. . . . [23]

August 24, 1942. They're thinking of raising the number of residents in the ghetto to seventy thousand. They want to prepare lofts in the roofs and put people there. A very silly story was circulated as a "present" on the birthday of the camp commandant: a mentally sick man died. The doctors listed eight causes of death.

nearly 25,000 people died of disease, starvation, brutality, or despair, a death rate estimated at thirty times that of an ordinary Central European community of the same size (Adler, 527, and Lederer, 143-44).

18. If Terezin were truly to be a *Reichsaltersheim* (home for the aged), somebody younger had to be sacrificed. Redlich's four hundred teachers, counselors, physicians, etc., labored to protect the children. This meant that able-bodied workers would have to go. In the end, many of the Jews who left Terezin in the fall of 1942 came from the sick and elderly.

19. A member of Maccabi Hatzair who underwent agricultural training with Redlich.

20. There was much distrust and opposition among Jews in Czermna when Eichmann authorized an official of Aliyah Bet to organize the transport.

21. One thousand Jews left for Maly Trostinec on Transport Bc. One returned.

22. The number is unclear. It may be N or IV. Under the Nazi numbering scheme, incoming trains bore prefixes with Roman numerals. Berlin was I, Munich II, Cologne III, etc. Each was designated further I/4, I/5, etc. Transports IV/6, IV/7, IV/8 did arrive from Vienna in August. Redlich may have recorded the number incorrectly.

23. With so many women involved, Redlich apparently despaired of placing the woman with her own group.

August 25, 1942. Three transports will go. Rumor has it that they are deciding how many Jews will come, at what pace the old will die.[24] Much work, and sadness fills the soul. I am lonely, even if good people like me.

August 26, 1942. Night. A summer's night. The barrack sleeps. People sleep. Worries leave them. They have passed to the world of dreams. The electric light bulbs cast their gloomy light on the hallways. A large shadow looms over the house, over the ghetto, over the world. People sleep and dream of a better tomorow.

August 27, 1942. They want to organize private households. Every family will cook for itself. Perhaps some may improve their situation this way. But for the majority, it will be a disaster. Where to cook— without stoves, without coal, without room. Friday, they will decide on important matters in the ghetto.

August 28, 1942. Very hot. Today they are issuing summonses for the transport.[25] Those summoned come in tears. The fate of hundreds of poor souls whom they send from a shaky situation to a world where the dangers are even greater. That's the fate of the Jew—how many times have these Jews switched their places?

August 29, 1942. Shabbat. They want to put seventy thousand people in Terezin. What will happen in the winter? There aren't any furnaces. Already the attics are completely taken up. An attic like this on a summer's afternoon is a true Hell. Suffocating air and a stench hover like a cloud above the people, trapping their souls.

This week, I started to learn Arabic.

Before us, in a wide yard (the yards of several connected houses) a meeting takes place—a cabaret.

A strange time, strange people, a cabaret of life.

August 30, 1942. I have started learning Arabic. Before I get to Eretz Yisrael I want to master Hebrew. Then I could read the papers, the

24. Informed that the daily death toll was between 75 and 100 in a ghetto population of 58,491, Commandant Seidl declared: "The clock ticks well" (Lederer, 49).

25. The Secretariat of the *Ältestenrat* later issued summonses under the signature of Rudolf Prochnik. Individuals who wished to volunteer for transport could report to the Magdeburg barracks the day before departure. House and block leaders were charged with the responsibility of getting designated people to the Hanover barracks for transport (Announcement of Central Secretariat, October 20, 1944, Transport File, Beit Terezin Archives, Microfilm II). The system did not always work, as many people hid. See entry of October 27, 1942.

literature, speak. Then I would have time to study Arabic. It won't hurt if I lay foundations to study Arabic in the Diaspora.

August 31, 1942. An interesting debate. Is it better to separate children from the Reich or to educate them together with the children from the Protectorate? I considered this problem and it isn't clear.[26] A transport from Prague will be arriving with 1,100 people. I don't think my beloved will be coming with this transport. Two children again stole watches and other things.

September

A noteworthy month because of Rosh Hashanah (Jewish New Year), the arrival of Redlich's fiancée, Gerta Beck, and their marriage on the 22nd. What should have been a festive time was marred by the continued deportations of the aged, the blind, and orphans. Four thousand people died in the ghetto this month, the largest death toll in Terezin's history, but the Nazis directed their attention to the creation of a number of shops that were to be photographed for a propaganda film dealing with the wonders of the Jewish town.

September 1, 1942. The Arabic language is very hard. I don't know if I will have enough patience to study such a difficult language in addition to Hebrew. I visited the room of members of the [Maccabi Hatzair] movement today.[1] Normally I stay at the home after I return from the office.[2]

26. Separate kindergartens were established for Czech-speaking children (three hundred students) and Hebrew (seventy to one hundred), and there were some children's homes specifically reserved for Czechs (L417 for boys ages ten to fourteen, L410 for girls ages ten to sixteen) or Germans (L414 for Germans ages ten to fourteen). But others (L318 for sick children ages four to ten, CIII for children ages four to twelve, and the *Lehrlingsheim* for youths ages fourteen to eighteen) held mixed populations (Adler, 563). Hanka Fishel complained about the poor attitude of German children who were so influenced by Nazi songs and power (Fishel testimony #94, Hebrew University Oral History Project).

1. Various groups of girls had rooms in L309 next to the Hamburg barrack.
2. Of one thousand Jews on transport Be to Raasika this day, forty-five survived.

September 2, 1942. We are settling the young girls in another barrack.[3] There will be many counselors there whom I respect very much. I think this barrack will be an interesting experiment.

I admit that my behavior toward my father isn't good or proper.

September 3–4, 1942. The views of people who have returned from Eretz Yisrael are very interesting.[4] It seems to me that members of a certain generation (for example Placzek,[5] Engländer,[6] etc.) went to Eretz Yisrael because of a strong belief that they would find a better world, a new and righteous world. People were enthusiastic. They did not see the reality, did not recognize man as he was. It is no wonder that the hopes of each of these men were dashed. They have not been able to forget this great disappointment. They started to look for a new spiritual vision. It seems to me that if they cling to their current vision, another disappointment will befall them. Who knows? Perhaps this one will be greater than the first.

September 5, 1942. Shabbat. The number of dead: one, then ten. After that, tens, fifties, sixties. The number grew and grew. It became nearly 100 per day. Now it has reached nearly 130. It's hot here, as it never was before, and there is no one to dig graves. The struggle for life here is immense. A disease means a worse classification and the possibility of a summons to a transport.[7]

September 6, 1942. A committee of three people will be arriving, high-ranking German officers, to determine which of the elderly Jews from Germany should register for transports. A procession of death and sickness. . . . I am tired. My beloved will be coming. Will she like me?

September 7, 1942. I am sick. A high fever. I don't want to see people. I have a great need to rest, just to rest. . . . Perhaps it's only a reaction

3. There were 450 Czech girls in L410, situated next to Terezin's church, which formerly had been used by the military administration.

4. Members of Zionist groups like "Bar Kochba" and "Techelet Lavan" who emigrated to Palestine in the 1920s and, unable to cope with conditions in the Holy Land, returned to Czechoslovakia. Many, including Redlich's brother Robert, dabbled in idealistic communism.

5. Redlich's diary opens with reference to Friedrich Placzek, father of Joseph Placek-Alon, the Israeli attache murdered in Washington in 1973. See entry January 1, 1942.

6. Arthur Engländer (1899–1944). His wife Rosa was a counselor in L410.

7. That month, 3,941 persons died in Terezin, the largest death toll in the ghetto's history.

to the amount of work lately. It's not good to be sick here—but perhaps I will find a little rest.

September 8, 1942. The old people, men and women, went to register all night. If it were only possible to have a little faith in the Germans, I might believe they want to better conditions for Jews from the Reich, for they only are sending Jews from the Reich. But it is impossible to believe Germans. They are terrible, strange enemies.[8]

September 9, 1942. It's possible one of the highest officers will visit the ghetto—Himmler. The camp commander has ordered us to open some stores in order to mislead the officer. A Potemkin Village.[9] After the officer leaves the ghetto, the stores will disappear. My [health] situation is improved. I want to have my dearest here near me.

September 10, 1942. They are fixing up stores for shoes, toiletries, clothes, food and cooking utensils. All the inhabitants of the ghetto are curious to see what will happen, how long the stores will be open. They assume not much time will pass before the stores are closed.

September 11, 1942. Rosh Hashanah: a time to review the past and hope for the future. My beloved will be coming on Rosh Hashanah. How eventful this year was. I was privileged to witness things I had never seen before. Time has passed quickly, like a raging stream whose waves threaten to drown people. I escaped, thank God.

September 12, 1942. Shabbat. Well, you have arrived, my love. See how we live. See the difficult aspects of life and what may be learned from them.[10]

The stores have captured the attention of the ghetto. A high-level visit will take place. Potemkin Villages.[11] Perhaps something of this will remain. They have already issued vouchers. It is hard for a man to believe. My love, I will be happier when you are near me, after the wedding, after everything. All of this is bad for me.

8. Four persons survived Transport Bk to Maly Trostinec this date.
9. See entry September 12, 1942.
10. Redlich's fiancée, Gerta Beck, arrived from Prague this date.
11. Sham villages named after Grigory Potemkin, onetime adviser to Catherine the Great, who in his exuberance to impress the Czarina on a tour of the Dnieper region, constructed a number of towns with false fronts. The whole purpose of the Embellishment in 1944 was to supply the Red Cross Commission with a fantasy world that did not really exist. See also Kulisova, *Terezin*, 85-91, and entries November 10, 1943, February 27, May 9, and June 19, 1944.

September 13, 1942. I received permission to buy wares in the stores. This week I am permitted to buy [writing] paper. In the coming weeks there may not be other wares. Perhaps I am mistaken. If the Germans start something. . . .

September 14, 1942. My dearest. I haven't seen her for nine months. But she is just as she was. Generally, I have noted that people I haven't seen for a while haven't changed much. My dearest, my dearest, I am happy, God willing, we will be together, happy together.

September 15–16, 1942. Relationships between the old and young aren't good. I see this with my father and mother-in-law. We don't pay enough attention to the problems of the elderly. We are so tense that our behavior toward the elderly isn't good. For example, we want to be alone, only the two of us. But it is impossible. Always visitors come, and new aquaintances, friends, family. My dearest still does not live with me. In the evening, she always rushes straight home.[12] During the day I have a lot of work. What to do? We are looking for each other.

September 17, 1942. Two thousand old people will leave the ghetto. They will travel in cattle cars which lack benches.[13] A terrible life, a terrible struggle for survival. Yesterday, orphans from Frankfurt arrived.[14] We didn't know where to place them. But in the end, we found room.

September 18, 1942. I looked for the address of a prominent person.[15] He died a few days ago. My relationship with my dearest is good.

12. With an early curfew, only physicians, police, or other key personnel were permitted on the streets after sunset.

13. Two thousand aged persons went to Maly Trostinec on September 19. Another 2,020 Jews of all ages left on the 21st, 1,000 on the 22nd, 1,980 on the 23rd, 2,000 on the 26th, and 2,000 on the 29th. Of the more than 11,000 deported at the end of September, only one is known to have survived, a man who leaped from the freight trains near Dresden.

14. On Transport XII/3, 1,369 youngsters arrived this date.

15. *Prominents,* as they were known in the ghetto, had roomier quarters in six special blockhouses where they enjoyed larger rations of food and were generally immune to deportation. There were two kinds of Prominents in Terezin. Type A Prominents were designated by the SS and included collaborators of the Mandler group as well as men of international reputation (French minister Leon Meyer, Heinrich Stahl, and Rabbi Leo Baeck of the Berlin community, Dr. David Cohen, onetime head of the Amsterdam *Joodse Raad,* members of the Bleichenroder banking family, even the vice-governor of Indonesia). Type B Prominents were afforded temporary protection by the Jewish community and numbered less prominent scholars as well as officials and families of the *Ältestenrat.*

Today a transport from Ostrava will arrive.[16] We don't know where to put the children. There is no room. Next week, I will marry my beloved.

September 19, 1942. Shabbat. Ostrava has arrived. Again a transport leaves and there are appeals. A woman is brought here straight from jail, sick with consumption, with a four-year-old child. The husband is in a concentration camp, and she traveled on. Again the resumption of conflicts over appeals for relatives.

Chaos, shouting, people in the attics. Pictures that will never be preserved on film, dramatic pictures, naturalistic, terrible.

September 20, 1942. The attics. A blind woman has been registered for a transport.[17] She has been sitting without help for many hours. They are bringing her to the attic. A small child, ten years old, helps her. A spectacle not to be believed. Anyone who has not seen it would not believe it.

September 21, 1942. Evening. I accompanied my dearest and returned home. A transport from Berlin arrived.[18] They traveled all day, Yom Kippur. Nevertheless, some women fasted all day. Now they have brought the elderly women to an attic in one house. The women did not want to lie on a stone floor in the dust in a dirty attic. In Berlin, they were told they were coming to a sanatorium.[19]

September 22, 1942. Wedding Day. The wedding was simple and nice. Only my father, mother-in-law, brother-in-law, with my sister-in-law and an old aunt. Weddings in the ghetto, interesting weddings.[20]

16. The first of four incoming transports from Ostrava that brought more than thirty-five hundred new deportees to the ghetto in September.

17. There were anywhere from 150 to 445 persons living in Q319, the *Blindenheim*, most of whom were over the age of sixty. Dr. Karel Fleischmann, a dermatologist from Budweis, worked with these people and in the spring of 1944 offered a poetic dirge to the blind. In it he wrote: "You don't see the miserable quarters in the blocks. You don't see the contaminated rooms, the well walls and the riddled pavements. You don't see all this sadness, unhappiness and doubt. You don't see the sickrooms, the ambulances with the endless rows of waiting patients. You don't see the tempo of difficult work and cannot appreciate the obstacles which must be overcome, and how the primitive state of medical facilities have deteriorated" (Adler, 534-36). Fleischmann and his family were deported to Auschwitz in October 1944.

18. Group I/66 numbered only one hundred persons. By way of contrast, one thousand arrived from Berlin with I/65 on September 15.

19. Many aged German Jews, believing they were going to a *Reichsaltersheim*, signed away their life insurance to the Reichs Main Security Office.

20. Marriages for confessional Jews were performed, with simplicity, by rabbis.

September 23, 1942. The head of the police from Minsk will take on himself the command of the police here.[21] He came here a couple of weeks ago, to the prison, but had a separate cell. He alone was allowed to read newspapers, and they gave him a double portion of food. He related that the Jewish situation in Minsk is very bad.[22]

September 24, 1942. My beloved has arrived. The room was prettied, given a new look. I am happy, but. . . . They are permitting the writing of letters.[23] People may request letters, food packages.[24] It is possible they may improve the situation. In spite of it all, I ask when will it end?

September 25, 1942. Orphans, children in the attics. It's impossible to find another place for them. The people who are in charge don't have enough energy. There isn't enough authority among the others. It goes without saying that there is a connection between the first phenomenon (lack of energy) and the second (lack of authority).

September 26, 1942. Shabbat. A convention of the movement [of Hechalutz].[25] A debate concerning the activities of the organization and relations between "the young" and "the old." Both sides are stupid and unsure in their opinions. The young are immature, and the old are unable to understand that it is normal for the young to be immature. Generally, I almost prefer the energy of the young (much as there is) to the lack of will of the old toward everything. Perhaps there is a difference between the doubts and a lack of energy.

Individuals labeled Jews by race could acknowledge their "solemn engagement" by notifying the registrar in the Department for Internal Administration. Couples could then live and be deported together. There were 463 religious and 96 civilian marriages in the ghetto (Lederer, 67).

21. Dr. Karl Löwenstein had been naval aide-de-camp to the German Crown Prince in World War I. Deported to Terezin in May, he was given a special cell in the ghetto jail, with numerous privileges of the kind reported by Redlich. When the SS decided to reorganize the *Ghettowache*, Löwenstein was placed in charge of the four-hundred-man unit. For his undoing, see entry January 1, 1943.

22. An understatement. *Einsatzgruppe B* under Wilhelm Kube murdered more than seventy-five thousand Jews in Minsk in 1941–42.

23. Prisoners could now write one fifty-word postcard every three months.

24. Outgoing letters were censored by the SS. The SS delivered parcels weighing no more than twenty kilograms, provided they were registered and addressed to specially protected individuals (e.g., Prominents, Danish Jews, or partners in mixed marriages).

25. Preparatory for the first conference of the united organizations of Hechalutz, which was to be held in November 1942. Nearly five hundred persons would attend that later meeting, which would establish committees to supervise Hebrew culture, education, stores, self-defense, etc. (Schmiedt, 113).

September 27–28, 1942. A convention. A debate on many questions. I spoke on the subject of *Histadrutarbeiter* [Hechalutz officers who did no manual work]. I tried to explain that a worker in the organization is not a "necessary evil" but a fundamental part of the organization. I also spoke of the relationship between us and "A.I." [Eretz Yisrael]. What do we learn from the flawed life of the ghetto? The answer is easy—there is much to learn when we get to the building of the land. We have encountered obstacles here that we shall never see again. What do we see here? Different types of Jews. What can we learn from the realities of life here? How tired we will be of life here in Europe.

September 29, 1942. We came as Zionists. It is our desire to leave as Jews. How many mature comrades are dissatisfied with the conference.[26] They say that from the standpoint of the young, the youth movement is a fire department whose members feel no partnership with the firefighters.

September 30, 1942. The Prominents will get new quarters. They have the right to write abroad several times a month. An interesting conversation with Aaron Menczer, the head of the movement in Austria.[27] He related various things concerning the youth movement in Austria.

Two youths stole suitcases. Tomorrow I will sit at the head of a court which will judge these youths.[28]

26. Among the least tolerant of the youth was Professor Adler, who subsequently accused leaders like Redlich and Fredy Hirsch of being vain, ambitious, and dictatorial young men who succeeded in infusing children with a Jewish national spirit (Adler, 548-49). Here, as elsewhere, Adler's criticism seems excessive.

27. Menczer was the head of "Gordonia" in Austria. In 1938, he returned to Vienna after accompanying a group of Jewish youth to Palestine. He arrived in Terezin from a work camp in Doppel, Lower Austria, in September 1942. Subsequently, Menczer was given responsibility for a transport of children from Bialystok. See entries August 24–September 8, 1943. Ruth Bondy maintains it was Menczer who informed Gonda Redlich of the plan, if not the mechanism, for Hitler's "Final Solution."

28. On June 1, 1943, a special juvenile court was established. Till then, children were tried in regular tribunals where administrative leaders like Redlich served as judges.

October

*After months of talking about the possibility of another ghetto in Po-
land, Redlich's entries are filled with gloom about "blood being
spilled in the East," the "death sentence" that accompanies each
transport, and how his fellow Jews are "sheep led to the slaughter."
Yet he never abandons hope, noting that German defeats on the Eastern Front may lead to a quick end of the war. That same desperate
optimism informed his attitude toward the conference of Zionist
youth groups that was trying to develop a program for postwar activities in Palestine.*

October 1, 1942. To write a book and describe in it the character of all
the people that a man meets in his life—an interesting subject. Aaron
Menczer told me some interesting things about the development of
the movement in Germany, about his experiences and views. He saw
much in Poland in a few seminars of Hechalutz. He also traveled as
a guide with a youth group to the land [of Eretz Yisrael].

October 2, 1942. We will be a model ghetto in order to cover up the
blood that is being spilled in the ghetto in the East,[1] the great injustice, the dead. . . . And we are forced to write and read: the situation
of the Jews in Germany isn't bad. Not. . . .

October 3, 1942. Shabbat. A celebration of Z's [Zucker's] birthday. An
interesting speech by Y. [Yaakov Edelstein]. A special ghetto . . . a
coverup of blood, of the victims of the ghettos in the East. A special
ghetto where more than a hundred people die in it daily. My dearest,
we are together now. Yes, there are many sad and hard times. It is
better that we are together. I don't know what will happen after
Terezin, but I suppose that we will stay together.

October 4, 1942. A continuation of the convention [of Hechalutz]. A
great dissappointment. There is no special goal, no set work, no
problems. They have stuck to their old patterns without any change.

1. It is difficult to gauge exactly how much Redlich knew of events in the East.
Survivors in Israel's Beit Terezin insist that people believed there was a single ghetto in
the East. Because of his contact with either Aaron Menczer or other independent
sources, Redlich expresses a legitimate cynicism in this passage.

My relationship with my dearest is unusual, uneasy. But in spite of this, I am happy because she has arrived.

October 5, 1942. A transport of elderly will be leaving.[2] Father, mother, a grandfather of people who have worked here for months. This is the reward—a ghetto in Poland. A death sentence. The mood isn't good. Fear and despair, anger, anger. Sheep led to the slaughter. Without the possibility of defense.

October 6, 1942. I am a married man. Ask if I am happy? It's difficult to answer. I am happy that I have a companion with whom I can speak concerning all aspects of life, of work, of people. But there are also difficulties. I love studying, but I do not have enough time to study.

October 7–8, 1942. We find ourselves in a big trap. If we ever escape, we should remember with a fearful and trembling heart all that we have seen here, all these terrible things. On one transport, for example, they are sending an entire family except for an aged mother who is more than sixty-five years old. This mother will go with another transport to another ghetto.[3] They tear the family apart, kill, torture, and they give to this a semblance of order. I would like to sleep and wake up at the end of the war.

A transport of elderly. One of the worst things is the transport of the elderly.

October 9, 1942. Hours of happiness trade off with hours of despair. It's not easy being jammed into such a tight place, even with my wife. Nervousness gives way to anger, to shouts. Both of us work hard, and many problems are still unclarified. Still I believe it will all be better in the end.

October 10, 1942. Shabbat. Transports of very old people, citizens of the Protectorate. The children must remain in Terezin. This is noth-

2. Six transports bearing a total of 9,866 persons left Terezin in the month of October. On this date, October 5, a train designated Bt departed for Treblinka. It was the first of five transports bound to the death camp fifty miles from Warsaw, and there were no survivors.

3. Despite what he had written earlier this month, Redlich clings to the fantasy that people may be going to the ghetto in the East. In reality, the transport mentioned (Bu) departed for Treblinka on the 8th. Of one thousand persons, fifteen were selected to live. The others were exterminated. Two of the fifteen survivors were among the inmates who destroyed Treblinka on August 1, 1943. Subsequently recaptured, they were liberated at war's end in Mannheim.

ing but a device for the destruction of nerves. . . . We are trying to create a curriculum of Jewish education. We want to conduct morning prayers with the small children. And behold—they say that this is reactionary, outdated, and God knows what else. They don't understand that "Shema Yisroel"[4] does not have to be an expression of religious faith but can also be an expression of national faith. The debate on this one is at times very severe.[5]

October 11, 1942. A great debate on the forms of "Jewishness" in the children's education. Many assimilationist and indifferent counselors are opposed to Hebrew education. We tried, for example, to conduct morning prayers with the small children. Many were opposed to it. In their opinion, it was reactionary.

October 12, 1942. Yesterday, we worked all day. Everyone has a lot of work now. Ten thousand people will go eastward on transports. In my opinion, the camp commander received instructions to send 10,000 old people. But there are only 7,600 old people here. The commandant wanted to fulfill his order and so he is also sending young people.

October 13, 1942. We composed lists, with comments about work. We have to take into account that they will take almost 40 percent of our assistants and clerks.

The mood in coming weeks will be very bad. Autumn doesn't bode well for us. We have to hope that next autumn, perhaps, will bring redemption.

October 14, 1942. They are setting up seminars for the counselors. Different scholars will lecture on various subjects.

The Germans aren't having success with their battles on the Eastern Front. But how much longer the war will last no one knows.[6]

4. The basic expression of Jewish monotheism, literally "Hear O Israel."

5. The *Jugendfürsorge* encountered opposition from the assimilationists, modernists, and socialists, all of whom had objections to the introduction of religious services. Hence the reference to the "Shema" (the profession of monotheism). Redlich and aides were trying to make the daily routine, which centered about a morning (9 A.M. to noon) educational program, more meaningful. Despite the terrible influences of the ghetto, official reports note some success. Children from a variety of backgrounds worked together in their homes, friendship circles, and collectives and "changed for the better" (Adler, 566).

6. The Nazi advance into northern Russia had already stalled outside Leningrad and Moscow before the end of 1941. A new campaign launched in the summer of 1942 to reach the Caucasus oil fields had also been stymied. By the end of October, the Nazis had also failed to capture Stalingrad on the Volga. When German generals urged a

October 15, 1942. Here in the Terezin ghetto we do not stand in the frontlines of the war, but this place is pretty close to those frontlines, for here the old, the weak die, without assistance. Battles where men do not fight with men. Instead, strong men, heroes, kill the weak masses, without pity, without compassion.[7]

October 16, 1942. All day, I felt a great fatigue. Perhaps I'm finally feeling the effects of malnutrition, the lack of milk, eggs. I thought the war would end in the fall. Even now, I think it's not unlikely the end may come quickly.

October 17, 1942. Shabbat. Evening of my birthday. Twenty-six years—ten months of the past year in Terezin, marriage.

Beczulkah told me about her family. She had two other brothers. Both of them have died. The other two were handsome, and she had been the "ugly one." From this all her complexes.

A debate on developing Hechalutz. We need a political movement that will prepare people to meet the future. A movement—but how to build it?[8]

A Hebrew circle. Many people participate in it, a committee of Hebrew experts. Still, it gives the impression of an academy spreading Czech culture during the period of the Enlightenment.[9] We are 150 years behind.

cessation of the offensive on October 29, Hitler took personal command of the army from General von Brauchitsch and instructed General von Paulus to resume the assault on Stalingrad. When von Paulus's army surrendered on January 31, 1943, fewer than eighty thousand of the five hundred thousand men in his Sixth Army were still alive.

7. Transport Bv left for Treblinka this date with 1,998 persons. None survived.

8. The Hechalutz movement, which had as its goal the preparation of youth for settlement in postwar Palestine, was illegal in the ghetto. It was also opposed, for obvious reasons, by assimilationists. Still, nine hundred youngsters between the ages of twelve and sixteen belonged to underground cells created by leaders like Zeev Shek (Adler, 703-4). Total membership (to age thirty) numbered two thousand.

9. Redlich likens his sessions with Yehudah Steinberg, Eng. Fausta, and thirty others in the Hebrew club to the Czech Enlightenment. Terezin was a closed society but one with unusual cultural activity. Its *Bucherei* (library), created by the SS and off limits to the general populace, held two hundred thousand volumes of Judaica, science, and fiction by 1944. A single month, July 1943, saw the following public lectures delivered: Dr. Carl Castelin, "Early Assyrian History"; Rabbi Leopold Neuhaus, "Midrash"; Professor Emil Utitz, "Overcoming Expressionism"; Professor Maximilian Adler, "Aristotle" and "Socrates and the Sophists"; Rabbi Leo Baeck, "Spinoza"; and Dr. David Schapira, "The Blind and their Environment." The ghetto could also draw upon the resources of poet George Kafka, a distant relative of Franz Kafka; George Einstein, the nephew of Albert Einstein; painter Peter Kien; or Viktor Ullman, a disciple of the Schoenberg school of music (Adler, 595-623).

October 18, 1942. We are establishing a Hebrew kindergarten. We already have enough registration. The Hebrew club is very interesting now. Yesterday, I received the letter *Ayin* for Hebrew speakers.[10] Several experts who know the language exceedingly well have come to the club.

October 19, 1942. Not an easy period for the ghetto. Now people who have been working at hard labor will be leaving. The parents of these people will also go. And regarding the children, the question remains: to travel with them or stay in the ghetto.[11]

October 20, 1942. Sometimes it seems to me that nearly everyone in the ghetto is a thief and the only difference is in the amount one steals. Someone steals less and another more. It happened, for example, that a man attempted suicide and cut his wrists. They brought him to a hospital and saved his poor life. Meanwhile, all of this poor man's possessions were stolen.[12]

October 21, 1942. At the last minute, they took the Jews who were German subjects out of the transport and put Jews from the Protectorate in their place.

October 22, 1942. Confusion, muddling, difficult and great arguments. Thousands of nervous people live with fear in their hearts. They are afraid and struggle to remain here. They race, race back and forth during the day and at night, without rest.[13]

October 23, 1942. Every man tries to exempt his friend. Every man is a special case, and there aren't enough people to send with the transports.

October 24, 1942. Again a crisis. All week, day and night we make up transports without stopping. Tension, fear, and confusion rule those designated for travel and, at times, also those "who decide."

10. The first letter of the word "Ivrit" was awarded with a certificate of honor to persons who demonstrated fluency in the language. Redlich was one of the few to receive this distinction. At Hanukkah that year, Dr. Kahn offered an inspirational address that ended with "Am Yisroel Chai." See Rothkirchen, 432, and Schmiedt, 122.

11. Redlich wrestles with his own responsibility. This day 1,984 persons left via Transport Bw. None survived Treblinka.

12. Redlich needed to look no further than his own *madrichim* for encouragement of theft. Yehuda Bacon recalls that there was such a shortage of fuel in L417 that the youths sneaked out after dark to steal coal or wood. The counselors actually awarded points for this competition, to what was known in ghetto parlance as *Schleusen-stehlen* (Adler, 552).

13. Aboard Transport Bx, 2,018 persons went to Treblinka. None returned. It is noteworthy that Redlich's entries are cryptic in this troubled time.

Sometimes one unit or another sends typists they want to keep to the Transport Committee and makes a request to keep them in order to protect them. The two committees are operating here.[14] And once again there is "Sergeant Grischa" in hundreds of variations.[15]

I want to write a monologue: "A woman in the *Schleuse*."[16]

October 25, 1942. All the people are tired, the "senders" and those who are "sent." On several occasions, "Sergeant Grisha" comes and goes. For instance, a woman works in my bureau. They registered her with her sister for the transport. Then afterwards they took her sister out, and she remains in the transport.

October 26, 1942. A big visit in the ghetto. It is forbidden to go out. (When did they ever permit this?) We have been ordered to be strict about cleanliness.

They want to open a coffee house.

In order to save their parents, the transport clerks included the old, sick, and bedridden.[17]

October 27, 1942. One hundred eighty people did not come to the transport.[18] The entire city was punished because of it:

(1) it is forbidden to go out in the street after 6 P.M.

(2) lights must be out after 6 P.M.

(3) all gatherings are forbidden

(4) the ghetto police have been ordered to carry truncheons.

October 28, 1942. It isn't a pleasant affair to arrange different things for my dearest and our apartment. My dearest rebuked me for not concerning myself with this.

I was x-rayed for tuberculosis. Thank God, I am healthy, fit, nothing turned up. The examination was negative.

14. Transport and exemption committees.

15. Arnold Zweig (1887–1968) wrote his satire of bureaucracy *The Case of Sergeant Grischa* in 1927.

16. Literally "floodgates." In the ghetto, it represented the staging barracks for deportations. See entry August 15, 1942.

17. The transport mentioned is By with 1,866 persons. This was he first of twenty-five death trains from Terezin to Auschwitz. Of 350 healthy men who were selected to live in Monowitz, 28 survived the war. The rest were gassed immediately. Of the nearly 87,000 persons sent east from Terezin between 1942 and 1944, 44,839 went to Auschwitz. Only 2,747 returned (Lederer, 223).

18. One hundred eighty persons either hid or ignored summonses of a kind mentioned in note to entry of August 28, 1942. For that, the entire ghetto was punished.

October 29, 1942. K.R. [Kamila Rosenbaum] told me she hadn't had her period for a long time. The doctor said it still isn't clear if she is pregnant. She told me this with great indifference.[19]

The people who did not report for transport are all imprisoned. There are almost one hundred people.

October 30, 1942. They haven't given the prisoners food for three days.[20] The prisoners were given twenty-five lashes. The days go by and are short. Winter is coming—the second winter in the ghetto.

October 31, 1942. Shabbat. Punishment for the 180 for failing to report to the transport:

(1) Lights out at 6 P.M.

(2) It's forbidden to go out after 6 P.M. on Shabbat and Sunday.

Everyone who did not report was imprisoned. The men did not receive food for three days and were punished with twenty-five lashes. Even Fredy [Hirsch] is afraid of L. [Löwenstein].

November

With these entries, Redlich dutifully noted the anniversary of one year in the ghetto. He could not be heartened by the constant squabbles between Zionists and non-Zionists, the additional burden of complaining relatives, or the behavior of a mean-spirited Jewish officer, Dr. Karl Löwenstein, who assumed command of the ghetto police. As the bitter cold froze milk in its containers, Terezin was beset with new outbreaks of typhus and typhoid.

19. Female survivors of the Holocaust testify that their systems, too, had become irregular, some believing that the Nazis put medicine in the food. Physicians, however, point out that the menstrual cycle may be upset by tension, malnutrition, and other factors. See Friedman, *Amcha: An Oral Testament of the Holocaust* (Lanham, Md.: University Press of America, 1979), 343. Whatever the case, the announcement by Kamila Rosenbaum must have unnerved Redlich as much as the ongoing transports.

20. A reference to the 180 who refused deportation in the entry of October 27, 1942.

November 1, 1942. What is the difference between our situation here in the ghetto and that in Prague a year or two ago? Here the struggle is not merely between those who pursue glory for personal sake but frequently the decisive question is one of life and death.

November 2, 1942. Caring for small children is not an easy task. Frequently, such and such mother complains that the counselors do not take proper care of the children. In truth, the children are dirty and the counselors are sometimes negligent.[1]

November 3, 1942. A lot of theft has been uncovered. The new police chief [Löwenstein] is very militant. He is Prussian to the hilt. He acts against thieves with a vengeance and great energy. But he is a dangerous fellow, a typical assimilationist and German to the core.

November 4, 1942. One of those imprisoned was a cripple.[2] The Jewish police did not want to beat him. "He was wounded in the war," they said. "He lost his arm for Germany." "Indeed," replied the German commandant,[3] "He must get twenty-five lashes." Such is the reward of the Fatherland, Germany's reward.

November 5, 1942. Our work is great, and it isn't easy to urge people to compromise, to resolve differences. Even my Hebrew work is not so intensive. Again and again, people want to establish a Hechalutz movement throughout. A question of unity. In my opinion, there isn't another movement here except Maccabi Hatzair.[4]

November 6–8, 1942. The *chaverim* in charge of Netzach are not reliable. It is difficult to promote them and give them important responsibility in the matter of unity for they are a head without a body.

After the end [of the war], millions of Jews will remain in Europe, without possessions and without money. What will happen to them? I suppose that the Jews of America will invest their money helping the European Jews. Perhaps there will be a great Aliyah, the

1. Washrooms in Terezin with their limited supply of water were to be treated with lime or chlorine three times daily. Soap, which did not lather, was issued to the children. Individuals might launder three kilograms of laundry every six weeks. With thirty to forty children in a room, many of them sick, it is little wonder that many of the children's rooms were "infested with rats and vermin" (Adler, 109).

2. Another reference to 180 Jews punished for running away October 27.

3. Ordered by SS Obersturmführer Karl Bergel.

4. According to Ruth Bondy, Maccabi Hatzair was allied with Gordonia. Others, like Hashomer Hatzair, Bnai Akiva, El Al, and Netzach (see entry March 28) were rivals for membership and leadership.

rapid development of Eretz Yisrael, and a new Eretz Yisrael will emerge from the crisis, stronger internally and externally. But "AI" Eretz Yisrael alone will not be the answer for millions.

November 7, 1942. Shabbat. Some relaxation, but another committee. . . . Will money be introduced?[5] Of course it could be. The thing could be an interesting experiment in national economics. Anyway, a coffee house has been opened. (They say there will even be music there, a bank, a reading room.) Five thousand people reside in the attics and have to move to other living quarters.

They are now taking serious measures against stealing. The new director of the O.W. [*Ordnungswache*], Dr. Löwenstein, rules with strict discipline. He is an experienced German officer.

November 9, 1942. They are making a film. Jewish actors, happy, satisfied, happy faces in the film, only in the film. . . . [6]

Yesterday, I spoke to Yaakov [Edelstein] face to face, with great candor. I think it's been a long time since I had spoken to him in this manner. Perhaps I hurt myself. What to do?

November 10–11, 1942. One must contend with the view held by many of our members who believe their task in taking part in the Hechalutz convention is to preach. In my opinion, we will not create a new movement this way. It is only possible to create such a movement with people that really work physically. For a new movement such as this, it isn't necessary to have a chairman from the *Shtadlanim*.[7] From a political perspective, this isn't the right way. All the *Shtadlanim* will be interested in the new movement if it is shown to be united and has power and great energy directed outward.

November 12–13, 1942. We spoke today with *chaverim* about our relationship to communal life. The difficult questions are, in brief: first, our relation to physical work; and second, the relationship of our

5. See entry January 13, 1943.

6. A personal project of SS Hauptsturmführer Hans Günther, this preliminary film was much like footage shot in the Warsaw Ghetto, designed to show Jews living the good life while Germans were sacrificing for the war effort. Later, SS Obersturmführer Otto would direct a finished product titled "Der Führer gibt den Juden eine Stadt." Designed to deceive the free world, the film was replete with scenes of members of the *Ältestenrat* discussing administrative matters, lectures on philosophy, a soccer match, and Jewish workers moving to and from their toil. The twenty minutes that have survived in Yad Vashem's archive are singularly lacking in happy faces.

7. Traditional intercessors on behalf of Jews toward Gentiles. The word has a negative connotation and is applied here toward assimilationists, collaborators, or other ego-bent individuals who wanted to be leaders.

wives to community life. For women, communal life is harder. Every woman likes to control some private property, and not just in the negative sense. The women want to influence every small detail. They want to cook, to arrange their apartments, etc. Another thing is important to them: children's education. The impression that the meeting of the *Chalutz* [future Zionist pioneers] made on people was not good. It really was not good.

November 14, 1942. The Hechalutz convention. I have no faith in these people. An education committee. How to deal with the problem of stealing? Where is the difference between theft for the collective good and theft for personal gain? It is hard to offer a 100 percent moral education here, for lack of models. (For who doesn't carry off something?) There are problems whose solutions are very difficult, even if they are very interesting from an educational perspective.

November 15, 1942. The Jewish police freed a sixteen-year-old girl who stole and was punished with three months in jail. The police brought the youngster to the girls' quarters. What to do with her? The girls that knew her before she came to the ghetto aren't sympathetic. We brought her to another unit. She will live with a female clerk who works in the police.

November 16, 1942. A young boy came to me and cried. He wants to travel to his parents who left the ghetto a long time ago and were sent eastward.[8] How do you explain to a child that it isn't worth traveling to the East because his parents are surely in another ghetto?

November 17, 1942. I received information that my sister[9] was very sick and attempted suicide. I have a lot of worries now, for family, for children, for the future.

November 18, 1942. A policeman was accused of taking a bribe and the camp commander ordered him registered for the next transport. But the policeman was actually innocent of any wrongdoing. They are now asking clemency for him. The camp commander agreed if the doctor decided that [the policeman's] small child could not leave on a transport.[10]

8. The *Ältestenrat* had managed to protect children under twelve from the massive deportations that fall. The age limit was lowered until *Wickelkinder* (literally newborn babes) were sent east in October 1944.

9. Wilma Goldstein returned to Olmutz after the war.

10. Obviously a sick child. If a doctor declared a child sick, the family was exempted from the transport.

November 19, 1942. The danger of lice is very great. The possibility of [contracting] communicable disease is very great, and it is difficult to battle this multifaceted danger.

There still are no stoves in the rooms of many childrens' houses. Sick children lie in the rooms. There are all kinds of worries and much energy is required to overcome them.

November 20, 1942. My uncle has arrived. My cousin is a doctor. He is sick with consumption. Opposing viewpoints continue to grow between the Zionists and assimilationists (and, perhaps, between the communists).[11] The situation now is not conducive to political debates. Our first task—first and foremost—is to tend to the health of the children.[12]

November 21, 1942. Shabbat. Great worries—children with lice, disease. This is complicated by defective work which comes from the conflict of [political] viewpoints.

Uncle Bertik, Frantik, the Langer family, etc., have arrived.[13] Gerty [Gonda's wife] admonished me on my cold relations and ill manners toward people who ask for my help. It's true. But in the end, I always help with everything in my power. The coolness is part of my character, Gerty. I am not especially keen on people. I certainly could live alone with you. You may not understand this.

November 22, 1942. One day here is enough and a healthy man would die. These things happened in other times, but here, such incidents aren't unique. Rather, they occur periodically. My mother-in-law is an odd one. She is good-hearted. "People would not believe it, if it were told." She is sick, because she worked too much.

November 23, 1942. Prager is sick.[14] Fredy [Hirsch] also is sick, and I have to run my department alone. It isn't an easy task, and the work is complicated. A political debate is going on now among us. Our detractors sometimes use unfair methods.

11. In the first years of Terezin, the communists were a small but influential group drawn from Czech Jews like the engineer Jiri Vogel. Their existence as a political unit was kept secret from the SS.

12. Documents from the *Jugendfürsorge* note outbreaks of scarlet fever, diarrhea, jaundice, measles, whooping cough, and stomach typhus in the children's barracks by the fall of 1942. In some periods, as many as 30 to 35 percent of the children lay sick (Report of L417, July 1943; Adler, 565). Adler also reports as many as seventy children per month sick with mumps (519).

13. Relatives and friends from Prague who reached Terezin on November 20.

14. Fritz Prager (1909–1944), a member of Maccabi Hatzair and one of Redlich's lieutenants in the childrens' services department.

November 24, 1942. My brother-in-law's sister was listed with her children for a transport. Her husband died in a concentration camp. I will appeal, but will I succeed? If not, what will my brother-in-law say? Certainly he will speak badly about me. My uncle also is a standby for the transport.[15] My quarters have become nicer. They reflect a woman's touch.

November 25, 1942. Today, the milk froze in the pot. The cold is very dangerous. The children don't undress, and so there are a lot of lice in their quarters. Today, there was a premier performance of *The Bartered Bride*. It was the finest one I had ever seen in the ghetto.[16]

November 26, 1942. I am working by myself now. It is difficult because there is no room. The number of ghetto residents has risen to over forty-seven thousand people. They put men, women, children, old people in the attics, where temperatures go down to four degrees below zero. The transport that was ready did not leave the ghetto, and it is not clear if it will depart.[17]

November 27, 1942. They searched the workers in the factories and found a lot of money and cigarettes. Even in the childrens' hall, there were searches. Even in there, they arrested some people. The opposition between the Zionists and assimilationists extends also to art.

November 28, 1942. Shabbat. Fritz Prager is sick for a second time. Fredy [Hirsch] is suspected of having typhus. Maybe today it will clear up.[18] I remained alone throughout. There is much work, much

15. Redlich's concern was premature. No further eastbound transports deported Terezin until January 20, 1943.

16. Karel Ancerl, Rudolf Freudenfeld, Raphael Schachter, and others conducted performances of operas (*The Bartered Bride, Marriage of Figaro, The Kiss, Carmen,* and *Brundibar*) while dramatic groups staged *Cyrano de Bergerac* and works by Gogol, Moliere, Shakespeare, Shaw, Molnar, and Herzl (Adler, 590-97). See entry July 18, 1942.

17. See entry November 24, 1942.

18. There is some confusion over the exact disease to which Redlich makes reference because the same word, "typhus," is used for typhoid fever and typhus in Hebrew and German. Some survivors of Terezin insist that it was typhus, a rickettsial disease, generally transmitted by an arthropod vector, e.g., fleas or lice. Related to Rocky Mountain spotted fever, exanthematic typhus or *Flecktyphus* normally was not fatal among children. It did, however, manifest itself over the body with dark red spots, which may have been mistaken for typhoid rashes. Typhoid, known as "Unterleibstyphus" or Typhus abdominalis, is a bacteria that enters the body through contaminated food or water (*Encyclopedia Britannica,* [1960], vol. XXII, pp. 646-48). Adler and Lederer insist that the principal "typhus" epidemics in 1942 and 1943 were actually typhoid. According to Adler, there were 1,165 cases in 1942, of which 153 proved fatal. A more serious epidemic broke out in February 1943. As with most typhoid cases,

work. One transport was set to leave on the 25th and still has not. Again, forty-seven thousand people live here, many in the attics in cold of four degrees below zero. The danger from lice is greater in a situation such as this than in the summer. People don't take their clothes off because of the cold, and they sleep in their clothes. We have had many instances of contagious jaundice and some instances of stomach typhus. Searches in Lautscharna. Also in building 414. They arrested three people.

November 29, 1942. In a few days, we will have been here one year. In all my life, I never saw as much as in this past year! Worries, sorrows, experiences, hope for victory.

November 30, 1942. An interesting and burning problem. Where to put people who will be coming? In the attics? But what will happen in the winter, in the severe cold? Sheets of artificial wood.[19] Maybe they can renovate the attics, but this will take a lot of time.

I liked the rehearsal of my play.[20]

blood was taken from the sick and sent to the Hygiene Institute of the German University in Prague for the "Widal test." By the end of summer 1943, "the danger was overcome." Adler insists that *Flecktyphus* did not become a real threat until 1944 with the arrival of a carrier from Berlin, then again in 1945 when 502 deportees from concentration camps died (Adler, 515, 520). Lederer states, "Typhoid occurred first in the autumn of 1942 and spread quickly; in January, 1943, the incidence of this disease was reduced to manageable proportions, only to flare up again with greater virulence soon afterwards; at the end of 1943, however, this outbreak was overcome apart from some isolated cases." His figures show 127 dead of 1,234 cases. As for the other "typhus," Lederer notes that pediculosis was always a threat among incoming prisoners. With delousing, however, it was contained, until April 1945 (Lederer, 138-40). For the integrity of this manuscript, we shall keep Redlich's references to "typhus," pointing out discrepancies where they arise. See entries February 4–5 and March 12, 1943.

19. The *Raumwirtschaft* used plywood and pressed wood (plaster, wood shavings, etc.) beneath the roofs and as dividers in the attics. The makeshift arrangements offered little privacy or protection from the cold.

20. Redlich had written a play called *The White Shadow*. The story concerned an assimilated Jewish woman who was married to a Christian officer. Old and abandoned, she was sent to the ghetto, where no one knew her and she felt estranged, reminiscing on her past. The music was written by Gideon Klein. The performance was directed by Vlasta Schoenova, later of the Habimah Theater in Israel.

December

Expressions of frustration and disgust become more common in the diary as Redlich tries to cope with the continuing jealousy among various factions. Like most of the fifty thousand Jews in Terezin, he is disturbed by efforts of converts to observe Christmas in the ghetto. Faced with bitter criticism for his leadership in the Jungendfürsorge, he contemplates resigning his post as the month closes.

December 1, 1942. As long as I stay in the ghetto, I am interested in political developments. Reading papers is not merely a pleasure but also work, a subject for debate, the basic substance of life.[1] When will it end? What will happen then? What will be?

December 2, 1942. Tolerance is a great and searing issue. Do we have the right to put off someone or other for political or religious reasons? Should a "Christian" Jew be a cook or clerk?[2] Is he to blame for leaving Judaism? (Sometimes he was converted when he was a baby.)

December 3, 1942. The first presentation of the play was not favorably received by the public.[3] The assimilationists especially were annoyed that I dared present the problem of a converted old woman on stage. For the most part, I was interested in the problem from a humanistic, rather than nationalistic, perspective. The assimilationists don't learn. They don't learn from circumstances.

December 4–6, 1942. One year. Already we have been in the ghetto one year. The time has passed quickly, very quickly. . . .

1. Radios were forbidden in the ghetto. When the Nazis suffered their defeat at Stalingrad, newspapers also were prohibited. Residents of Terezin were forced to rely upon materials smuggled in by Czech gendarmes or word of mouth carried by incoming transports. Such information (telling of Russian counterattacks or Allied invasions of Western Europe) was generally inaccurate (Adler, 580-83).

2. According to Adler, no ghetto in Europe had such a large Christian minority as Terezin. Initially perhaps 9 percent of the ghetto's population were people defined as Jews under the Nuremberg Laws. By the end of April 1945, the figure had risen to 36.6 percent (6,194 persons). There was a good deal of animosity between practicing Jews and those who had been thrown into Terezin according to racial decrees. Catholics, the best organized sect even though they never had a priest, tried to maintain an aloofness (Adler, 308-9, 609-11).

3. Redlich's play *The White Shadow.* See entry November 30, 1942.

The news coming from the East isn't good. They tell of thousands of Jews killed. The head of the Jewish police here [Löwenstein] used to be the head of the Jewish police in Minsk. Now people come and ask him how someone or other is doing. He answers: "They are well." But after these people leave, he lowers his head and says: "This one or that died before my eyes."

The situation in the ghetto still is terrible. The number of residents has risen to more than fifty thousand. If we compare our situation in the winter with that in the summer, we have lost our living places which have been converted into stores, coffee house, offices.

December 5, 1942. Shabbat. A year in the ghetto. What to write about it? Again we will have fifty thousand people. Now in the winter. . . . They are ready to build cabins for those with contagious diseases. (There are more than one hundred cases of typhus.)[4] But when will this be? Dr. L. [Löwenstein] is an interesting character, mysterious. A naval officer in bygone days, according to rumor, an adjutant to the German Crown Prince, afterwards he served as a Jewish police officer in Minsk. Now he is here. Everyone is afraid of him. Because of the crowded population, the situation is catastrophic, worse than anything till now. Cold, typhus, hunger among the aged. If Dominik Eisenberger asks for a slice of bread. . . . [5]

December 7, 1942. Sometimes the question is asked: what about later on? Will we be satisfied with a difficult life, a life of physical labor? Will my dearest be satisfied with a life like this?

December 8, 1942. People aren't satisfied with the child care program. The male and female counselors aren't happy with their work. The shelters are overflowing, and it is impossible to place orphans or motherless children in them. Many of the aides are sick. Add to this more political opposition, etc.

December 9–10, 1942. The question of space is more volatile than any other. The food isn't so bad now, especially for the workers. The aged who do not work do not have enough food.

4. For note on stomach typhus, typhoid, and spotted fever, see entry November 28, 1942.

5. Eisenberger had owned a factory before the war. He and his son Honza were both active in the Zionist movement. Redlich is saddened by the spectacle of a once wealthy man reduced to shame by hunger. Another survivor, Zdenka Fantlova, saw her weight dwindle from seventy-five kilos to thirty-seven on the Terezin diet of soup sauce, potatoes, and, rarely, slivers of meat. Wrote Ms. Fantlova, hunger was a "cruel enemy, destroying and deceitful," "a psychological affair." See twenty-nine-page memoir titled "Modernes Mittelalter" in Beit Terezin Archives, pp. 3-4.

We were told to present *The Dancing Doll* before the Germans. They want to film it. They also ordered dancing on stage, actors in costume. K.R. [Kamila Rosenbaum] will dance. Her mother is in prison. She hopes that the Germans will release her if she dances. A subject fit for a play.

December 11, 1942. By chance, I visited a room of old, sick people. The stench in the room was terrible. The sick relieve themselves in their beds. Caring for the sick isn't easy. Those who look after the sick and aged are forbidden to act badly toward them. Truly not easy work.[6]

December 12, 1942. Shabbat. A lecture in WIZO.[7] Really irrelevant. A debate on the question of who needs to go to a G.A.[8] It's sickening. A man can despair of his "friends." But I am too much a skeptic to despair. The "politicians" of the youth movement who make politics out of a nonexistent base are truly awful. I am ashamed of them. I don't deny that I also like politics, though I understand it is always a dirty [business]. Because of this, I always try to place politics on a realistic base.

December 13, 1942. A discussion as to whom from Hechalutz will go to the G.A. [General Assembly]. I don't lean toward those people who make politics merely for the sake of politics, that is, for their own sake. Yesterday, there was a lecture in WIZO. I didn't especially like the woman.

December 14, 1942. A national debate in the toilets. They lock them from the outside. There is a special guard [unit] on the toilets. The members of this guard frequently are German Jews. Everyone that goes to the toilet calls out the number of the toilet where he sits. But the guards don't go to open them because they don't understand the Czech numbers. Thus bizarre and funny arguments frequently start. Why don't the guards learn Czech?

A Jew whose daughter was a spy in the German service asked for a personal favor on this account.

December 16, 1942. Political activity is increasing a lot in all ghetto matters. Despite all the troubles, Jews are beginning to divide up into

6. There were approximately 550-560 doctors and 1,300-1,500 nurses in the ghetto in 1942–43. They tended a daily sick count of more than 10,000 patients (Adler, 509-11).

7. Women's International Zionist Organization.

8. Redlich is referring to the *General Ausschuss*, plans for a meeting of the Zionist Executive in Terezin. Among the groups participating were WIZO, Maccabi, Hechalutz. He mocks the ambitions of some leaders.

hundreds of factions, one against the other. All of this would be comical if the situation weren't so serious.

December 17, 1942. Jealousy. I despise this jealousy. Why do people cherish their honor so much? Why don't they appreciate human values without regard to their own viewpoints? I am very tired of these battles.

December 18, 1942. A small child looks at a photograph of a municipal building in Prague and says: "This is a very lovely barrack. . . ."[9]
   A difference of opinion between Fredy [Hirsch] and Otto [Klein] that is impossible to reconcile.

December 19, 1942. Shabbat. Disputes and intrigue everywhere, with the higher-ups and lower echelons. Also with us, also with us.
   Fredy [Hirsch] and Otik [Klein]: differences. Both are right and not right. And so their arguments take on a political tone, a personal tone, and who knows what else. Disgusting, really disgusting. They argue, and we have fifty thousand people here in the midst of a merciless conflict. All of this is repulsive and bothers me terribly.

December 20, 1942. I came to one of the childrens' homes and my beloved heard the children call out: "Zionist pigs." Arguments and a difficult situation. It's very difficult.
   My beloved. I love her. Our sexual relationship is also improved.

December 21, 1942. My relationship with my brother [Robert] and sister remains very good. There were moments that strained this relationship. But today, even though I haven't seen my brother for over a year, I always think of him with great affection.

December 22, 1942. Yaakov [Edelstein] visited me today and asked if there is something wrong between us. I haven't been to see him for a while. I will visit him this week, because our conversation was cut short.

December 23, 1942. They have placed many children in the attics. During one inspection of the children's homes, I heard a child revile: "Zionist pigs." I mentioned it to a counselor, and he sent the child to

9. Trude Groag, a nurse who taught art to children, recalled a similar experience. As she told Anita Engel, "The 3-4 year olds couldn't make anything that resembled flowers or animals, for they had never seen any. When a cat ran across the road once, the children went wild with excitement" (undated interview, Herzl File, Beit Terezin Archive, III).

me. I explained to the child that everyone has the right to his opinion, but that great tolerance is needed, especially for us.

December 24, 1942. A new discussion about celebrating the birth of Jesus Christ. My position isn't simple. I am ashamed of the celebration of Christian festivals, not only from a Zionist perspective, but in my opinion, it is a great shame to celebrate any holiday without feeling the sanctity which is the basis of that holiday.[10]

December 25, 1942. A woman came to our office to complain that in one of the houses, parents had beaten their son. I was sent to investigate the complaint and the child was moved to (a children's shelter. Political arguments have not ceased. They still continue.

December 26, 1942. Shabbat. A debate about Christmas. It's really a shame: not only from the Jewish standpoint, but also from the Christian. The dying Christian world. Here the Jews profane it by celebrating Christmas.

The continual arguments incense me. It isn't worth getting so angry. On both sides there is a great deal of insincerity, personal grudges, egoism. How is it going to end? I still don't know.

December 27, 1942. We go to bed at a very late hour every day. . . . My wife is a very good person. I love her very much. Next month I want to visit the children's quarters.

December 28, 1942. How many days till the end of the year 1942? What will happen next year? All of us hope the coming year will bring us redemption. Maybe the situation is better today than last year. But what will the future bring?

December 29–30, 1942. Two people have sent the head of the ghetto police a memo. In it, they complain that the administration of the child care division is unable to organize youth activities. One of the two has been my deputy clerk for a long while. . . . I remember an examination of his handwriting.[11] The expert did not recommend

10. Redlich's position is remarkably similar to that of American rabbis who have tried to combat the influence of Christmas. Among Jews from Slovakia, observing the day would have been unthinkable, for Christmas, like Easter, connotated a time of tension, and possible pogroms. Many German and Bohemian Jews, however, observed it as a secular holiday. There is a tragic irony of ghettoized Christians (Jews by "race") celebrating the birth of Jesus before many of them were shipped out to their deaths.

11. For the importance of psychological evaluations of handwriting, see entry February 18–19, 1942.

him and said he had a two-faced personality and could not be trusted. I wrote a response and handed it to Z. [Zucker]. In general, the work is hard and people do not make it sweeter for me.

December 31, 1942. Today is the last day of the year. A year ago, I had been in the ghetto for almost a month. The children's kitchen is ready to go. Tomorrow they will start cooking in it. The counselors who live with the children will eat with them. Even other clerks want to eat the children's food. I cannot fulfill their requests.[12]

12. Children received slightly larger rations than did regular workers (243 grams of meat for children, 225 for regular workers; 543 grams of flour for children, 418 for regular workers; 217 grams of margarine for children, 187 for regular workers; 228 grams of sugar for children, 193 for regular workers; 2,638 grams of potatoes for children, 2,195 for regular workers), enough to prompt some adults to seek admission to their mess. Even with rations of skim milk, the children's portions could not compare with those of heavy duty workers, officials of the *Ältestenrat*, or Prominents (Adler, 346-47). See also diary entry June 7, 1942.

1943

January

Conceding that there was too much crowding in the ghetto, Adolf Eichmann ordered the Auflockerung, a thinning out of its population. The dispatch of transports, suspended in October, was resumed January 20. Children who previously had been exempted were now sent directly to Auschwitz. One week later, the Nazis shuffled leadership in the Ältestenrat, replacing Jacob Edelstein with former Heidelberg sociology professor Dr. Paul Eppstein. The move signaled a shift in power from Czech to German Jews and was designed to disrupt whatever harmony existed among Terezin's inhabitants.

January 1, 1943. A parade of Jewish police going about goose-stepping.[1] A spectacle worthy of the new year. Also, a child died today.

I wanted to give up my administrative position. My beloved opposed it. I will not give up, even if I am tired.

January 2, 1943. Ambition. The struggle for power. For whose good? From the smallest to the greatest here, the same thing—a struggle for position of power, for the most part striving for personal reasons rather than objective authority. And, again, a paradox possible only in the ghetto of Terezin. A hall: up front, on stage, a revival of Wolker's *Hospital.* In the back, Jews are praying.[2]

1. Redlich employs the German term "Hochschritt." The SS, too, expressed surprise at the arrogance demonstrated by Löwenstein's revamped *Ghettowache.* By September, the police chief would be back in jail (accused of dealing fraudulently in meal tickets) and most of his men would be on their way to Auschwitz. Löwenstein, however, would survive the war in a Prominent barrack (Lederer, 60).

2. The play mentioned was written by Jiri Wolker. Terezin's residents were not pleased that they had to split large halls between cultural and religious affairs (Religion File, Beit Terezin Archive). See appeal to *Ältestenrat* dated September 15, 1944, complaining about "the clamor of children" disrupting prayer services.

January 3, 1943. A power struggle everywhere, from the littlest to the biggest. I don't feel the need to have more and more power. What is life here? I hope it is only a brief interruption of normal life.

January 4, 1943. Transports from Zlin and Mlada Boleslav are going to arrive.[3] Relatives of my brother-in-law will be coming. That will mean new worries about their stay in the ghetto. I would like to visit the children's house next week or in the coming weeks and stay in each house a week. Perhaps in this way I will be able to assess the practical situation in education and youth activities.

January 5, 1943. We will be given all the floors in an additional children's home. We hope to settle 450 children there. Our situation may improve in this way. I am not very active now. I don't understand the people here who seek more and more influence and power. I also have my pride, and for this reason I use influence, but only when necessary. I have my self-respect.

January 6, 1943. There was a small child whose birth was very difficult. The doctors said that either the child or the mother would die. By chance, both survived. Then the child took sick and died. The mother wept inconsolably.

January 7, 1943. The graphology circle is very interesting. The teacher has a good way of instructing, and it's possible to learn much from him.[4] Generally, the ghetto's main characteristic nowadays is the continual power struggle within the administration.

January 8, 1943. An astronomer, whose daughter was our friend before being sent eastward, lies sick in a hospital.[5] He has new ideas about the structure of the moon that are completely different from contemporary science. I heard him speak, though I did not understand the subject.

January 9, 1943. In January, ten transports.[6] Fifty percent from the territory of Germany, 50 percent from the Protectorate, 50 percent young, 50 percent old. Surely, for a while, the arguments will stop.

3. Two incoming transports from Bohemia-Moravia on January 13 and 16 brought 1,041 persons to Terezin. There really had been no letup of incoming transports. Six transports in December brought over 2,400 Czech Jews. Several hundred others arrived from Berlin, Oppeln, Drava, and Usti (the latter two Sudeten districts).

4. See entry February 18–19, 1942.

5. Redlich does not name the astronomer. One of the tragedies of the Holocaust was the slaughter of artists, musicians, writers, historians, theologians, and scientists. The loss for humanity and civilization in new ideas is incalculable.

6. Incoming transports.

Already children have died here in the ghetto. Sending a child to Poland means sending him to his death. Last year the age limit was twelve, this year three years.[7]

A year has passed since they hanged nine Jews in the ghetto, a year since the first transports left. A subject for a drama: a man or a group of men who control a certain collective, play a prank. The collective is threatened with a certain punishment. The same member of the collective who is the victim of the prank believes in a miracle.[8]

January 10, 1943. I wanted to visit the children's homes and stay a week in each one. Yesterday, I found out that transports will be leaving and that I must not leave the office. Last year, nine Jews were hanged. May their memory be a blessing. When, when will it all end?

January 11, 1943. So the days pass, one after another, in a long line. In the greater world, a terrible storm is brewing. And here, the Jews wait under hard conditions, hoping for the future. It still isn't known when the transports will go.

January 12, 1943. Winter has come, and with it a great chill. I remember how much we feared the winter. The situation truly is very bad. People are living in the attics where the temperature often falls below zero. Still more transports will be coming.

January 13, 1943. There isn't any news. The question of where to hide money is not simple. We must assume that money will be very dear to us.[9] A few days ago, they started to cook in the central chil-

7. Already the Nazis were lowering the age limit for deportation. Redlich understood, intuitively, this would mean death for the children.

8. Another case of self-doubt. Redlich repeatedly wonders whether he is doing the proper thing.

9. Deportees were supposed to turn over all valuables, including money, when they reached Terezin. In return, they received vouchers, with which they might acquire goods. Work was compensated with food coupons. Despite threats of punishments, many people attempted to conceal money when they entered the ghetto, and a thriving black market developed in cash and goods (cigarettes, sugar, margarine, bread). In January 1943, the SS announced that a special ghetto *Krone* would be issued beginning in May. Designed by two Jewish artists (and modified by authorities in Berlin), the currency bore a stereotypic image of Moses with the Ten Commandments and was signed by Yaakov Edelstein. The Nazis also created a new Bank of Jewish Autonomy and opened accounts for all residents of the ghetto. Now, automatically, salaries would be deposited in the bank, one hundred *Krone* per month for a worker, seventy-five for a Prominent, fifty for a child. Rena Rosenberger worked in the bank and reckoned that there were seventy-nine thousand accounts, of whom 4 percent survived the war (Rosenberger memoir, p. 16, Beit Terezin Archive). See also Adler, 124 and 152.

dren's kitchen. People aren't satisfied with the new kitchen.

It happened that a mother with three children has to go to three kitchens. Her kitchen (for adults), the children's kitchen, and a dietetic kitchen for a sick child.[10]

January 14, 1943. A letter from my brother. He speaks harshly to me and writes that I don't concern myself with his family. He isn't correct. I lodged an appeal for the sake of his wife's family. I am unable to care for her. I have such a large family that I could sacrifice myself for my family alone.

January 15, 1943. They inspected the houses of the Prominents and discovered that one hundred people were living in one room. The Germans ordered that the quarters of the Prominents be enlarged for an inspection that will be coming from Berlin. It will visit these houses. The Germans want to create a Potemkin Village. They won't show the old people living and dying in the attics to the visitors.

January 16, 1943. Shabbat. In the homes of the Prominents: it turns out they are too crowded and the furnishings are bad. A deputation from Berlin is coming that will want to see how good it is for everyone here. Today they removed forty people in order to expand the rooms of the Prominents. No one knows when the transports will leave.

January 17, 1943. Two youths ran away from a children's house. One was badly ill with a vitamin deficiency.[11] This thing isn't very pleasant. The camp commandant ordered the Jewish Elder [Edelstein] to pay attention to the children's houses.

January 18, 1943. I visited the children's houses. Through these visits, I want to know the existing conditions of the houses and their problems. It still isn't clear when the transports will go.

January 19, 1943. Today they announced that tomorrow evening a transport will be going. We have a very short time to prepare the transport. The mood isn't good now.

10. There is some confusion concerning the exact dating of this paragraph. The original text is clearly marked "13/1 'hamshech' " (continuation).

11. As a result of vitamin A or D shortages, there were numerous cases of bone deformities, spontaneous fractures, and osteoporosis in the ghetto. Shortages of vitamins C and B led to anomalous cases of scurvy and pellagra, a lack of iron to anemia (Adler, 520–21). Some wags noted sarcastically, "You can do without all these vitamins if you have Vitamin P—Protekzia" (Schmiedt, 117–18).

January 20, 1943. We worked all night. They exempted the orphans and the sick from the transport. The transports are a flock of lambs. Sheep sent and cast aside, sheep whose taskmasters are also lambs. Jews driving Jews. An eternal circle.[12]

January 21, 1943. Transports. Five thousand people up to the age of sixty will leave the ghetto. It appears they really want to send them to a work camp because the age limit up to which you can register for the transport is sixty.

In the morning, they placed many counselors into the transport of German youth. We succeeded in extricating almost all of them.[13]

January 22, 1943. A transport from Zlin arrived. Once more, my brother is sending people and promising them my help. They come and I haven't a chance of supporting them because the situation is very bad, as bad as it ever was in the past. Frequently, chance decides who is to go and who will stay.

January 23, 1943. Shabbat. Transports up to the age of sixty. The first time one thousand youngsters from Germany proper. Tension, great responsibility. Frequently the hand of chance decides. Hugo[14] again sent me people in order to help them. How can I? Afterwards, they revile me and speak who knows what about me.

January 24, 1943. They put my mother-in-law into the transport.[15] I removed her one hour after they put her in. But in spite of this, I was frightened when she came to me at night and announced she was included in the transport. A friend of my brother, who brought me food, said after he saw that I could not exempt him: "The food he took. Now he doesn't help me."

January 25, 1943. A young man fled from Vienna in a cattle car to the Swiss border. There they caught him and returned him to a concen-

12. What had been a relatively peaceful interlude was now ended. There had been no outgoing transports since the one to Auschwitz on October 26. Henceforth, all trains (with the exception of four small groups bound to Bergen-Belsen in 1944) would make the one-day journey to Auschwitz. Of the 2,000 persons who departed this date on Transport Cq, 240 were chosen for work. Two survived the war.

13. A loose paragraph in the diary, which some suggest should be joined to January 22. The reference is to an outgoing transport, while the entry of the 22nd relates to an incoming transport of Czechs from Zlin. The entry is penciled "1/21."

14. Another of Redlich's brothers, born in 1904.

15. Transport Cr carried two thousand Jews to Monowitz. Of two hundred young persons selected from various labor tasks, three survived the death camps.

tration camp. From there, they sent him to the ghetto. Now they send him eastward. Much work, nervous tension. . . .

January 26, 1943. Eppstein came today, the head of the *Reichsvereinigung* [Association of Jews in Germany].[16] It's possible he will be appointed Elder of the Jews. I have been told they will abolish the concentration camps and send the wretched prisoners east to build fortifications.[17]

January 27, 1943. What is going to happen? Every one of us is waiting for the end and hopes it will come quickly. Still, two more transports will go. I had hoped there would be a break for a few days, but I was mistaken.

January 28, 1943. A great deal of tension. Transports will be arriving. No one knows what is going to happen. Perhaps they will close the *Zentralstelle* offices and send the Jewish leaders here.[18] I am sorry for Yaakov [Edelstein]. But in my opinion, he has nothing to regret.

January 29, 1943. The change in ghetto leadership has brought great confusion.[19] Today they decided that Murmelstein would take Zucker's place. Edelstein would be second, Murmelstein third.[20]

16. Dr. Paul Eppstein (1901–1944) was a Zionist socialist from Mannheim. Redlich was correct in anticipating he might replace Edelstein as Elder in the ghetto. See entry January 29, 1943. The arrival of German Jews prompted the SS to designate Dr. Henrich Stahl of the Berlin community as Edelstein's deputy in October. When he died, Dr. Desider Friedmann from Vienna was his successor. Eppstein proved to be an unpopular choice with many of the ghetto's residents who considered him weak and theatrical. He would be shot in the Little Fortress in October 1944 (Lederer, 43–44, and Adler, 116).

17. Eppstein arrived with incoming transport I/86, one hundred persons from Berlin. At the same time, Transport Cs departed with one thousand persons. One hundred were taken to the Goleslov quarry. Thirty-nine survived. The rest were exterminated immediately. Redlich's optimism was misplaced.

18. The Nazi's *Zentralstelle für judische Auswanderung* in Prague, which functioned as a unit of Eichmann's Office IVB4 of the RSHA. In August 1943, the name was changed to *Zentralamt zur Regelung der Judenfrage in Böhmen und Mahren*. Jewish leaders in Prague, as well as in the ghetto were under its supervision.

19. On January 27, SS Sturmbannführer Möhs informed Terezin's Jews that Dr. Eppstein would now be *Judenältester* assisted by Edelstein as his first deputy and Dr. Löwenherz of Vienna as his second. Four days later, Dr. Benjamin Murmelstein replaced Löwenherz.

20. Murmelstein was a rabbi who taught ancient Jewish History (including Josephus) in Austria. The only major figure to survive Terezin, he succeeded Eppstein as Elder and was interrogated after the war about possible collaboration. The charges were dropped. Lederer compares his behavior to that of Josephus: "It appears that he saw himself as another Flavius Josephus, who undeterred by the vociferous contempt of his people, worked for its salvation" (Lederer, 166–67).

There is a great turmoil because they want to give a hallway where Prager and Brammer currently live to Dr. Kahn.[21] If they do this, it will be an act of injustice. The best children's ward is L417.[22]

January 30, 1943. Shabbat. A bombshell. A directive to change the leadership. Eppstein, Lowenherz, Edelstein. Today a change: Eppstein, Edelstein, Murmelstein. This fact as well as the arrival of the Prominents from Prague caused great commotion in the ghetto. Never were Edelstein and Zucker as popular as today. There may be some jealousy toward those who lived these past fourteen months in relative calm. Or perhaps the work of those people who have been here fourteen months has been recognized. I'm not enthusiastic about these developments.

January 31, 1943. My brother has arrived. I am so tired. I have been working day and night for ten days. I may be getting sick.
My attitude toward my beloved is very good now.

February

The cold winter months, overcrowding and malnutrition brought on one of Terezin's deadliest epidemics. Redlich employs the generic term "typhus," but the nature of the malady and the hunt for its locus suggest that it was typhoid.

February 1, 1943. The Germans sent the different "leaders" here only to cause quarrels and confusion in the ghetto. Perhaps they think if the situation continues without rancor or strife it might pose a danger to them.

21. Fritz Prager (see entry November 23, 1942) and Honzo Brammer worked in the *Jugendfürsorge* and lived together in an enclosed hallway of the Magdeburg barrack. They were to give up this room to Dr. Franz Kahn (1895–1944), a leader of the Czech *Histadrut.* Kahn had lost an arm in combat fighting as an Austrian officer in World War I. Kahn postponed emigrating to Palestine when the Nazis seized Czechoslovakia. Ruth Bondy salutes his spiritual force in Prague and Terezin.
22. On the 29th, Transport Ct with one thousand passengers began its odyssey through Monowitz, Buchenwald, Oranienburg, and Ohrdruf. Twenty-three persons survived.

February 2, 1943. Mandler was beaten "bloody."[1] He is lying down now in a sick room. Some Jews are glad. Revenge against the wicked. I am not pleased. Of course he sinned. But who is fit to cast the first stone?[2]

February 3, 1943. Now what will happen? Yesterday Mandler was beaten. What will happen tomorrow? Perhaps "Avengers of Israel" will rise up and attack every man against whom there is a personal grievance. A dangerous precedent.[3]

February 4, 1943. A dreadful epidemic. Typhus [sic] among children.[4] Generally typhus isn't harsh among children. But here it is very severe. There is great excitement among parents.

February 5, 1943. Discussions, consultations, how to protect oneself against typhus. Everyone expresses his opinion, suggests, writes memos. Everyone wants to supervise. Everyone wants to uncover the source of the disease.

February 6, 1943. Shabbat. Typhus. Two children have died. We have reached the danger point which I feared. Everyone—Löwenstein, Morgenstern,[5] and all the other Prominents want to know the reason, to find out what is the focus of the disease. Parents are frightened. They are looking for guilty parties. Everyone blames the other. Today a meeting took place without a concrete program.

February 7, 1943. In my opinion, the fundamental mistake in health matters is that each department is sending representatives to supervise. The result is tension. We urgently need a single, central supervising body which knows the limits of what is possible.

1. Mandler collaborated in the deportations from the Protectorate. Later he was sent to the ghetto where some Jews were waiting for revenge. See entry March 5, 1942.

2. Transport Cu carried 1,001 persons to Auschwitz this date. Of 219 selected for labor, 29 eventually were liberated at the Gusen labor camp in 1945. The transport was the last until September 1943.

3. There is sarcasm and some private fear in Redlich's reference. Those who knew him indicate that as a humanist Gonda disapproved of beating as a form of revenge.

4. The entry says "typhus," and survivors insist that this was the disease. Curda-Lipovsky mentions an outbreak of spotted typhus in Litomerice at this time (208). All evidence, however, points to typhoid. To prevent the spread of the disease, the Nazis halted outgoing transports, something they never did when faced with typhus. They also expressed concern over the water supply and possible contamination of the Ohre River. Redlich's diary indicates a general hunt for "the person responsible." See entry February 10, 1943. For a comparison of typhoid and typhus, see also note to November 28, 1942, entry.

5. Dr. Paul Morgenstern, a professor who worked with the hygiene unit.

February 8, 1943. Some children have died. I fear the disease will not pass. But I hope the overall effect of the disease will be easier, that the children will not die.[6] The dying children, the future of the people—even if the end comes, they will not survive.

February 9, 1943. The infants' dormitory. One mother nurses her infant. She has enough milk for another child but doesn't want to breast-feed another baby. Even if she suffers great pressure in her breasts which are filled with milk. Now her husband drinks the milk instead of other infants who are dying for lack of milk.

February 10, 1943. They are looking for the center of the contamination. They thought the focus might be in the children's kitchen. But a strange fact—no kitchen attendant is sick. Only two helpers who handle the food. Perhaps the utensils and pots were contaminated.[7] Who knows?

February 11, 1943. Today a high-ranking German doctor from Prague will be coming. We were ordered to secure a white coat for this guest who will inspect all the sick who are ill with contagious diseases. A few days ago, there was a discussion about what to do. How to defend oneself against the disease. The suggestions were childish. They demonstrated that many of us do not fully comprehend the situation.

February 12, 1943. Many children have died. But we are living through the fourth year of the war. In the last year of World War I, thousands of children died of tuberculosis. I know this fact will not console the parents of the dead children.

February 13, 1943. The constant arguments among the leadership are meaningless and frequently dangerous. It drains you. Add to this the constant threat of typhus. It may have abated, but we still don't know what the incubation period is and when the next wave will come.

February 14, 1943. The disputes between the leaders of the ghetto continue to grow. If we argue so much today, what will happen afterward? There is a chance, at least, that the arguments among the Zionists won't be as serious, for the assimilationists will attack the Zionists and this may prompt the Zionists to unite.

February 15, 1943. The workers here are not really workers in their hearts. They don't appreciate the significance of their class. For ex-

6. There were 80 deaths among the 839 cases of typhoid in 1943 (Lederer, 138-40).
7. Another indication that the sickness was typhoid.

ample, all day they criticize the new Jewish leader [Eppstein] and at night they applaud when he speaks to them.

February 16, 1943. What have I learned in Hebrew here in the ghetto? First of all, I have learned Talmudic literature (Mishnah, sections of Gemara, etc.). I have learned much with [Rabbi] Weiss.

February 17, 1943. They imprisoned Friedmann[8] because they caught a guest of his smoking. It's a shame not only for him. I had hoped he might be a mediator between Yaakov [Edelstein] and Zucker. Now I don't know who will be able to work out a compromise between them.

February 18, 1943. Judgment of the court. A man who spat in the street was sentenced to forty-eight hours in jail. This is vital for the general welfare. Nevertheless, we don't have the freedom to spit on the streets.[9]

February 19, 1943. Several of my acquaintances have died. Typhus is a harsh disease. Much news. Tomorrow will be census day.[10]

February 20, 1943. Shabbat. A small quarrel with Gerti. Maybe it happens to every married couple. Eichmann's visit: typhus must disappear from the ghetto or it will be bad.[11] Census day was successful.

February 21, 1943. We have moved our office. The Germans ordered that typhus must be stamped out soon. One of the counselors left the city with a group of children, and the commandant met him and ordered him to be imprisoned.[12]

8. Redlich uses the Hebrew "Ish Shalom" for Dr. Desider Friedmann (1890–1944), who served as Edelstein's aide in the *Ältestenrat* from November 1942 to January 1943.

9. Among Commandant Seidl's greatest sources of anger were smoking, *Papierschnitzel* (discarding paper), and spitting. Violators were threatened with severe punishment. A major duty for artists (Bedrich Fritta, Otto Ungar, Leo Haas, Alfred Kantor, etc.) was to draw up signs warning the ghetto population to "wash your hands after going to the latrine and before eating" and to "guard yourself against typhoid!"

10. Instead of the traditional monetary "shekel," Hechalutz members paid in food to be used for sick members of the movement (Schmiedt, 113).

11. Eichmann personally had been responsible for the *Auflockerung* (thinning out) of the ghetto to Auschwitz in January 1943. The outbreak of typhoid threatened shipments eastward as well as the existence of his *Musterghetto* (model ghetto). See Arendt, 81.

12. Some youths farmed or were allowed walks outside the ghetto walls. Apparently this leader was not carrying his permit.

February 22, 1943. There was a barrel that was almost empty. Only a little millet on the bottom. Two men were fighting in order to get at the grain. A sight for tears. And outside the sun is shining. The weather is radiant.

February 23, 1943. A man has arrived from Vienna. A few days after he arrived, the Germans ordered us to give him two rooms, one in which to live and the other for study. The man promised to come up with the medicine against all types of diseases. A high-ranking officer whose wife was cured by this man announced that this Jew was a great researcher. The Germans believed him. But after a while, they found out that he was a fraud. They had him beaten, then imprisoned on the pretext that they wanted to protect him.

February 24, 1943. How did the camp commandant [Seidl] become an enemy of the Jews? When he was fourteen years old, his parents lost their wealth. A Jew cheated them. This Jew came here. The camp commandant struck him and punished him with imprisonment. As a personal revenge, this Jew was deprived of food every other day. An old man.

February 25, 1943. They don't imprison Jews in the basement of camp quarters because they imprison German soldiers there.[13]

February 26, 1943. Rumor has it that people in the factories will work twelve hours a day, seven days a week. There won't even be a day of rest on Shabbat. An interesting thing that evil rumors are spreading and they contain no truth.

February 27, 1943. Shabbat. A day of twelve hours work without the Sabbath rest. It's not certain that this thing will be implemented. An

---

13. Jews could be sent to the *Kleine Festung*, the earth-covered fortress that served as the original base of Terezin. Prisoners marched out the *Schleusenmühle*, across a viaduct, and disappeared through a stripped brick entry. More than thirty thousand prisoners passed through the Little Fortress. Thousands were tortured, shot, or hanged. Women were placed in solitary confinement, while four to six hundred men were squeezed into Death Cell 44 (Vaclav Novak, ed., *Terezin: Dokumenty* [Archiv Pamatniku Terezin, 1974], 70-71). Watching the sick inmates from afar, Ruth Bondy commented, "I sat many hours without guard, opposite the Little Fortress, and in my heart I felt great pity for [them]" (Bondy Testimony, Hebrew University Oral History Project, #47). From a cell within the Little Fortress, Rostislav Korcak wrote: "My heart is in a jail, from summer to winter. I hold my head high. Who persists will win a prize." See "Mam Hlavu Zprima," 12, in *Mala pevnost terezin.*

interesting psychological fact. Rumors are being spread.[14] For example, they say that Churchill is dead, etc.

February 28, 1943. A dispute with the head of the Jewish police [Löwenstein]. He interferes everywhere. He wants to oversee every department of the ghetto. The ghetto administration does not block him and he thinks he's all powerful.

March

Whether because of official duties, family matters, or simply the size of paper he was using for the diary, Redlich's entries became much shorter, some no more than a dozen words. Still, it is possible to gain glimpses of manpower shortages, the infusion of Viennese Jews, and the staging of cultural events in the ghetto. Several entries highlight once more the dilemma of converts who were forced into the ghetto.

March 1, 1943. My brother's mother-in-law wrote a letter home filled with anger against me. I don't know, but it seems to me that after the war many of my acquaintances will vilify me because I did not concern myself with them or help them.

I am starting to like serious music more. Today I attended a performance of *Ein Lied geht um die Welt.*[1]

March 2, 1943. German women are now searching our barracks.[2] They have already found money with people who were [actually] innocent and imprisoned them. The weather is so nice. It seems spring is coming earlier than usual.

14. Redlich employs ghetto slang, "J.P.P." signifying "jedna pani providada" or "one woman said."

1. A song popularized by the Jewish tenor Josef Schmidt (1904–1942). A refugee interned in a Swiss labor camp, Schmidt suffered a fatal heart attack when he was denied admission to a hospital by the Swiss.

2. Random searches had been conducted through the year. See entry March 6, 1942, for punishment of women in Room 34 of the Dresden barrack.

March 3, 1943. Next to our barracks is a pile of wood. Boys play war games around it. They don't know that outside, in the big world, tens of thousands of soldiers are paying for this desperate game in blood.

March 4, 1943. The [German] women who searched the Jewish belongings have been imprisoned.[3]

A transport will be arriving from Prague.[4]

A number of youths who worked in the post office stole food from packages. We wanted to dismiss them from the post office, but the camp commandant forbade this.[5]

Two young men stole potatoes. They didn't eat them themselves but passed them on to their commune. The counselor knew it. The police investigated the incident and handed over the counselor to us for punishment. We know the guilty parties, who are, by nature, decent people. So we limited the punishment to a strong rebuke. But the chief of the Jewish police is not pleased, and he is demanding a stronger punishment. Another matter: a youth killed a cat and ate it. What is the reason? hunger? cruelty?

March 5, 1943. There aren't enough workers to build huts for those sick with typhus, to pave the highway that runs around the city so that Aryans will not pass the ghetto,[6] to work with disinfection of lice, etc. There aren't enough people, and the departments are required to send their clerks for this work. It goes without saying that the clerks aren't happy and are angry with me.

March 6, 1943. Shabbat. There is a shortage in manpower for different jobs. The department releases people, but they aren't happy. Their anger falls upon my head. It's said that some youths caught a cat somewhere and ate it. (Afterwards, it turned out the animal was a rabbit.) Is this cruelty or what? And what, in fact, can be done about

3. The women took goods for themselves and were punished.

4. Lederer notes the arrival of 1,021 persons from Prague on March 6, one of the last large contingents of Czech Jews to enter Terezin until January 1945.

5. Approximately two hundred persons worked in the postal service, which had been sanctioned when ghetto residents were permitted to send and receive mail on September 24, 1942. Many employees were, as Adler calls them, "Lumpen" (bums) who intercepted parcels and turned the contents over to the SS. How else explain the light punishment meted out to individuals who hosted a December 31, 1942, New Year's gala where each guest received a two-kilogram package of food. Apprehended on February 16, they were placed in custody for three months (Adler, 128).

6. Originally the Litomerice-Prague road passed through Terezin. To prevent contact with Jews, a detour was constructed around the walls.

it? Or the stealing of potatoes when the thief (should the word be placed in quotes?) hands the potatoes over to his commune?

March 7, 1943. Now they are sending youngsters here, fourteen years and older, sons of mixed families. They told us that Christian mothers, whose husbands are Jewish and whose children were taken from them, protested against the evil at the railroad station.[7]

March 8, 1943. For the first time, I attended a gay, happy cabaret. There is almost no leadership in the ghetto now. We miss the absence of a strong [leadership] core.

March 9, 1943. The weather is nice. When you go out of the barracks, you see the high hills from afar. For sixteen months, the mountains have been standing out there waiting. When will the gates of the city open?

March 10, 1943. The nursery sits on the street which automobiles pass on the way into the city. Perhaps the passengers hear the cries of babies who suffer blamelessly.

March 11, 1943. A young married woman. A young man from Transport Ak[8] married her in order to save her from the [outgoing] transports. After a while, they became acquainted and found happiness with one another. Now they have imprisoned the young man because they found money on him. What will happen? Will the woman (who is sick) go with him to the East or not?

March 12, 1943. The matter of those recuperating is very difficult. No one knows if they are still typhus carriers. There are differences of opinion among the doctors on this subject.[9]

March 13, 1943. Shabbat. Wonderful days. But everyone is terribly tired, tired of arguments, intrigues, callousness.

7. Jewish husbands of Christian women were protected until the fall of 1944.

8. Three hundred forty-two persons came into Terezin from Prague on this transport, November 24, 1941. Redlich's concern is misplaced here, since there were no outgoing transports till September.

9. As the typhoid epidemic subsided, several barracks were set aside as convalescent homes. L216 near the Brunnenpark was reserved for children. Later, the *Ältestenrat* would designate Sudstrasse 1 as the *Kindererholungsheim.* One hundred children recovering from tuberculosis would be moved and gassed in Birkenau in the fall of 1944 (Adler, 563).

Many *Bnai Ta'arovot*[10] have arrived. They haven't the faintest idea of Judaism. They simply were taken from their Catholic parents, Lutherans, etc., and brought here. How can these children grasp the fate of a people to whom they don't belong? What links them to us?

March 14, 1943. What do children from mixed families (the father or mother is a Gentile) have in common with our fate? Most of them did not even know of their Jewishness till they arrived here. And now they must bear the fate of their blood, the fate of the Jewish people that comes and goes forever, from generation to generation.

March 15, 1943. Four years of hard persecution. Almost four years of war. The time goes by quickly.

March 16, 1943. What are we to do with the young people who stole turnips twice from the basement? Is it sufficient to lock them up for five hours? Or what to do with the youth who steal from the mail?

March 17, 1943. Herzl's daughter died.[11] We want to set up a juvenile court.

March 18, 1943. Bubatron [Puppet Theatre].[12] A simple Czech story without meaning. In spite of this, the children enjoyed it. They applauded. The question of orphans is heartrending because we have approximately five hundred children without parents.[13] A feud between Fredy Hirsch and Inq. Zucker. It isn't pleasant for me.

March 19, 1943. Berlin. They took children from a mother who worked in a factory for the sake of Germany's victory and brought them here.

10. Redlich employs the Hebrew for mixtures, of *Mischlinge*, children of mixed marriages. Mentioned in his March 7 entry, the largest contingent came in among 1,342 persons from Berlin on March 18.

11. Trude Herzl Neumann left a pathetic ten-page diary, chronicling her journey from Vienna to Terezin. She meticulously notes all of her belongings and the difficulties she had in retrieving them in the ghetto. Before her paper gave out, she wrote about the food, visits of nurses, and proposed meetings with Yaakov Edelstein. One letter to the *Ältestenrat* invoked the memory of "the deceased Zionist leader Dr. T. Herzl" in order to obtain help with her accommodations in L124. She was cremated with twenty-three others. At her funeral on March 17, Rabbi Albert Schoen declared, "Had we appreciated Herzl's personality and acted according to his leadership, we would not have been in our present situation." See Trude Herzl file, Beit Terezin Archives.

12. Eva Sormova claims that Gustav Schorsch of the Prague Dramatic Conservatoire staged the premiere of Peter Kien's puppet theater for the children ("Theatre under the Hardest Conditions" in Pechova, 35).

13. Technically, the *Jugendfürsorge* was responsible for designating guardians of children whose parents were either deported, in concentration camps, or dead (Adler, 475).

An interesting club with Dr. Baumel.[14] The teacher Weiss tells of his life.

March 20, 1943. Four people died after the disinfection.[15] The room was not aired out properly.

Celebration of Purim.

Today I wanted to stop a man that was about to enter the ghetto without a star.[16] When he turned to the Aryan street, I saw he was an Aryan.

March 21, 1943. They beat a man to death. Four people died after the disinfection in their rooms. Today I wanted to stop a man who had no Jewish badge. We aren't used to seeing people without a Jewish badge.

March 22, 1943. The weather is nice. Springtime is very pleasant. At night, the moon shines. A bright light and a chill is cast over this city filled with the wretched and diseased.

March 23, 1943. I worked in the garden till after noon.[17] I was happy. I played soccer.[18]

March 24–25, 1943. I saw the opera *Das Ghettomadel* yesterday.[19] The play was a shame, from a cultural perspective. To venerate a policeman in the ghetto is a strange and disgraceful thing. Young girls participated in the play, and this was a worse shame. It would have been

14. A psychologist who with his wife started a program in Terezin for exceptional children, from the disturbed to morons. See also entry April 1, 1943.

15. Until it was damaged by a fire in August 1942, the former Brauhaus at L506 was used for decontamination. One thousand people could be processed each day. Clothes and other items were deloused in two kettles and eight gas chambers that used the same gas (Zyklon B, hydrogen cyanide) employed at Auschwitz. When the typhoid epidemic became rampant, some of the HCn was used in barracks. Lingering traces may have killed some people (Adler, 132 and 511).

16. Another reference to the mandatory Jewish badge.

17. For this garden tended by youths ages thirteen to sixteen, see note, February 4, 1942.

18. Apart from schoolwork, the children kept busy with a number of competitions—gymnastics, chess, even a form of table football played with buttons. Most important, however, was soccer. Every unit had its own team, uniforms, pennant. Children collected all sorts of things—razor blade wrappers, money, programs of cultural events—but the most prized memento was a soccer pennant (memoir of Jehuda Bacon in Adler, 553-57).

19. An operetta composed by members of the Jewish Police and performed by their families. Written with support of Loewenstein for the sake of improving the image of the police. Two girls from L410 participated.

right to stop the play, but those responsible did not have sufficient authority to do so.

March 26, 1943. A house of prayer. Jews pray in the *Freizeitgestaltung* [free time or cultural activities] hall. In the back of the hall are dancers, actors, a stage. There aren't any orthodox among us, for the real orthodox would not pray in a hall such as this.[20]

March 27, 1943. Shabbat. One day, I would have wanted, like Kisch,[21] to collect the oddities of the ghetto: prayers of Catholics, evangelicals, Jews, a play *Das Ghettomadel*, interesting types from the houses of the Prominents, etc.

March 28, 1943. People worship God in strange ways here. Terezin may be the only ghetto in the world where prayers are said according to the rituals of Catholics or Protestants. Catholics and Protestants pray under one roof. Here those two churches have made peace with one another. The Protestants pray before a picture of the Holy Virgin that was placed there for Catholic ritual. The two churches are reconciled. When things deteriorate, divisions give way before the victorious cross.

March 29, 1943. There is no news. They are organizing the *Freizeitgestalung*[22] and want to divide the department into several subdivisions.

March 30, 1943. I want to start a new newspaper of criticism and cultural matters.

March 31, 1943. I am currently reading a book called *Gehinom shel Matah*,[23] on prisoners in the Great War. How like our situation. I find many expressions which I can use for my diary.

20. See also note to entry January 2, 1943.
21. Egon Kisch was a popular journalist from Prague who escaped to Mexico.
22. The Nazis were sticklers for slogans and regimentation. As Adler points out, they exhorted Germans to "Kraft durch Freude" and Czechs to "Freude am Leben." Jews were also to have their "organized free time." One hundred thirty-one full-time employees and many volunteers worked with Professors Emil Utitz and Dr. Maximilian Adler coordinating different cultural activities. Among these were theater (in German, Yiddish, and Czech), music (opera, vocal, orchestra, piano and popular), lectures (on everything from the Talmud to chess instruction), libraries, and sports (soccer, volleyball, basketball, handball) [Adler, 240, 276, 586-87].
23. "Hell of a Lower Depth" written by the Hebrew author Avigdor Hameiri.

April

As the Passover festival of freedom was commemorated, the residents of Terezin were confined to quarters, without access to lights for two weeks. The only concession granted by the Nazi Referents: the Jews might supplement their normal daily ration of 370 grams of bread by baking fifty thousand leavened rolls in the former military bakery. Redlich also notes the arrival of Dutch Jews who were deceived about conditions in the ghetto.

April 1, 1943. In one of the girls' rooms, you can see signs of sadomasochism.[1] The teacher wanted to punish the girls and spoke with them about the punishment. The girls suggested slaps, pinching, striking the legs. It's difficult to determine at first glance if the matter is serious. Doctor Baumel wants to inspect the children's drawings.

April 2, 1943. It seems I have gotten used to deciding too quickly, without proper reflection. This habit crops up everywhere.

April 3, 1943. Shabbat. A woman who arrived here last year in Transport H was sent on a transport to Riga.[2] She apparently escaped, becoming pregnant in the meantime. At present, she is locked up in the ghetto. The child is in the infants' home.

April 4, 1943. One woman came here with Transport H and left the ghetto in Transport O. Now they have brought her from Vienna to the ghetto a second time.[3] Meanwhile, the woman became pregnant and gave birth to a girl a few months ago. The child is in the infant house. The mother is in prison.

April 5, 1943. A barrel contained remnants of dried peas. Old people circle the barrel and want to scrape out the remnants. The cook chases them away saying: "I don't want to catch lice."

1. For the psychologist Dr. Baumel, see entry March 19, 1943. It appears Redlich and others detected ominous signs in the drawings.
2. H was the second transport from Prague with one thousand deportees on November 30, 1941. The woman was on Transport O to Riga in January 1942. One hundred two persons survived. See entry below, April 4, 1943.
3. Two transports, IV/14f and IV/14g arrived from Vienna in the first two days of April with 101 and 72 persons respectively.

April 6, 1943. Tomorrow, an inspection [team] will come from Prague. I don't like these inspections.

April 7, 1943. Erich[4] described the situation in the hospital for us. Those sick with high temperatures see visions and leap out of bed. A terrible sight.[5]

April 8, 1943. Six men ran away.[6] For this reason, it is forbidden to go out into the streets, to put on lights, or perform any cultural activities.[7]

April 9, 1943. There is a city in the Protectorate. A Jew with three children was left there to wind up affairs for the community. One moment, in the evening, there was a knocking at the door. He opened it and was attacked by some men. He managed to shut the door quickly and phoned for help from the Czech police. After a couple of days they summoned him to the Gestapo and sent him eastward. The reason: he used a telephone but not for official purposes. His three children, whose mother had died, were left alone. The community's administration promised they would not be sent here [to the ghetto]. Yesterday, the children arrived.

April 10, 1943. Shabbat. Last night, an official delegation inspected the childrens' quarters. Everything was found to be all right.

April 11, 1943. Sometimes it's difficult to tell where the [limit of the] "ordinary man" ends and "the chief" begins. The man in charge of the children's kitchen gets his food from this kitchen. Officially he doesn't deserve it, but his wife (who worked with me for fourteen months) is very sick.

The son of one of the clerks wants to work in the bakery. We forbade it. I don't permit exceptions. What will happen? The clerk will seek revenge at the expense of the children or, better yet, will not treat them nicely.

4. Dr. Erich Munk (1910–1944), director of health services in the ghetto. See July 17, 1944. There are contradictory assessments of this man. Adler claims (500–501) Munk was an unfortunate choice to head this vital department because he was vain, dictatorial, surrounded by corrupt elements. Other survivors recall him more favorably as a man whose integrity was irreproachable. Like most of the *Ältestenrat* leaders, Dr. Munk was deported to Auschwitz in the fall of 1944.

5. The diary does not specify the disease, which probably was typhoid.

6. It was possible for people working outside of the ghetto to slip away from the gendarmes who supervised them in gardens or along highways. A hostile and frightened Czech populace made escape virtually impossible. See the tragic entry of January 25, 1943.

7. The punishment remained in effect for a month. See May 11 entry.

April 12, 1943. Yaakov Wurzel[8] is going to be "a pioneer." He will work in agriculture. Members of the inner circle think that thereby they have reached an important decision. Actually, this is nonsense. Sometimes they are like little children.[9]

April 13, 1943. There are many people here who want to work hard so they won't have to think too much. Unfortunate people. Through work, they forget.

April 14, 1943. Sonya Okun is an interesting young woman.[10] She is forty-three years old but looks thirty. She has a scar on her neck and cancer. Twenty years ago, they tried to heal her with X-rays, but did not cover her neck. They burned it badly with a deep wound.

April 15, 1943. Sonya [Okun] related how she came from Russia at age five. Her parents fled during the pogroms [of 1919]. Sonya was a member of the young socialist movement. But after a few years, she joined a Zionist youth group. She knows Kathe Kollwitz,[11] Erich Kastner,[12] and others.

April 16, 1943. The day after tomorrow is the first day of Passover. The spring festival, a festival of freedom—in the city which is surrounded by high walls, in the prison camp where captives are forbidden to light a light in the evening or go out of the houses.

April 17, 1943. Shabbat. Passover—a festival of freedom, of light, of freedom. Around the city are walls and barbed wire. In the evening, lights are forbidden. And during the day, you cannot go out.

April 18, 1943. There isn't any news.[13] But I forgot: if they imprison someone because of money matters, they beat him to death.

8. Nicknamed Jackie, a member of the Hechalutz leadership. A Hebrew teacher and a good counselor, he worked with Gonda in a Prague school for Youth Aliyah.

9. The ideological disputes among various Zionist groups had not subsided. Some favored physical work over education.

10. A relative of Dr. Eppstein, she molded scouts into the "Helping Hand," groups of five who secured food, put up shelves, and even washed the aged and crippled (Schmiedt, 122, and Bondy Testimony, Hebrew University Oral History Project, #47).

11. Kollwitz (1867–1945) was a German artist whose paintings made a powerful antiwar, anti-Nazi statement.

12. Author of *Emil and the Detectives* and other novels.

13. Redlich's diary reveals no knowledge of the Warsaw Ghetto uprising that took place during this Passover. Much has been written of the struggle of fifty thousand Jews from April 19 until the middle of May or June. It was not a significant military triumph (as SS Oberführer Jurgen Stroop portrayed in a seventy-five-page report to Berlin), nor a "bloody murder expedition" (the words of General Alfred Jodl). Rather, it was the final, heroic act of a desperate people in this particular Polish ghetto.

April 19, 1943. The festival of Passover. "Seven days where leavened must not be found in your houses."[14] Long lines of old Jewish men and women requesting matzos and Pesach food from the rabbis. They didn't get it. The lists were misplaced. Even in this matter *Protekzia* reigns.[15]

April 20, 1943. "In all your habitations you shall eat matzos." But here in the ghetto, they celebrated the seder and ate—rolls.[16] A strange act, a strange ghetto—strange Jews, a strange world. A celebration of Passover and for the seder they eat [leavened] bread.

April 21, 1943. The counselors who have been teaching the children for more than a year are very tired. They don't know what to do with the children. A difficult problem.

April 22, 1943. A transport from Germany will be arriving today.[17] The commandant is going on vacation and still has not canceled the ban on lights [in the evening] or going out [of the barracks]. If he doesn't cancel the ban this afternoon, we will remain dark another fourteen days.[18]

April 23, 1943. Yesterday, Jews arrived from Holland.[19]

April 24, 1943. Shabbat. Discipline continues to erode considerably. I mean discipline toward Jewish institutions. It is a sad phenome-

14. Redlich may have intended to use the word for light rather than leavened bread. There was a ban on lights at this time. See April 17 and 22 entries. Bondy attributes the mistake to a misspelling by Redlich.

15. Limited supplies of matzos were available for important people. Adler points out that it was virtually impossible for people to cling to traditional dietary laws in the ghetto. As he phrases it, "Religious life rarely deepened in the ghetto" (Adler, 609).

16. To commemorate the holiday in some way, the *Ältestenrat* circumvented the Nazi ban on baking of matzos by having the central bakery prepare fifty thousand rolls, one for each resident of the ghetto.

17. Only partially correct. The transport came via Germany but was made up of Dutch Jews. See following entry.

18. Redlich is vague about the lifting of the ban. See May 11 entry.

19. Two hundred ninety-five persons came from Amsterdam, the Hague and Naarden via the Westerbork transit camp on transport XXIV/1. They were the first of eleven Dutch transports to November 1944. Most scholars (Levin, Gerald Reitlinger, Raul Hilberg) estimate as many as 100,000 Dutch Jews killed in the Holocaust. Because of the typhoid epidemic, 35,000 were shipped directly to their deaths in Sobibor. The 4,897 in Terezin were the remnant of a deeply integrated, modern, progressive community (Nora Levin, *The Holocaust: The Destruction of European Jewry, 1933–1945* [New York: Schocken, 1973], 413). Adler notes that Dutch Jews were split into cliques (native-born vs. refugees) and had a superior attitude toward their kinsmen from Germany or Czechoslovakia (305-6).

non, the blame for which must be shared by two sides: the leaders that did not succeed in maintaining honor in a proper fashion without recourse to force and the masses who do not have enough inner discipline.

April 25, 1943. A woman from Holland related: "My child was with a Christian. He behaved well with him. I had the opportunity to leave the child with him and come here alone. Before the journey, the Germans told us that the ghetto was very beautiful, a large city with play areas and gardens, and that it was permitted to stay within twenty-five kilometers of the city." On the last night before the journey, she decided to take the child with her. Now she sees and is sorry.

April 26, 1943. The Dutch Jews brought chocolate and butter in their suitcases. Obviously when they got here, all of these things were taken from them. German officers[20] were not permitted entry into the ghetto.

April 27, 1943. Food is being distributed according to ration cards. A paper full of squares, each square for a day. If someone loses a small square, he doesn't get food. Those who lose their ration card get sent from office to office. In the end, they get hungry from running here and there and don't get the food anyway.[21]

April 28, 1943. Obedience to the administration is not great.

April 29, 1943. Sometimes, it seems to me you can see all the good and bad characteristics of democracy here. Orders often are carried out slowly. In spite of this, there is much tolerance here, sometimes too much.

April 30, 1943. A transport from Prague. They asked: how many Jews will be coming? Janeczek[22] answered: three boxcars of Jews.[23]

20. The SS apparently stopped the *Wehrmacht* from visiting.

21. The *Wirtschaftsabteilung* of the *Ältestenrat* employed more than one thousand people, whose duty it was to see that no one went hungry in the ghetto. The "Zentrale Essenkartenstelle" issued monthly ration cards bearing the name of the recipient, his barrack, and the kitchen where he was to eat. Each day, one stub would be removed from the card. If an individual lost his card, he was to receive a temporary one for three days (Adler, 372-73). Redlich's assessment is probably more accurate.

22. Oberleutnant Janeczek, head of the Czech gendarmes, was a collaborator and a brute. A Viennese who spoke only German, Janeczek accompanied SS Obersturmführer Bergel on his forays into the women's barracks to ferret out illegal visitors or smokers (Lederer, 78, and Adler, 84).

23. Forty-seven persons arrived this day.

May

The Nazis permitted the creation of a twenty-two-team soccer league, to perform along the ramparts. Against that excitement and the return of spring, Redlich also offers brief vignettes of personal tragedy. Note, however, references to petty squabbling and his repeated use of the word tolerance. In Hebrew, sovlanut *(tolerance) is quite similar to* savlanut *(patience) and it is clear that Redlich's patience has been exhausted.*

May 1, 1943. Tolerance. How far can it go? And later, who among those that we have put up with would believe that we have been tolerant? How would it all look if our situations were reversed?

May 2, 1943. The lager supervisor [Bergel] shot a cat and shouted: "This is how a camp supervisor shoots."

May 3, 1943. The administration does not act wisely on some matters. It isn't wise. The Eisinger affair[1] should be looked into and a solution found. The administration fears appearing intolerant. An administration needs strength, not fear. Even fear seems like a lack of tolerance. Surely, fear is nourished by weakness.

May 4, 1943. A man came to the office and showed us his papers: during the First World War, he was an Austro-Hungarian spy in the United States.

May 5, 1943. One of the young girls stole a head of lettuce.[2] Her punishment is five weeks in prison.

May 6, 1943. The sister of Walter Rathenau asked for a job.[3]

1. Redlich may be referring to Walter Eisinger (1913–1945) who had been a Czech language teacher at the Jewish Secondary School in Brno. In Terezin, he served as a counselor in barracks L417. A communist, he antagonized some officials by trying to develop a "Republic Skid" based on a similar children's commune in St. Petersburg after the Bolshevik Revolution.
2. Garden vegetables were produced for the German commandant. The girl was punished when gendarmes found her smuggling.
3. Rathenau (1867–1922) was a Jewish industrialist who served as Germany's Foreign Minister in the wake of World War I. Credited with engineering a diplomatic coup

May 7, 1943. The Red Cross sent a boxcar full of condensed milk and dried vegetables to the ghetto.

May 8, 1943. Shabbat. Mother's Day. How many mothers are celebrating this day without fear for their chlidren?

May 9, 1943. There is great anger in the room of the Hechalutz. Rudy Sachsl, a foolish and ridiculous boy, used the pages of the *siddur* [prayer book] for toilet paper. Now you can see the difference between the East and West. We view this as an improper act. But this thing strikes at the very soul of *chaverim* coming from the east, and even those people who are not Orthodox.

May 10, 1943. I don't have time to work outside now. Yesterday, I was at the "Bastei" playing field.[4] The field is very nice.

May 11, 1943. They canceled the order against going out. They are permitting *Freizeitgestaltung* [free-time activities] again.

May 12, 1943. Yesterday, for the first time, I attended an experimental theater. The performance took place in an attic. You can learn a lot here.

May 13, 1943. I wondered today: will we ever see forests or hills again? Will we ever see nature in its full glory? We have become accustomed to this cage. We have lost our desire for the great world outside.

May 14, 1943. There isn't any news. I am writing a story which takes place during the Children's Crusade.[5]

May 15, 1943. Shabbat. The start of soccer championships on the ramparts. Twenty-two were chosen in different uniforms.[6] Sometimes it is possible to forget we are in a ghetto.

at Rapallo in the spring of 1921, he was vilified and subsequently assassinated by right-wing extremists.

    4. Redlich had strolled the ghetto's walls a year earlier looking for possible fields for recreation. Each of the earthen ramparts at the corners of Terezin fortress offered potential as a playing field for soccer. The best was situated at Sudberg, just behind the *Jaegerkaserne* for men. Guards in watchtowers kept an eye on the activity lest a youth pursuing a ball decided to escape. But, as Eli Bachner noted, "We had no interest in fleeing" (Bachner Interview, Hebrew University Oral History project, #19).

    5. 1212–1256.

    6. Each group of workers subsidized a particular soccer team. The games offered a break from the melancholy life of the ghetto. For young people, they were an opportunity for a rendezvous with the opposite sex (Bachner Interview, Hebrew University Oral History Project, #19).

May 16, 1943. This is a typical Jew's fate. Professor Aaron died at age eighty-six. After the Great War, the French imprisoned him in Strasbourg because he was a German supporter, and he spent some time in jail. From there, the French exiled him to Germany. Till 1935, he was a professor in Germany. His first son was an officer on the Eastern Front. His eldest daughter made Aliyah to Eretz Yisrael. The second was sent with him here. That is the fate of a Jew: a son fights against the Bolsheviks. A daughter makes Aliyah to Palestine.

May 17, 1943. I read the book *Yerushalayim Mechakah [Jerusalem Waits]*. The author is a Revisionist,[7] and the book was written as a polemic against the Histadrut. In spite of this, you can tell the author is a true believer. In many ways, he is right. But in principle he is wrong.

May 18, 1943. More on *Yerushalayim Mechakah:* How does the author blame the Histadrut? He deals with them roughly because they blind the eyes of the people—the eyes of the workers who are hoping for the messiah. And they, the clerks of the Histadrut, administrators of the organization, say the messiah will not come. The messiah is dead. Only a token redemption will occur, the legacy of the messiah. The author becomes bitter about this and uses it to lash out against the Histadrut. Here is his mistake: the messiah surely will not come, only a slight or great improvement of the situation. We hope it will be great.

May 19, 1943. There is no news. They are preparing a grand opening for the "Bastei." I have been studying Hebrew for a while. Nevertheless, I am still frustrated in composing some opening words.[8]

May 20, 1943. My brother's father-in-law is very sick, and they want to move him. I filed an appeal on his behalf.

May 21, 1943. A woman received a package and in it was a key to her apartment. She doesn't know what it means.

7. Written by Joshua Heschel Yevin (1891–1970), a follower of Zev Jabotinsky who split with the World Zionist state with a Jewish majority on both sides of the Jordan River in Palestine. Jabotinsky was a fiery orator who argued for a mass movement of Jews from Europe during the interwar period because, as he saw it, "the town was burning." Revisionism stressed the virtues of bourgeois society (including a capitalist economy) as well as the need to engender *hadar* (pride) among Jewish youth. It is not to be confused with Marxist Revisionism (usually associated with victims of Stalinist purges) or the pseudohistorical claque that claims the Holocaust never happened.

8. Redlich was asked to make a statement at the opening of the soccer field. See entry May 23, 1943. His concern about what he was to say may have caused him to omit the entry for May 22.

May 23, 1943. Shabbat. A dedication of a sports field at the ramparts. A speech in Hebrew-Czech. Six thousand people. Certainly the only occurence of its kind in Europe.

May 24, 1943. Yesterday one of the elders remarked about the mass of youth: "They are the young. Now it is all right to die."

May 25, 1943. The weather is terrible. There is no news.

May 26, 1943. In a flyer today: "Be careful! Someone lost a small ring in a cake[9] today. Be careful in eating."

May 27, 1943. The fate of a Jew: a blind person, lost his sight in the war. His wife married him in order to save herself from the transports east, but now she does not care for him.

May 28, 1943. Today someone said to me that the blind man was a liar. Whatever the case, he is miserable. A man and a woman came from Amsterdam, only the two of them.[10] She is elegantly dressed in an expensive fur.

June

Instead of increasing the food allowance for people who were starving on a diet of mash, bread, potatoes, and coffee, the Nazis opened a library for Judaica in Terezin. During the last week of June, Commandant Seidl was replaced by another SS officer Anton Burger. Equally ruthless, the Austrian Burger was more meticulous than his predecessor.

May 29–June 5, 1943. [1] The railroad track has been completed.[2] The Jews have built [it]. The camp commandant [Seidl] has ordered an

9. *Buchta* was a small pastry, the national delicacy of Bohemia. Baked of ninety-five grams of white flour, five grams of sugar and margarine, it was considered a delicacy by some people.

10. Redlich is correct. Transport EZ brought two Jews from Holland on May 27. No more arrived until January 29, 1944.

1. A unique, weeklong entry.

2. The spur from Bohusovice now ran via Sudstrasse to the Frontier regiments'

especially nice steam engine and, with several Nazi officers, opened traffic on the railroad. At night, the officers celebrated so much they didn't know where they were. One of them called ghetto administrators and forced them to stay with him all night.

The production of crates for anti-freeze equipment has begun.[3] There is a serious shortage of workers. The juvenile court issued a judgment: ten days in prison for two youths who counterfeited Jewish police documents. After this judgment, it was learned that these two boys had stolen many packages. It is now necessary to have a juvenile prison.[4]

They have banned electrical [hot] plates and imprisoned their owners.

June 6, 1943. A mother writes to her son: I am sorry that I am a Christian. They took you from me, as if I were a bad animal. But even bad animals don't have their children taken away.

June 7, 1943. Yesterday, two German officers slapped each other. Both were drunk. A wonderful spectacle for the Jews, the "subhumans," according to racial law.

June 8, 1943. What is this in my blood? Is it not a drug that yearns for the forbidden? Is the forbidden truly forbidden?[5] We're looking for a room for young prisoners and cannot find a place.

June 9, 1943. I am sick. What do I have inside? A warm heart or a body of ice? Many people are being imprisoned now. It seems Jews have their spies that relay information to the Germans.

June 10, 1943. A lovable, pleasant child, adored by everyone in the children's house. Things have been disappearing in the shelter and they haven't found the thief. Yesterday one child said: "My candy has

barrack, thereby eliminating the two-kilometer walk for transports. See also entry March 11, 1942.

3. The *Wehrmacht* needed new starter units for its mechanized units, which had been devastated by the Russian winter. A makeshift assembly line was set up in Terezin's main square and the residents pressed into service assembling starting gear that came from Lodz and Germany. All told, 120,000 boxes were assembled and disassembled, as the SS used the *Kisten* boxes to impress visitors. Production ended in November, and few components ever made it to the front lines (Lederer, 89-90).

4. The Jewish jail, where punishment was primarily detention, was located in the Dresden barrack. The Jewish police were inconsistent in their law enforcement. In 1942, for example, there were 156 convictions for theft, 62 for "insults to the guard." By way of contrast, there were no murders and no rapes in the ghetto (Adler, 486-88).

5. All of this may refer back to Redlich's affair with Kamila Rosenbaum.

been stolen." Another child replied: "Candy. Today I received candy in trade for other food." So, they found the thief—the sweet, dear child.

June 11, 1943. More on the dear child. . . . The other youths wanted to hit him. Finally, the counselor succeeded in appeasing them. The child was reprimanded. They disciplined him, and the child said: "Forgive me." But in his heart, he did not care. A dear child. A child thief. A child in the Terezin ghetto.

June 12, 1943. A walk with Rabbi Baeck.[6] He truly seems to be a special, moral personality, a man of exceptional depth.

June 13, 1943. I am now the censor of the children's paper.[7] The literary value of the newspaper is really very great. But anyone who looks for a jot of Jewish spirit in the paper will look in vain.

June 14, 1943. I am learning Gemara now, the tract on idolatry. An interesting study.

June 15, 1943. A young girl tried to commit suicide. There were two young girl friends who loved each other. One of the friends disclosed her secret to me. Lesbian love. Another attempt at suicide.[8] A young man. Feelings of inferiority. Feelings of guilt.

June 16, 1943. The counselors don't know very much. One female instructor in geometry said that the area of a square is larger than its circumference. Her comparison is one between apples and oranges.

June 17, 1943. If you go to the place where food is distributed, you will always witness the same scene. People ask for soup, which is only warm water. People who receive parcels don't take the soup.

6. A Reform rabbi from Berlin, Baeck (1873–1956) helped organize the *Reichsvertretung der Deutschen Juden* when Hitler came to power and urged German Jews to wear the Star of David with pride. In Terezin, he lectured on Plato and Kant, served on the Altestenrat, and, after October 1944, assumed responsibility (with Frau Elisabeth von Stengel) for the *Jugendfürsorge* and *Altersfürsorge*. Adler (253) called him "the most profound thinker" and honorable leader in the ghetto. Gerald Green offers a more troubling image. Rabbi Baeck supposedly had information on mobile gassing vans as early as 1941 and on the operations of Auschwitz in 1943 and suppressed it, writing later: "Living in expectation of death by gassing would only be harder" (148). Baeck amazed even Eichmann by his capacity to stay alive. After the war, he taught religion and philosophy at the Hebrew Union College in Cincinnati. For another view on Rabbi Baeck, see Leonard Baker's *Days of Sorrow and Pain* (New York, 1978).

7. Possibly a reference to *Vedem* ("We're Leading"), a journal founded by Walter Eisinger and youth in L417.

8. For suicide statistics, see entry July 14–15, 1942.

June 18, 1943. What a wealth of material we have here for a sociologist. What you can see here with the care of youth alone![9] Where else can one find so many children who were taken from their parents to children's homes?

June 19, 1943. Shabbat. There is a daughter from a mixed marriage, adopted. She did not know until a short while ago that she was Jewish and adopted. Only after the journey here did her adoptive parents disclose it. Here in the ghetto, the girl of fourteen met her two brothers who did not know until yesterday that she existed. At the time of her meeting with her sixteen-year-old brother, they cried, "How could father do a thing like this?" And the girl that didn't feel anything toward her natural parents said: "Surely, they wanted to get rid of a bastard." She loves her adoptive parents and cannot understand that she is only an adopted child. "Indeed, Mother said that I inherited many of her characteristics." Mother said. . . .

June 20, 1943. There is no news. It's difficult to work in the ghetto. The administration is indecisive. They don't want to implement what we have decided. Or they generally cannot decide.

June 21, 1943. I am starting to play soccer.

June 22, 1943. An order to eliminate the group of policeman under the age forty-five in the ghetto police.[10]

June 23, 1943. Among the belongings of a dead Jew, they found a swastika. One of the youths wanted to leave the ghetto. Before his departure, he handed over ghetto money to a policeman at the gate. (It is forbidden to take this money out of the ghetto.) Because the boy gave the money of his own free will, he was imprisoned for three months. We will try to gain his release.

June 24, 1943. We were ordered to improve and beautify the administrative offices of the bank. They have ordered the cleaning of the windows in the houses. It seems they are expecting an inspection.

9. Ruth Bondy estimates that Redlich's charges in the *Jugendfürsorge* included one thousand children under the age of seventeen. Divided by sex and age into groups of twenty or thirty, they lived in barracks L417, L414 and L410 under the care of counselors and baby-sitters who based activities in a room dubbed the *Heim* or home.

10. The corruption and strutting of the *Ghettowache* had become too much even for the SS. See entry January 1, 1943. Löwenstein's police would be a factor in the replacement of Commandant Seidl. See June 27, 1943.

June 25, 1943. The food continues to worsen.[11] A sack of ten moldy cookies were found on a girl. Her parents work in supplies. They found two rotten lemons. They say that in the hospital, a girl who is critically ill lies next to her. They asked her for the lemons, but she didn't give them to the sick girl.

June 26, 1943. People who know Hebrew were ordered to translate and catalog books. It seems they want to send Hebrew books here for cataloging.[12]

June 27, 1943. The camp commandant [Seidl] will leave the ghetto.[13]

June 28, 1943. A delegation of newspaper men visited the ghetto.[14] They sent only young men to the hot showers. It was forbidden to answer questions of the delegates or to volunteer information. Only the camp commandant was to respond.

June 29, 1943. A boy from Agram [Zagreb] has come here. There, he lived with another man whose business was very mysterious. The youth's mother (he speaks ill of her) turned the man in to the authorities. They imprisoned both of them and brought the young man here.

11. Kathe Goldschmitt Starke also reported a decline in the diet during the summer months of 1943. Twenty grams of margarine were issued every other day, seventy grams of sugar every third day. Meals consisted of soup, potatoes, and a spoonful of what the Germans called goulash. Fruits were virtually unobtainable, leading to vitamin deficiencies noted in entry January 17, 1943. See also Starke, *Der Führer schenkt den Juden eine Stadt* (Berlin: Haude and Spenersche, 1975), 238.

12. The *Ghettozentralbucherei* (GZB) at L514 contained volumes ranging from classical music to Zionism, religion to science. Its importance to ghetto life was reflected in the number of patrons (115 in December 1942; 3,775 in October 1943). Jews in Terezin were to serve as a special *Bucherfassungsgruppe* for the museum planned in Prague (Adler, 606-7).

13. Lederer maintains Seidel's downfall stemmed in part from a clash between Eichmann and Hans Günther. As Seidl was considered Günther's man, it was relatively easy to exploit his blunders (namely, the creation of the paramilitary Jewish police, the typhoid outbreak, incidents of drunkenness). Seidl's successor was SS Obersturmführer Anton Burger, another Austrian Nazi who was notorious for his hatred of Czech Jews. In 1940, Burger helped clear Brno (Lederer, 75-76 and 90).

14. Members of the German Red Cross were included in this first visit to the ghetto. Despite a tour of workshops, homes of Prominents, the bank, and courts, Walter Hartmann relayed his shock at conditions to a Swiss colleague on the IRC (Meir Dworzecki, "The International Red Cross and Its Policy vis-a-vis the Jews in Ghettos and Concentration Camps in Nazi-occupied Europe," *Rescue Attempts During the Holocaust: Proceedings of the Second Yad Vashem International Historical Conference* [New York: Ktav and Jerusalem: Yad Vashem, 1974], 96).

June 30, 1943. They wanted to beat up Heinze Schuster.[15] Yaakov [Edelstein] "intervened" and persuaded the people not to hit him. But why is this intervention [necessary]? Why do they want to hit Heinz or Bondy?[16] Perhaps their manner toward the people wasn't good. Nevertheless, they only did what they were ordered.

July

Among the first decrees of Commandant Burger: a change in the names of streets from their previous lackluster numbers to Rathausgasse (Town Hall Street), Turmgasse (Tower Street), Badhausgasse (Bathhouse Street), etc. During the month of July, the Terezin grapevine worked efficiently, informing inhabitants of the invasion of Sicily and the ouster of Mussolini from power in Italy. Periodically, thereafter, Redlich had to suppress hope that the end of the war might be near.

July 1–7, 1943. My family has arrived.[1] It isn't easy to satisfy them. They don't understand the situation here. They simply do not understand. It's hard to explain reality to them. It's hard to explain. Today they beat to death a man who came on the transports.

July 7, 1943. It was commanded in the Order of the Day: all pregnant women are required to report their condition. They want to destroy the offspring of all women who are less than six months pregnant.[2]

15. Schuster (1915–1944) was a member of Maccabi Hatzair who eventually served on the Central Committee of Hechalutz. A work administrator in the ghetto, he was remembered fondly by Peter Lang, a member of the movement (Lang Testimony, Hebrew University Oral History Project, #181).

16. Bondy also was an official in the labor department.

1. A small trickle of Czech Jews continued to arrive in Terezin through the spring and summer months. Sixty came in from Brno on July 1 and were followed by 1,900 more before the end of the month. On the first transport were community leaders, some of whom were unpopular among ghetto youth.

2. Commandant Seidl had issued a similar order on April 8, 1943. It had no significance for Redlich at the time, for Seidl did not stringently enforce the rule. SS Obersturmführer Burger was a different story. He issued a follow-up decree in November.

July 8, 1943. Ruth Baeck has arrived.[3] I've heard her nerves aren't good.

July 9, 1943. Rumor has it that the camp commandant [Burger] has prohibited lipstick for the women.[4]

July 10, 1943. We learned about the *mitzvot* [commandments] of burying today. At this point, the instructor said: "There are many Jews who preferred to go eastward when they finished building the crematoriums here."[5]

July 11, 1943. People are saying that the American and British attack on Europe began yesterday.[6]

July 12–13. 1943. A young man ran away. He stole the citizenship papers of a friend and the permit of another to go outside the city. The farm workers can see the terrible torture [meted out] to those imprisoned in the Little Fortress.

July 14–15, 1943. Officials of the Prague community have arrived. I don't think that one is limited to useful work only in the ghetto. Our comrades in Prague have been working too. Despite this, I cannot relate to everyone nicely.

July 16, 1943. Three years ago, I loved a girl. (I'm not sure if it was love.)[7] Her father lived in a foreign land. Her mother, an historian,

Women in their seventh month aborted or faced deportation to the East. Only a handful approved by Burger were permitted to give birth. Gerty Baeck was among them. See March 16, 1944.

3. A relative of Leo Baeck, she was a former student of Gonda's. At one time, he may have been infatuated with this pretty, young girl (b.1925) who had a nervous breakdown. See entry July 16, 1943.

4. Even in the ghetto, apparently, some women tried to cling to their cosmetics. An equally tragic vanity was noted among French and Dutch women in Auschwitz by Polish-Jewish survivor Eva Fugman Jacobs (as related to a graduate seminar of Dr. Saul Friedman, Youngstown State, Oct. 20, 1971).

5. Some Jews preferred to be deported rather than participate in burning people who died in Terezin. Cremation is forbidden to traditional Judaism, which regards it as a desecration of the body. Burial alone is allowed according to Deuteronomy 21:23.

6. One more example of the underground ghetto news service operating with accuracy. On July 10, the British 8th Army under Montgomery and the American 10th Army commanded by Patton swarmed onto the shores of Sicily from Avola to Licata. With the knowledge that the Russians, too, were repulsing the Nazis, spirits soared in Terezin. That optimism may be reflected in Redlich's journal entries, which become even more cryptic.

7. Probably a reference to Ruth Baeck, noted July 8, 1943.

had an affair with another man. The girl discovered it. I took care of this girl for a long while. One day, she had a nervous breakdown. Later, she recovered. Now her sickness has returned. Her mother has cancer.

July 17, 1943. Shabbat. An exhibition of children's works. Interesting, very interesting! Terezin's problems come to full expression (a model of a bunk three stories high, repeated several times; the likeness of "the ghetto man";[8] sexual problems revealed in the drawings of a fourteen-year-old girl). Next to these are drawings in which the children express their ideals: a kibbutz, a beautiful model of an apartment, a plane, a train. One can find true artistic expression here. The Dutch boy Sapir, a youth of sixteen, sculpted a fisherman and his surroundings in Holland. The symbols and the mosaics are interesting, wonderful works. So are the rows of bracelets and a beautiful lampshade. The objects of German children have a little more Prussian flavor—a fortress, a tank—but also a row of pretty objects with no connection to war.

July 18, 1943. I opened the children's exhibit. The children and youth made many wonderful things. Pictures, carvings, sculpture, etc. Children's life in the ghetto is expressed in all their work.

July 19–21, 1943. A man of forty came to Yaakov [Edelstein]. His wife finally became pregnant after twelve years of marriage. He is unwilling to follow the directive concerning abortion. A few moments later, his wife came and admitted that her husband was not the father of the unborn child. She requested an abortion.

July 22, 1943. It is forbidden to dress in mourning garb.[9] They ordered us to announce this to the residents of the ghetto in an appropriate way.

July 23, 1943. The streets have new names. No longer the letters L or Q.[10]

8. Jewish police with their flat-topped caps, boots, and armbands.

9. It was customary for Jews to wear either black garb, a black armband, or a piece of black ribbon on their coat lapels if a member of the family had died. As part of the general policy to "brighten" the ghetto, Burger ordered such practices stopped.

10. Another example of Burger's sardonic wit. L2, where the railway line entered the ghetto, became Bahnhofstrasse. L4, with the Magdeburg barrack and the *Ältestenrat* offices, became Haupstrasse. Q1, at the main bakery, was renamed Backergasse. Q8, with its post office, became Postgasse. Real street signs replaced the old, wooden plaques (Lederer, 91).

July 24–25, 1943. A high-level inspection will be conducted. Rumor has it that each worker will receive four cigarettes a week. Yesterday there was an interesting discussion about the end of the war.

July 26–27, 1943. They have ordered the evacuation of the Sudeten, Zeughaus, and Bodenbach barracks. It may be that some of the high officers or government leaders want to take refuge here because of the bombing of Germany.[11]

Mussolini has given up his post.[12]

July 27–29, 1943. The Council of Elders: each one is more demagogic the next. Each man wants to curry favor with the workers or fight for the elderly. This, too, is demagogic. Why move the men's quarters to the quarters of women, children, the aged?[13]

It is a fact that the workers are better than the people who claim they are protecting them.

July 30, 1943. Nearly seven thousand people were moved from their quarters in two days. A large mobilization: in fact it compromised the moving of a small city, quickly, without arguments. They moved the quarters of the men and squeezed them among thirty-seven thousand others.[14]

11. With the Allied bombing of Germany stepping up, Nazi officials scoured Central Europe and Bavaria looking for potential retreats. Terezin's fortress architecture appealed. The six thousand residents of these barracks were given forty-eight hours to relocate. To avoid contact with the ghetto's Jews, the Germans constructed a bridge and an inner wooden wall between their quarters on the north and the Sudeten barracks on the west. Eventually, the archives of the RHSA were transferred to the Podmokly barracks. These included hundreds of thousands of index cards marked "an K.L.A." (to concentration camp Auschwitz) (Lederer, 92-93). When these records were burned in April 1944, one jubilant survivor wrote: "Alles verpackt Dokumente und Kartotheken Tag und Nacht verbrannt. Der Wind tragt die schwarzen Papierfetzen uber die ganze Stadt. Und eines Nachts geht es wie ein Lauffeuer. Wir sinnen frei" (All the packaged documents and file cards were burning day and night. The wind carried the blackened scraps of paper over the entire city. And one night it went like a raging fire. We were free). [Report of Dr. Edith Ornstein, Beit Terezin Archives, p. XII]. See also Starke, 161. Few of the ghetto's residents anticipated that the shifting of quarters would mean the resumption of transports in September.

12. Another example of the speed and accuracy of the ghetto information pipeline. With Sicily crumbling, Mussolini met Hitler at Rimini on the 19th to seek guarantees of support. Five days later, the Fascist Grand Council failed to give him a vote of confidence. On Sunday, the 25th, the very day before this entry, King Victor Emmanuel informed Mussolini he was taking over command of Italy's armed forces.

13. The Sudeten barrack was to be cleared of six thousand workers within forty-eight hours.

14. Adler puts the exact figure at 46,395, the average age of which was 46.6 years (697). With 10,000 people being treated for illness daily, the healthy were dumped into attics where their privacy was supplied by tarpaper or wallpaper separations.

July 31–August 1, 1943. The fate of Jews: it makes one laugh and cry. A Jewish policeman stands at a crossing. Two German vehicles approach. The policeman stops one vehicle in order to prevent an accident. One car crosses. The second car stops, and the driver slaps the Jewish policeman. Why? Whatever happens, the Jew is always to blame.

August

Terezin waffled between oppressive extremes—cold in winter and the heat of summer. There were some constants, however: the inadequate food, overcrowding, brutality, and inevitable transports. Redlich's last entry for August notes the movement of five thousand Jews, including his trusted coworker Fredy Hirsch. Together, with those who would be shipped out in December, they constituted the Family Camp, Jews who managed to live quasi-charmed lives as families in Auschwitz until March 1944.

August 2, 1943. Hamburg was bombed a couple of times.[1] A few [Aryan] women whose children are here in the ghetto fled to Bohusovice. They have now been arrested.

August 2–16, 1943. The heat is oppressive. It's impossible to sleep in the crowded barracks. The rooms are filled with bedbugs and fleas. Most [of the people] sleep in the hallways. We were told to evacuate three barracks.[2] Afterwards, they promised a day of rest. A promise which was not kept. New decrees and suddenly a new order to register people between the ages of fourteen and sixty. No one knows the reason. They are promising that the registration is not for a trans-

---

1. Another accurate, if understated, entry. Beginning on July 25, Allied B-17s and B-24s pounded this Baltic port six times in nine days. Incendiary bombs devastated the city, leaving fifty thousand dead, thirty-seven thousand injured (Charles Whiting, *The Home Front: Germany, Time Life,* World War II series [Alexandria, Va.: Time-Life Books, 1982], 144-45).
2. See entry July 28, 1943, for this order.

port eastward, but who believes? Some people think they want to organize a work force. They hope the work area isn't far away, but no one knows. . . . [3] No one knows how many have been registered. Two thousand people are being registered every day. (They only requested thirteen hundred.) They registered ten thousand people and chose sixty-six hundred for work. Now, none of those registered want to work.[4]

They registered my brother-in-law and my sister-in-law. I wasn't able to release them immediately. My wife spoke harshly to me. The whole family spoke harshly. . . . Now they are released, thank God. My wife is sick in the hospital . . . as if I weren't nervous enough.[5]

August 18–22, 1943. A short respite—a new registration. Next week, another new registration, of people over sixty, from sixty to sixty-nine. A new catastrophe is looming.

My wife is sick. She has been in the hospital for a week.

August 22–24, 1943. Great commotion. They have called for a general census and included members of the first two transports for registration. Who is the informer who implicated these men? Why are they doing this? It isn't fair toward these men who built the ghetto.[6]

August 24–September 8, 1943. How many days have passed? What has happened? They incarcerated Fredy [Hirsch] and Janowitz[7] and put them on a transport. A transport of five thousand people. They sent five thousand in one day.[8] Children have arrived from the East.[9]

3. From September, all outgoing transports were dubbed "Arbeitseinsatz."

4. Adler reports 29,603 able-bodied workers at the end of August (697).

5. Redlich's summary for two weeks reveals great personal pressure brought on by both his family and the amount of work he must have done in helping to arrange these registrations.

6. Reference is to incoming transports from Prague Ak1 (November 24, 1941) and Ak2 (November 30, 1941), which had first organized Terezin. Redlich himself had come in on the latter and knew most of these people. The selection was probably deliberate, given Commandant Burger's special hatred for Czechs.

7. Dr. Leo Janowitz, a Zionist who was Edlestein's top aide in the Central Secretariat.

8. Transports D1 (2479) and Dm (2528) were sent in family units to Auschwitz on September 6. For six months, they were treated reasonably well in the quarantine section of Birkenau. Fredy Hirsch continued his education work in what came to be known as "the Family Camp." On March 8–9, 1944, approximately thirty-eight hundred of these Jews were marched off to the gas chambers. Hirsch committed suicide with Veronal. Thirty-seven were spared for Dr. Mengele's twin experiments (Gerald Reitlinger, *The Final Solution* [New York: Barnes, 1961], 169-70).

9. Fifteen hundred children arrived from Bialystok at the end of August. Ranging

They ordered us to put in some men and 150 police.[10] The fate of the men: they cast lots to see who would go. They paid the doctors to give them injections, to make themselves sick. And in the end, they also were sent.

September

Less frequent entries than usual this month. Redlich noted the arrival of several hundred Jewish children from Bialystok. Some had witnessed the killings of their own parents. Segregated in specially built huts, they harbored few illusions about what would happen to them when they were deported—which they were in the first week of October.

September 12, 1943. A coffee house, with empty tables.[1] Each man may linger two hours. Melodies—but one can order only tea or coffee. In the houses nearest the street where the Germans walk home, it is forbidden to open windows. They are only allowed to have lights on in the houses for one hour.

September 14, 1943. We asked for fresh vegetables for several infants, but the request was denied. A department head went out of the city.

from six to fifteen, some were barefoot, without any belongings, in a pitiable, half-starved state, according to Adler. They were the remnant of a Jewish community in a textile center of more than one hundred thousand people. With the exception of a massacre in July 1941, Jews in this region enjoyed a relative degree of immunity until February 1943. At that point, several transports carried thirteen thousand Bialystok Jews to Treblinka. More were killed behind barbed wire at Jurowiecka Square. When the Nazis resumed deportations in August, Mordecai Tenenbaum ("Josef Tamarov") led an armed uprising in the ghetto. Much like the heroic stand in Warsaw, the Bialystok resistance lasted in the bunkers till September 15 (Reitlinger, 285-86). For more on the Bialystok children, see also Redlich's entries for September 14 and October 5, 1943, and the testimony of Otto Kraus, Hebrew University Oral History Project, #176.

10. Those with past exemptions found they were useless. The transports included 285 children under the age of fourteen, 3,925 persons between fifteen and sixty, and 797 over sixty-one (Adler, 697).

1. The entry was made several days after the massive transports to Auschwitz and reveals a melancholy mood. Redlich evinces no knowledge of the Allied landing at Salerno September 10. Instead, he speaks of coffee made from turnips and herb tea.

He had work to do in one of the wood huts. They met him and ordered that he be jailed and removed from his position.[2]

A game: "a small girl travels to Eretz Yisrael." One of the children polishes shoes—polishes the shoes of Elijah the prophet. . . .

September 19, 1943. It is forbidden to talk with or have contact with those who live outside in the huts. So, people sometimes go near the children's camp just to hear their voices. A mother listens for the voice of her daughter. The distance isn't great and they see each other, a mother sees her loved one.

September 24, 1943. Not all the counselors in the children's quarters were selected carefully. Some of them call the children "Polish pigs."

It is forbidden to cross the street which the Germans use to return home. There is only one crossroad that a Jew can use, if he has permission. The others must circle the entire city. Today, I requested permission in writing for a Jew who was wounded five times while a German soldier in the First World War.

September 29, 1943. Gershon Zentner had a son.[3] On this occasion, someone said: "It's not hard to have children in Eretz Yisrael." Not really.

October

Terezin received its most privileged inmates this month—the few hundred Danish Jews that were rounded up at Rosh Hashanah. The object of repeated inquiries by King Christian, his government and

2. The Bialystok children (entry August 24–September 8) were not admitted to Terezin proper. When they first arrived, the children were taken to the brewery to be deloused. As they entered the baths, they panicked and screamed, "Gas! Gas!" thinking they were about to be murdered. Afterward, they were segregated in a barbed-wire compound behind the West barracks. Placed in makeshift huts, they were guarded by gendarmes who were instructed that no one was to have contact with them except one physician and several nurses. And even those people were not to return to their normal duties in Terezin (Adler, 154-55, and Lederer, 95-97).

3. A member of Maccabi Hatzair who made Aliyah to Palestine before the war.

relatives, most of the Danes received packages during their detention and survived the war. Entries this month (October 3) and next (November 24) reflect earlier Nazi preoccupation with abortions (July 7, April 8).

October 3, 1943. In the middle of the night came an order to evacuate a building which till recently was used as a *Schleuse* [collection point for transports]. Fear that more transports will be going. Later, the order was rescinded.

Now I recollect: they have forbidden having children here. But it's also forbidden to use contraception. A young man was incarcerated and charged with [possession of] contraband when a condom was found in his gear.

October 5, 1943. The children from the wood huts traveled with their counselors out of the country. Once outside the country, the counselors have promised they will not fight against Germany.[1]

Danish Jews have arrived.[2]

We are the only city under German occupation where summer time is kept also on October 5. It is forbidden to read newspapers here, so it is impossible to know when winter time officially begins. The camp commandant forgot to announce the change to winter time and we were late for work by one hour after the Germans.

They brought the Danish Jews to a room and served them food on a table prepared with a white tablecloth. They even gave them postcards to write home.

1. Transport Dn left Terezin with the remaining 1,260 children from Bialystok and 53 adults. The latter, counselors and medical staff, were under the impression they were bound for Switzerland, then Palestine. The transport went directly to Auschwitz where all were gassed.

2. Eighty-three Danish Jews arrived on October 5. They were followed by 198 the next day, 175 a week later, and 10 more individuals in 1944. They were the unfortunates who either did not heed warnings or were trapped when Hitler ordered the roundup of Danish Jews at Rosh Hashanah in September 1943. From the moment of their arrival and greeting in Terezin by Burger, Rudolph Haindl, and other SS leaders, the Danish Jews were treated as a special group. Initially housed in the West barracks, they were issued food and accommodations fit for Prominents. Such treatment reflected the singular concern demonstrated by Danish Gentiles for their fellow countrymen. Better than 90 percent of Denmark's Jews managed to escape Eichmann's roundup thanks to the assistance of fishermen, pastors, students, housewives, etc. Those who were sent to Terezin received registered food parcels, money, letters. King Christian X and the Danish Red Cross badgered Gestapo chief Rudolf Mildner until the Nazis finally agreed to permit an international delegation to visit the ghetto in the summer of 1944. See entry June 19, 1944. See also Harold Flender, *Rescue in Denmark* (rpt.; New York: Holocaust Library, 1963), and Philip Friedman, *Their Brothers' Keepers* (rpt.; New York: Holocaust Library, 1978), 149-58.

I spoke to one of them. (He was my student in the Prague school.) This meeting was very disappointing for me. I spoke with him for just a few minutes. I saw an uncouth young peasant. And he is one of a hundred. Perhaps these people are needed in Eretz Yisrael more than us "Intellectuals." We shall see. . . . [3]

October 13, 1943. They jailed officials who were in charge of the bread supply. They had contact with the outside world. We were ordered to cut each loaf of bread. [4]

Yesterday, I was in charge of the blackout. It was a nice night. The moonlight spilled over the autumn air of the city. A deep serenity permeated the city. Why do people kill each other? Why do they hate each other? Why has the war lasted four years?

October 14, 1943. I received a package with another package inside. I learned that the man to whom it belonged had died and had no heirs. Everyone had gone eastward.

Porters sit on carts next to the post office and offer their services.

October 24, 1943. Why does man take pleasure in killing his fellow man? Does he really feel happy and content? The war has lasted more than four years. We don't dare suggest that the end may come soon, even if it is possible to foresee its end.

October 31, 1943. A debate in the *Ältestenrat* regarding crime in Terezin. Who are the judges—the men of the *Ältestenrat.* Are they *tzaddikim* [saints]? Can they judge the others? Walter Löwinger[5] said yesterday that members of the administration argue whether one man can cancel the order of another. Why is it that people don't respect anyone but themselves?

Jews—a strange people.

---

3. A Czech Jew who was sent to Denmark via Youth Aliyah for Palestine.

4. Ruth Bondy suggests that someone may have been smuggling letters out of the ghetto in loaves of bread.

5. Director of the *Raumwirtschaft* (Housing Office) and a powerful figure in the Central Administration.

November

Because an official census came up missing fifty persons, onetime Judenältester *Jacob Edelstein was jailed. The Nazis then ordered a day-long counting for November 11. Redlich notes the demoralizing effect and loss of life of that infamous* Zählappel *in an open field.*

November 3, 1943. The *Ältestenrat:* a group of people who, on the one hand, cherish honor; conceited men; on the other hand, old men who stutter and are unable to comprehend.[1]

An argument: what is better, to render light or harsh sentences? Who is qualified to issue a judgment? Who is guilty and who is innocent? Who is unclean and who is pure? An argument concerning the rights of the Council of Elders. There is no right to have better food. Big talk, and the one who says it knows he is talking to the wind. The "elders" will never agree to cutting back on a morsel of their rights.

Is a man who is given two portions of food fit to judge a thief who is given only one portion, when he tries to take another from the kitchen?[2]

November 9, 1943. From Polaczek's lecture:[3] "An optimist says: 'The end is coming soon.' He returns to this sentence again and again, like a magician uttering a charm in order to get something. The pessimist says: 'The end is coming, but not so soon.' Like a man afraid of rousing the jealousy of the gods."

November 10, 1943. They imprisoned Yaakov [Edelstein].[4] Tomorrow there is to be a great census. There is a connection between these occurrences and the great tension that exists in the ghetto.

They ordered us to remove the three-tiered planks. Especially in places they will visit during different inspections.[5]

1. When the Czech government permitted snips of the Redlich diary to be published between 1972 and 1974, it seized upon frustrated statements such as this to discredit Terezin leadership and Zionism.

2. One of the most poignant questions Redlich raises.

3. Karel Polaczek (1892–1944) was a celebrated Czech author and longtime friend of President Tomas Masaryk. In the ghetto, he gave lectures to the children.

4. Edelstein was arrested when Nazi census figures came up fifty persons shy. One hundred thirty people in all supposedly escaped from the ghetto.

5. The Nazis already may have been contemplating the so-called *Verbesserung* or

The theft of coal is on the rise. The children are stealing it in order to heat the youth houses a bit more.[6] Adults also are stealing. Education is difficult when examples cannot be found among the teachers.

November 14, 1943. An order was issued forcing all the inhabitants of the ghetto outside the city into a large, open field. Only the sick who are unable to move remain in the ghetto.[7]

It is written (Exodus 10:9): "We will all go, young and old." This verse has been fully realized, verbatim. Children two years old went with old people of seventy. They went and stood all day, from 7 A.M. till 11 P.M.

They went and were counted. As if we were cattle or sheep. Darkness came, and the Jews planned to spend the night in the open field. Thirty-six thousand people, as docile as little children or sheep—lambs, standing and waiting.

And when we were permitted to return, we went timidly, women, children at the front, going with great patience, awfully. . . .

There, outside, men were stripped of their shame, each acting according to his needs, relieving themselves like animals before a strange woman.

November 16, 1943. A tale of a man who wanted to get something. He tried to get it in the honest way but did not succeed. What did he do? He offered a bribe and got the desired item. After a while (during which time he became ill), he wanted to pay the promised bribe. He approached the man he had promised the bribe and said: "Excuse me. I was sick, but now. . . . " The [other] man didn't wait for him to finish his sentence, but rebuked him: "What do you want? I haven't time to listen to your request. . . . "

They jailed four youths along with one counselor. The Czech police found scraps of spinach among them. The prisoners swore the

Verschönerung (Embellishment) for an international commission that would tour Terezin in June 1944. To deceive the Red Cross, crowded conditions had to be eliminated in some barracks. These tiered planks that housed families had to go.

6. The *Jugendfürsorge* file of Beit Terezin contains a report dated November 26, 1942 on conditions in *Mädchenheim* L410. It notes that while the "Lager" is equipped with seven stoves, heat is inadequate. During the cold weather at night, the room is so chilly the young girls "complain about the cold."

7. During the *Zählappel* of November 11, most of Terezin's inmates were marched to the large meadow near Bohusovice that once served as a military campground. Many, fearful of losing personal belongings, were wearing layers of clothes. They stood in groups of one hundred as they were counted and counted again. Only the very sick were spared this roll call. Nurse Resi Weglein recalls she worked twenty-seven hours without relief. When it was over, nearly three hundred persons lost their lives to exhaustion or exposure, and still the Nazis had no accurate count. Two weeks later, commandant Burger ordered additional identity checks.

German commander permitted them to take the spinach. The matter was brought before the Jewish police (we have autonomy and the Jews take care of such things), and the Jews found the youths guilty without checking to see if their story was true. Just before the judgment was rendered, the German commander vindicated the accused.

November 19, 1943. Dr. Löwenstein makes threats from jail.[8] He wrote a letter to the [new] Jewish police chief: "I will still take my rightful place as head [of the police]."

November 24, 1943. They have forced us to agree in writing to infanticide.[9] There is fear everywhere. Its reign is terrifying—difficult to bear. Fear and depression turn men into evil animals. What am I saying? Even evil animals do not kill their children. What are they doing to us?

I signed [an affidavit] that I would kill my child. Then afterward, I sat down to hear the case of a young man who committed an offense with his friend's documents. I must judge. I who signed. . . . The other judges debate every formal point. For me, it's amusing. I am indifferent. Abortions. Yet they order the beautification of the city.

November 27, 1943. Beautify and decorate the city. A bitter mockery underlies these words. They forbid washing clothes during the day. (It's only permitted at night and now it is winter.)[10] It's forbidden to make beds after 9 A.M. Forbidden, permitted, forbidden, permitted. . . . They want to fix the cinema.

November 29, 1943. A young orphan girl of sixteen has become pregnant. What to do? I know she isn't the only girl to have lost her virginity. In spite of this, we have been forced to some conclusions. We may have to take her out of the dormitory.

November 30, 1943. A strange occurrence, sad and wonderful. They told an old woman that her husband had died. She went to his funeral, weeping aloud. And what happened? There she met her husband, alive and well. The announcement was a mistake. A strange story, sad and wonderful.

8. As noted previously, Löwenstein was jailed for possessing several meal tickets. He was subsequently exonerated.

9. Gerta Beck was nearly six months pregnant at this time.

10. For obvious reasons, it would be more difficult to hang clothes out to dry at night in the winter.

December

With the return of winter, rumors circulated of another visit by an important delegation. Food rations were doubled and photographs taken of the Council of Elders. Redlich was not heartened, though. His last entry for the year mentions the departure of five thousand more Jews to the East.

December 2, 1943. Yaakov [Edelstein] has been imprisoned.[1] They still have not released him. His wife paces back and forth before the prison. She cannot see him, but he sees her because his cell is in the basement.

A counselor's boots were stolen. What did he do? He sent the children from his quarters to look for boots. Really, the children found them with a person in the street. An occurrence like "Emil and the Detectives."

They say that Sunday we will receive a double ration. A Potemkin Village.

December 5, 1943. Sometimes, a man's pride takes precedence over his hunger. If I tell the counselors they are to be punished by canceling their rights to get food from the children's kitchen (you are good counselors, but I have to treat everybody equally) they will leave me and take their punishment gladly. They are the good ones.

I was at the German photographer. They want pictures of the ghetto administration.[2]

December 19, 1943. A few Jews defecated in the barracks before work, while they were raising the flag. An overzealous German soldier saw it and informed the police. The police didn't forward the information any further, and the soldier was sent to the front. The matter apparently was forgotten, but the soldier wrote back a letter

1. Edelstein and three registry officials (O. Faltin, E. Deutsch, and A. Gold-schmidt) were arrested in November when their figures failed to account for fifty-five missing Jews. Taken to the basement of SS headquarters, they were placed on one of the December transports and never seen again by ghetto residents. See entry January 1, 1944.

2. In anticipation of the visit of representatives of the International Red Cross.

from the front to the camp commandant asking what kind of punishment was given for the insult to the flag.[3] Now they have
punished the Jews with a harsh punishment. Lucky for the Jews, the
relationship between the security forces and the army isn't good.

Another Jew had his vision saved as a result of a dangerous operation. At first, they operated on one eye. The operation of the second was even more dangerous. The slightest mistake would have
endangered the life of the patient.[4]

December 19, 1943.[5] Five thousand people in a transport. [Comman-
dant] Burger requested a list and chose the clerks himself.

They sent those sick with tuberculosis and then children one year
old. They traveled in filthy cattle cars.[6]

3. How this occurred is not explained. Jews were not supposed to assemble before
the swastika flag.

4. There were several surgical units in Terezin. Serious cases were treated in a
ward with two hundred beds and two large operating theaters. In a bizarre twist of
Nazi treatment of Jews, one of the operating rooms was equipped with the most modern, sterilizing equipment. Eye, ear, and nose cases were generally treated in a smaller
operating room. In the year 1943 there were 343 eye operations, 302 in gynecology, 254
laryngology, and 136 urology. Patients faced the prospect of shortages of anesthesia,
power outages during surgery, and post-operative embolisms (Adler, 523). The chief
eye specialist was Dr. Richard Stein who replaced Erich Munk as head of the medical
service in the fall of 1944. Stein emigrated to Israel in 1949 where he worked at Tel
Hashomer Hospital.

5. Redlich made two entries for the same day, December 19.

6. Transport Dr left December 15 with twenty-five hundred prisoners who were
sent to Camp BIIb or the Family Camp in Auschwitz. Transport Ds went out on December 18, with twenty-five hundred more. It too arrived in Auschwitz where the Family Camp population temporarily reached more than twelve thousand. At the end of
June 1944, Mengele did a selection and seventy-five hundred were gassed between July
11 and 14. The rest went to work camps. Five hundred young men and women survived death marches and stays in Buchenwald, Gross-Rosen, Dachau, and Belsen.

1944

January-March

The stress of daily life obviously was affecting Redlich, whose entries in his journal became even more episodic during the winter. In January, he notes, in passing, the arrival of the first of nearly five thousand Jews who passed through Terezin. A month later, the appointment of a third commandant, Karl Rahm, barely merits a paragraph. Much of Redlich's concern and attention focused upon his wife Gerta who gave birth to a son, Dan, on the 16th of March. Thereafter, he kept a second diary dedicated to his son.

January 1, 1944. A new year, the third of Terezin exile.

Yaakov [Edelstein] . . . how the unfortunate suffered. How great were his tortures. On the night of the census in November, he wasn't able to sleep because he thought the people in the ghetto were all sleeping outside the city under the sky. He couldn't even talk with the guard because this guard was an anti-Semite. As an act of despair, Yaakov put on tephillin after midnight. The guard saw the strange scene, and it touched him. At first, he thought Yaakov was attempting suicide. He rushed into the cell, but Yaakov explained to him that he wasn't contemplating suicide but that it was a religious ritual. The guard's heart was filled with remorse. A wonder of the twentieth century occurred: an enemy of the Jews turned into a lover of Jews. A miracle taking place through the laying of tephillin.

Yaakov's family didn't know until the last minute if Yaakov would travel with them or not. When she went into the boxcar, his wife Miriam still didn't know. Then they told her he would be traveling. How great was her disappointment when they brought him to the last car for the prisoners.[1]

1. Five thousand persons were shipped to Auschwitz on transports Dr and Ds, which left Terezin December 15 and 18 respectively. Approximately seven hundred survived.

Terrible . . . on the train, a woman and child are traveling to an unknown future, and on the last train a husband and father is brought to a concentration camp.[2]

Life goes on. It passes like a stream of water, without pause, without end. . . . Last week, there were many weddings. Life goes on.

January 7, 1944. I have a new assistant: a German Jew.[3] Every department which has a Jew from the Protectorate as its head must have a German-Jewish assistant. There is no trust between the Jews of the Protectorate and the German Jews.[4]

January 8, 1944. A story of a child. His parents left him at the age of three. He lived with strangers, friends of his parents. The child is very edgy, loves his adoptive parents. Sometimes he soils himself because of his nerves. He is nervous and fearful that his adoptive parents may leave him. The child does not want to return to his real parents. He doesn't know them.

New people have arrived. They brought a mother to the ghetto and left her small children, who aren't Jews, outside.[5]

January 13, 1944. Youths who stole are testifying.[6]

How do you explain the difference to them?

They would say: "Yes, we regret that we admitted stealing some meat. If we hadn't admitted it, no one would have known that we stole it."

"And you are not ashamed that you are in jail?"

"No. Yaakov [Edelstein] is also in jail."

"How do you explain the difference!"

They say: "Here life is different from normality. When we return to normality, we will become decent again."

2. Edelstein was not united with his family. Placed in Block 11 of the main Auschwitz camp, he was shot to death in June 1944. His wife and son were sent to Birkenau where they along with families of other Terezin officials were executed before his eyes on June 20 (Lederer, 103).

3. Dr. Berthold Simonson (1912–1978), an aide of Dr. Eppstein. Simonson later dedicated a social work text to his mentor.

4. Friction was not limited to these two groups of Jews. See references to animosity expressed against Dutch Jews (April 23, 1944) and the children from Bialystok (September 24, 1944).

5. A sweep of arrests in Berlin, Dresden, Hamburg, Dusseldorf, Hanover, Breslau, Leipzig, Dortmund, Munster, Frankfurt, Darmstadt, Koenigsberg, and Vienna brought 999 German Jews to the ghetto in January. Among these were people who heretofore had been given immunity as *Mischlings,* including one former SS man (Lederer, 107).

6. An exchange between Redlich and youths in the juvenile court.

January 20, 1944. They ordered us to vacate the Hamburg barracks in four days. Thirty-three hundred women reside there. One day after they gave the order, it was forbidden to talk about it. An order of silence—woe to the man who talks. Three thousand women and children moved in four days. And what's more, in silence. Prepare everything and be quiet.[7]

The barracks will be deloused and then new transports will be arriving, Jews from Holland. They filmed their arrival.[8]

The ghetto administration received a present from the camp commandant [Burger]: a sausage, flour, sweets. Members had to carry these unwanted presents home.

The day before yesterday, an order came to remove all the pebbles in the street before the Hamburg barracks. The Germans worried that a Dutch Jew might throw his jewelry onto the street and it might break among the stones.

January 28, 1944. A young woman with TB married for the second time here. Her first husband supposedly died in a concentration camp after he was taken there a short time ago. One day, they informed the woman that her first husband was still alive in Birkenau. The woman went there with her second husband on the last transport. A strange twist of fate.

February 1, 1944. A Jew sent an emblem of Terezin to his beloved in Prague. The Germans found the memento in Prague and imprisoned both of them.[9]

February 11, 1944. A new commandant.[10] Will the situation improve? We hope so. We have been living in slavery in Terezin for more than

7. To make room for the 999 German and nearly 2,000 Dutch Jews who came to Terezin between January 20 and 26, residents of the Hamburg barracks (which had also served as the *Schleuse*) had to evacuate to prefabricated huts and lofts.

8. Burger staged a welcome for the benefit of Czech newsreels. When the Dutch Jews arrived, Dr. Eppstein made a welcoming speech, the SS helped the aged and young from the train, and the Dutch Jews were given postcards to write back how well they had been received. Then they were dumped into the filthy Hamburg barrack (Lederer, 107-8).

9. It was customary to give a tin medallion as a birthday present in the ghetto. The object dating to the eighteenth century, showed a lion holding a shield and sword atop the battlements of Terezin.

10. Burger was replaced by Karl Rahm, Eichmann's specialist with the Jewish Museum in Prague. Transferred to Yugoslavia, Burger escaped punishment after the war. Rahm, on the other hand, a onetime toolmaker from Klosterneuburg, Austria, was hanged in Litomerice in 1947.

two years. But the Jews who have arrived from Holland have been refugees for four years.[11]

February 13, 1944. A census with Günther.[12] He requested a report from the members of the *Ältestenrat* and the heads of departments.[13] Strange: he was interested in whether we had enough food, clothing, shoes. Strange! Our worst enemies in all of our history concern themselves with us. In spite of this, it is forbidden to give birth to children. Forbidden!

February 21, 1944. It's forbidden to give birth. But they permitted one woman to give birth to an unwanted, unloved child.

An interesting conversation with Polaczek.[14] He criticized my story. I could learn a lot from him.

February 27, 1944. A one-month child came from Berlin.

The camp commandant [Rahm] concerned himself with the wash basins in the youth quarters. It's funny![15]

March 6, 1944. The fate of a Jew: a Jewish girl, a *mamzer*[16] whose mother died in childbirth. The father did not concern himself with

11. Redlich refers to the fact that many Dutch Jews already had been interned in the Westerbork and Vught transit camps as early as 1940.

12. SS Haupsturmführer Hans Günther and his brother SS Sturmbannführer Rolf Günther, sons of racist anthropologist Professor Hans Günther, worked for Eichmann's RSHA IVB4 office. Hans Günther secured the first supplies of "blue acid" (Zyklon B) used at Lublin in 1942. According to Reitlinger (167), Terezin was his "private preserve," and he was responsible for making certain that the *Verschönerung* for the International Red Cross (see entries June 19 and June 25, 1944) was staged flawlessly. After the war, both Günthers disappeared.

13. The official count by the end of February was 36,912. The ghetto had to be thinned out; hence the deportation of 7,500 persons in May. (See entry June 1, 1944.)

14. Another reference to the writer Karel Polaczek.

15. It was this attention to detail that proved to be the reason for Rahm's promotion over Burger. Although the latter had attempted to beautify the fortress by renaming streets, improving cafes, and eliminating some of the worst attics, he apparently did not evince sufficient enthusiasm for Günther's Embellishment. Under Rahm, buildings were repainted and roads repaired. Better street lighting was introduced, sports fields tended, and seating built for fans. Rahm ordered the digging of a sham cemetery, imitation graves serviced by refurbished hearses. Terezin even received a new designation. No longer a ghetto, it was officially the "Judisches Siedlungsgebiet" (Jewish settlement.) See Adler, 161-62, and Lederer, 110-11.

16. Literally "a bastard." The word may carry with it a negative connotation. Redlich, however, has a special reason for using it for any child unfortunate enough to have been born in peculiar circumstances in that era. See "Yoman l'Dan" (Diary for Dan), the diary he began for his own son Dan, entry March 22, 1944.

his daughter because she was a *mamzer*. The young girl ran around begging. She lived among strangers who were pitiless. They were hard. They brought the girl from the orphanage to western Bohemia and gave her to a Christian peasant for education. Beatings and curses, rebukes were the only things she learned. Recently, they beat her badly and taunted: "If we kill you, it is nothing. We will not be punished. You are only a Jewess."

In the end, the Germans arrested her and brought her from one jail to another. Here [in Terezin] she has become ill. The first time she had slept in a bed while sick. A strange fate. Only [Charles] Dickens could describe it. She wrote the story of her life, according to the instruction of her counselor. She wrote it in the handwriting of an eight-year-old, even though she is fourteen.

March 7, 1944. An announcement came yesterday. It is no longer required to salute the Germans.[17]

March 13, 1944. A line of Jews are waiting for hot water. A Jew comes [along] whose accent indicates he is German. The Jews from the Protectorate start to rebuke him. Suddenly, a woman who speaks Czech cuts in to the head of the line. They stop rebuking the German Jew and start on her. There is no unity. Even common hatred is portioned out.

March 15, 1944. They check each man that is called to the Dienststelle[18] to see if he has lice or is free of infectious disease.[19] Heroes!

A violinist requested permission to live with his wife. After a while, it was permitted.[20] They lived together for a day. At night, their neighbors heard a great clamor. What happened? The violinist

17. As another sign of the Embellishment, Rahm relieved Jews of the obligation of tipping their hats or curtseying before the SS.

18. SS Headquarters, where Edelstein and his aides were imprisoned, was located in building DIV on the southwest side of the central plaza. Originally, the Germans used the post office next to the main church.

19. A definite reference to spotted typhus. Adler (520) claims that the disease first appeared with the arrival of a near-moribund Jew from Berlin. Despite efforts to contain the disease, it afflicted a number of the ghetto's "old-timers," including 200 doctors and nurses. With the arrival of deportees from concentration camps in 1945, the disease spread more rapidly. Before liberation, the epidemic afflicted 2,500 persons, of whom 502 died.

20. Another example of the SS trying to normalize Jewish relations before the arrival of the Red Cross delegation.

was a little crazy. He was overly concerned about cleanliness in his room. You cannot enter his house from the street with your shoes on. His wife suffers from an inflammation, and her urine [spilled] on the floor. This pollution angered the violinist, and an argument started that wakened the neighbors.

My wife is in the hospital. Labor pains have gripped her.

The Hungarians will leave the ghetto today.[21] Dov Revesz is among them.[22]

March 16, 1944. My son has been born. May God bless and protect him. I want to give my beloved a diary and write his history in it.[23]

March 19, 1944. Fifty people from the asylum will be sent east.

March 24, 1944. A young girl did not want to return a garment which was loaned to her by the administrator of a barrack. When her mother plied her with questions why she didn't want to go back, the girl began to cry and confessed that the official tried to rape her. The girl's parents are typically bourgeois and were embarrassed by the incident. Investigators could make a great sensation out of this incident.

A rumor has spread in the ghetto that the famous Dr. Stein has died.[24] The rabbis began to argue among themselves who would lead the mourners in the funeral. They quarreled, decided, called a memorial, and suddenly it was discovered that the doctor had not died.

March 30, 1944. Thus do people get punished. One man steals, a second fathers a child. My brother-in-law must leave his apartment and give up his job as a cook as punishment.[25]

21. An anomalous reference, as Redlich does not mention Hungarians in any of his previous entries. Until the Nazi occupation of Hungary in March 1944, Hungarian Jews like Revesz were immune to deportation. Now, they too were sent to Birkenau. Lederer mentions eighty who were deported in May, but most Hungarians entered Terezin as death camp survivors in the winter of 1944–45. See Adler, 298-301. It is possible that he is making a spurious reference to some ghetto residents, perhaps those mentioned on March 19, 1944.

22. Forty-five persons were sent on March 20 in Transport Dx to Belsen, where popular belief had it they were to be exchanged for German internes abroad. None survived.

23. From this day, Redlich devotes most of his literary energies to the diary dedicated to his son Dan. (See accompanying "Yoman L'Dan.") How his wife managed to avoid the abortion ban (entries July 7 and November 24, 1943) is explained in his son's journal, entry March 16, 1944.

24. On Dr. Stein, see December 19, 1943.

25. For a fuller explanation, see Yoman L' Dan, entry March 26, 1944.

April-August

Another spring in Terezin, with a different emphasis from the Nazi authorities. Heydrich's "Paradise Ghetto" for the elderly was to be purged of the aged, the sick, and overcrowding to impress a Red Cross delegation scheduled to arrive in June. Redlich's fear that Terezin might serve as a Potemkin Village became a reality after several months of Embellishment.

April 11, 1944. They took down the fence that surrounded the city square. But it is forbidden to walk in the square. We are awaiting an important commission and want to show the city in its beauty.[1]

A tale of a man who brought contraband into the city. They wanted to search among his belongings and asked him what he was carrying. He answered that in his pack was the excrement of people who had typhus. He was bringing it to the station in order to send it to the university in Prague for testing. The police were afraid of this contagious disease and allowed him to pass.

April 17, 1944. Two children arrived from Lublin. The children spent a year in a monastery with their Christian grandmother who brought them to the ghetto, then returned to Lublin.[2]

We aren't living in the ghetto, but in the Jewish *Siedlungsgebiet* (settlement).

April 23, 1944. The German commandant [Rahm] toured the park. Children followed him and called out: "Pane Rahm. Pane Rahm!" He smiled and swelled with pride: "You see how famous I am."[3]

April 27, 1944. They have handed some mothers from the infants' house, who did not want to work outside that shelter, over for judg-

1. To impress the Red Cross, some of the barriers segregating the Jews from German personnel (see entry July 26–27, 1943) were eliminated. As the visit of the international commission drew near, concerts were given twice daily from the pavilion in this idyllic setting.

2. Adler (699) reports some four thousand Jews of mixed ancestry in the ghetto at this time.

3. Leo Haas left a sketch showing the ghetto commander in a different time, when the barriers were up. The commandant, replete with jackboots and riding crop, is strutting through the wooded yard, while on the other side of a flimsy wooden barricade, Jews crowd by in despair (Frank, 81).

ment. I was called as an expert. It's hard to decide. On the one hand, it's hard for the childcare people to get along with the mothers. On the other hand, perhaps we should understand the mothers who don't want to give over the care of their children to caretakers because such care isn't good enough. Sometimes, the caretakers are too lax.

They are beautifying and improving the city. They fixed two children's homes and they look like nice sanitoriums.

May 3, 1944. A new hall has opened.[4] Festive speeches. Music, song. Two Germans stand on the gallery and look at the proceedings.

May 9, 1944. Barbed-wire fences have been forbidden. The password today is *Stadtverschönerung* [beautification of the city].[5]

June 1, 1944. Transports have gone. How many times already? Seventy-five hundred people traveled. Most had worked here for two years . . . [6]

---

4. While the post office and bank were merely refurbished, the *Sokolovna*, which had served as a hospital for encephalitis patients, was transformed into a community center. There were carpeted meeting rooms for the *Ältestenrat* in the *Haus der Judischen Selbstverwaltung*, Hebrew signs posted over the morgue, a library, a stage for cultural performances. And after all the aggravation about sharing space for religious services with other activities, the gymnasium became a prayer hall (Rosenberger statement, Beit Terezin archives, p. 21, and Dworzecki, 98-99).

5. Adler and Lederer concur that the process had been ongoing for several months, but the best testimony comes from Rena Rosenberger, who wrote: "For the children, a playground was laid out with sandboxes and swings, a 'children's pavilion' was built and painted from inside with big wooden animals as toys. Behind a glass veranda you could see a dozen of kribs (sic.) It was like a story book—but children were only allowed to enter this little paradise on the day the commission visited Theresienstadt. . . . That was it. Only bluff! The barracks and all the houses were painted from outside and inside. Only that part was painted where the Commission was supposed to make their inspection. Gazons (sic?) were laid out, an eating hall was opened which was only used during the time of the Commission's visit. There you were served by girls with white aprons and you were served on a plate. Forks and spoons you had to bring yourself. At the day of the Commission's visit, the tables were set with white tablecloths and flowers. The city now had a restaurant. . . . The windows of the stores also got another look with displays of things you couldn't buy and you could see suddenly sugar, margarine and vegetables in the foodstores. The butchers carried sausages, canned meat and liver sausages. Everybody looked with amazement at the windows" (Rosenberger statement, Beit Terezin Archives, p. 20).

6. Transport Dz left on May 15 with 2,503 persons bound for Auschwitz. In July, this group underwent selections and 119 survived. Transport Ea left for Auschwitz on May 16 and Eb followed on May 18, both with 2,500 persons. Some of the Hungarians (80 in the first group) and some musicians were spared. Most were gassed in the July selections of the Birkenau Family Camp. There were 5 survivors of Ea, 261 of Eb. The

A commission will be coming to inspect the city. They have been working for more than two months in order to improve the city.

The Germans took out two hundred craftsmen from the transport. Jews from Germany left, from Austria, and the Protectorate. There were many arguments among the *Landsmannschaften* [national groups].[7]

June 6, 1944.[8] The story of a young man: his mother died a while ago and a woman who did not like her wanted to assume custody of the child. Before her death, the mother asked that the son not agree to have this woman as a guardian. Very well and good, but this woman is the lover of an influential man who could exempt him from a transport. What to do?

June 12, 1944. A cripple wants to get something from a medical orderly.[9] The orderly says: the thing isn't available. I can't get it for you. The cripple gives the orderly a can of sardines. Suddenly the thing is found in storage. Suddenly it can be obtained.

June 14, 1944. An incident with a doctor: the doctor is a young Jew who loves his profession. He married a girl sixteen years his junior. The girl was rich and spoiled. After the wedding, she helped him in his surgery. The doctor did not permit her to go and have a good time in the coffee houses. They did not have any children because her husband did not want any.

When they came here, the wife was happy that she was not living with her husband. Then, finally, she and her husband got an apartment together. Then all hell broke loose. The doctor became very involved in his work. He was the only one who was loved by all the mothers in the infants' house. The wife saw the doctor taking care of all the other children. Her husband loved her passionately.

arrival of so many more Jews from Terezin probably hastened the end of the Family Camp.

7. It was during the registration for these May transports that Otto Zucker, his face bandaged, confronted Commandant Rahm and insisted that a number of personnel crucial to ghetto operations not be deported. Rahm was furious, but ultimately got his way, sending most of those who had temporarily been exempted to their deaths (Lederer, 112-14). The transports included 511 children, 3,601 persons between the ages of fifteen and sixty, and 3,391 over sixty-one. They were divided among 3,125 Germans, 2,543 from the Protectorate, 1,276 Austrians, and 559 Dutch Jews. When it was all over, the ghetto population was a manageable 28,090 (Adler, 699).

8. Redlich was aware of the Allied invasion of Normandy on this date. See entry for June 23, 1944, in Dan's diary.

9. Almost as amazing as the availability of sardines (which arrived in special Red Cross parcels via Portugal) was the existence of lame and handicapped persons (1,398 cripples, 333 blind) in the ghetto after the May transports (Adler, 699).

After a while, the doctor became ill with typhus. The disease lasted several months. The wife was left alone in the house because her husband was lying ill in the hospital. She was free.

During the same period, she got involved with a conductor and had sex with him. When the doctor was restored to health, she returned to him. Meanwhile, she became pregnant, and the doctor tried to force her to have an abortion. There were many reasons: it is forbidden to give birth in the ghetto, no security for the future, and the fear that the child she was carrying was not his. But the wife refused to listen to him. He urged her until, in desperation, she attempted suicide. Her husband did not want to save her. Instead, he wanted to join her. By chance, her father saved her. She went to the hospital, and there they performed an abortion. Afterwards, she refused to sleep with her husband. Her parents were put on the last transport. The doctor succeeded in saving them, and as a reward she slept with him. A few days ago, she left him for good.

June 18, 1944. Inspections by high-ranking officials (State Minister Frank).[10] They permitted the reconstruction of the school.[11] Jewish *chutzpah* [gall] is really too much. One Jew changed his name from Cohen to Coma twenty years ago. Now a package of sardines has arrived with the name Cohen and he wants it. Suddenly his name is Cohen, not Coma.

June 19, 1944. All events center around one thing: the visit of the commission. They rain down order after order. Kindergarten children are to sing during the visit, the workers are to return home. Plays and cultural events and sporting activities must take place. Even the few lambs left here roam about on the grass around the city. The children, the workers, the sheep—a perfect idyll.[12] An argument whether to teach Hebrew as a mandatory subject or an elective.

10. Obergruppenführer Karl Hermann Frank was Heydrich's successor as Protector of Bohemia and Moravia. He was executed in Prague in 1946.

11. Lederer tells how Commandant Rahm placed a sign "Boys' School" over the entry to a former hospital. The rooms were furnished with blackboards on which was written "closed for the holidays." See entry June 22, 1944.

12. There were numerous rehearsals before the commission arrived. In contrast with earlier visits, Terezin's Jews were told to answer questions put to them. Dr. Eppstein was supplied with an auto and chauffeur. On June 23, the commission made up of Frants Hvass of the Danish Red Cross, Dr. Juel Henningsen of the Danish Foreign Ministry, Dr. M. Rossel from the Swiss Red Cross, and D. Heidenkampf of the German Red Cross were accompanied by Everhard von Thadden of the German Foreign Office, Günther, and Commandant Rahm. Their tour, through specific areas of the ghetto, was, writes Theodor Mobs, very successful: "It [the commission] saw a soccer game with excited onlookers, exemplary rock gardens, interiors of buildings, the children's rest home, the steam laundry, sun-browned children singing and laughing with

June 22, 1944. A sign: school for boys and girls. Now, in vacation time! "Such is the teaching permit." It is forbidden to smoke in the city. This is a permit to smoke.[13]

June 25, 1944. "Do not smoke, gentlemen. Mr. Eppstein has imposed a ban on smoking."[14] The Germans told this to the Red Cross Commission.[15]

July 6, 1944. Today, two weeks after the committee's visit, they ordered the firing of the administrators of houses L417 and L318. These

shovels on their shoulders, white gloved bread distributors, the white bread bakery and the pharmacy. In the dining hall, it saw how well the camp inmates were fed and how they were served by white-aproned waitresses.

"During the noon hour, the guests were fed and the sightseeing quickly continued. They were shown the central swimming pool, the butcher shop, the fire department, the hospital and the boys' home. Then there was a long discussion with Dr. [Erich] Springer, the Surgical Director, and then they saw the steam kitchens, and the children's pavilion. The tour lasted six hours and it is no wonder that the individual commission members were extraordinarily influenced and had not the slightest suspicion of any deception" (Dr. Theodor Mobs, *Theresienstadt: Eine Philatelistische Studie* [Frankfurt: Philipp Kohler, 1965], trans. Dr. Carl Praeger, 6-7).

13. Redlich's comments are etched in sarcasm. After interfering with any semblance of an organized school curriculum, the Nazis furnished a building with benches and other materials to create the illusion that education was continuing in the ghetto. As for smoking, even the possession of cigarettes was punishable.

14. The charade would not last much longer. With more deportations looming that fall, Dr. Eppstein advised his colleagues on September 19: "We are like a ship that sees the long-awaited harbor from a distance. We can recognize our friends on the shore. But we still must steer through unseen reefs. We should not be deceived by premature celebrations" (Adler, 814). Eight days after making that speech, Eppstein was arrested by Rahm and thrown into the Little Fortress. He was shot there in October (Lederer, 148-50).

15. How much the Red Cross delegates were influenced by this sham is difficult to tell. In their reports, Hvass, Hennigsen, and Rossel described Terezin as an *Endlager* (final camp) where conditions were "relatively good." After the war, representatives of the International Red Cross explained they had not been deceived and that their very presence had eased conditions for the Jews. In fact, the IRC never made a formal representation on behalf of Jews in concentration camps who, it agreed in Nazi parlance, were *Schutzhaftlinge* (common criminals). See Arthur Morse, *While Six Million Died* (New York: Random, 1967), 325; *Report of the International Committee of the Red Cross on Its Activities during the Second World War*, XVIIth International Red Cross Conference (Geneva, 1948), Vol. I, p. 19; and Jean Claude Favez, *Une Mission impossible? Le CICR, les déportations et les camps de concentration nazis* (Lausanne, 1988). This particular visit led directly to the May deportations from Terezin, which in turn prompted the destruction of the Family Camp in Auschwitz. That the survivors in Terezin were not overjoyed, see July 6, 1944 entry. Apparently Hans Günther was delighted with what had occurred, for he now ordered the filming of a documentary on this so-called Jewish health spa. As noted previously, only forty yards of this film, labeled "Aktion Z" has survived. See Lederer, 119-21.

are people who have worked with me for more than two and one-half years. No one knows the reason for the firing.[16]

August 2, 1944.[17] A woman has arrived in the ghetto, bringing with her one thousand crowns of ghetto money. She brought them in Prague and paid over thirty thousand Czech crowns for them.[18]

16. The Embellishment was, said Edith Ornstein, "irrsinnig Vorbereitungen, irrsinniger Humbug" (insane preparations, insane humbug) [Ornstein report, Beit Terezin Archives, p. 9]. "We wanted so much to believe," wrote Resi Weglein, "that the terrible hunger would be past. But we saw our hopes dashed to the ground. Two days after the commission disappeared, our meals were stripped back for two weeks. The common cry resounded: 'Nie wieder Kommission!' (never again commissions)" [Weglein memoir, Beit Terezin Archives, p. 45].

17. Redlich's last entry in his own journal.

18. Ghetto *Krone* were useless outside of Terezin. Possession of large sums of Czech currency inside the ghetto was dangerous. Thus, the desperate exchange.

Diary of Dan

From March 16, 1944, when his son was born, to October of the same year, Redlich kept a concurrent diary for Dan. Like so many fathers, he hoped to have a record of his son's development that he could share in more peaceful times. This journal includes reference to major events like the Normandy invasion, the arrest of artists who tried to smuggle drawings of conditions in the ghetto out to Switzerland, aerial bombardments. Its essence, however, is the love of two young parents for their precious son. We share their concern for his weight (less than six pounds at birth, more than double that six months later), possible sickness, even the shape of his ears. We share delight when he makes gurgling noises and plays with his hands. Inevitably, however, Terezin must be restored to its original purpose of a ghetto for the elderly and Prominents.

Yoman L'Dan

"Dan is a lion's whelp, that leapeth forth from Bashan." (Deuteronomy 33:22).

March 16, 1944.[1] "And he said: "When ye do the office of a midwife to the Hebrew women, ye shall look upon the birthstool: if it be a son, then ye shall kill him; but if it be a daughter, then she shall live." (Exodus 1:16).

Perhaps one day you will read these verses and say, "My people's history from days of yore . . . the stories are nice, wondrous deeds, fables." A great mistake, my son.

"And a new Pharaoh arose. . . . " This is the fate of our people. That in every generation a new Pharaoh arises and brings disaster—destruction to the Jews, fear and dread.[2] Even in our generation a great enemy arose, hated and terrible, an even greater foe than Pharaoh in Egypt. The ancient pharaoh only wanted to kill male infants, but the new pharaoh did not even show compassion for the girls.

1. Redlich was writing concurrent diaries for himself and his son Dan for the remainder of 1944. The entries for his son are longer and more eloquent, as if he consciously was writing for posterity.
2. Taken from the Haggadah (Passover account), which notes the immediacy of threats to Jews in every generation and stresses the importance of freedom.

It was forbidden for Jews to be born, for women to give birth.[3] We were forced to hide your mother's pregnancy.

Even Jews themselves asked us to slaughter you, the fruit of our womb, because the enemy threatened to levy punishment on the community for every Jewish birth in the ghetto.

I hope that you will never have to encounter these degradations[4] and insults, the weakness of a people on foreign soil, a people without a homeland.

I admit that your mother was stronger than I. Remember this, my son, and honor your mother, the heroine, among all women. Without her, you would not be alive today. You would not play or be happy. You would not cry or laugh. You would not drink or eat. You would return to the nothingness that was before your birth.

For the light of the world, twice you should give thanks to her. Twice she gave birth to you. . . . [5]

They say that in our generation miracles do not occur. They occur, my son, for by a miracle were you saved, along with her.

Why did they cancel the order forbidding births when you and others were born? Do you know of the plagues that God sent upon Egypt? The last plague also came on our enemies. The wife of an enemy officer gave birth before her time to a stillborn child. Jewish doctors saved the woman. Our enemies felt for the bereaved mother and allowed your mother and other mothers to give birth.

An occurrence or a miracle? I believe that a miracle occurred.

March 20, 1944. Your mother had no peace and quiet during her pregnancy. In the outer world, a war raged fiercely, the fourth and fifth year. Men killed each other, without pity or compassion. Our enemies declared that Jews are responsible for the war. A heavy burden oppresses us like a dark and heavy cloud. [One] lightning bolt, and we, a small Jewish community among tens of thousands of Germans, would burn to ashes.[6]

You were born on a spring day. There was mud in the streets and the sun was reflected in puddles. Even your birth wasn't easy, as if you did not want to come out from the secure enclosure into this godforsaken world.

---

3. On the abortion decrees, see Redlich diary entries July 7 and November 24, 1943.

4. The Hebrew is overly formal in this phase in the original. It speaks of never being able to comphehend the indignities.

5. Possibly referring to her decision not to abort the infant.

6. With the evacuation of the Lodz ghetto in the summer of 1944, the last two major Jewish population centers in Central or Eastern Europe were Budapest and Terezin. Both were to be struck later in the year.

March 22, 1944. Every day, the *Judenältester* (head of the Jewish community and its spokesman vis-a-vis the Germans) informs the *Dienststelle* (the German office that supervises the ghetto) of births, number of deaths, and new incidents of dangerous and contagious diseases. After you were born, he [Eppstein] announced your name: Dan Peter Beck, along with thirty dead and another outbreak of typhus. You carried your mother's family name because our marriage was performed in the ghetto and such marriages were not legal according to the law of the land.[7]

I must acknowledge that you are my son and I your father. Formally, you are a *mamzer*. Please note that the public formality never was and never will be crucial. What counts is what's inside, the real, inner feelings and not outward appearances, even if they seem important.

March 24, 1944. In the first days after you were born, your mother was always tense and angry. During her pregnancy she knew that you were safe in her belly. She did not see you, just felt you.

But she has worried too much about a small baby, a naked and screaming child. If you did not want to nurse one day, she cried. If you did not scream for a long time, she was afraid that you had become sick and she was frustrated. You will never be able to imagine how much a woman, a mother, worries and suffers since you are a male, not a female. And you will not be able to imagine the happiness and pride of a mother over a healthy, smiling child.

March 26, 1944. Your aunt is also pregnant. She wanted to hide her pregnancy. She was able to do it for eight months. A few days ago, she was reported. The punishment is less severe now because the new German officer [Rahm] isn't as great a hater or zealot as the one before him. But the *Judenältester* wanted to show that the Jews are ever watchful and commanded that your aunt be moved from her apartment to smaller living quarters. In addition, she should be taken out of the kitchen where she worked as a cook. I write "commanded" because we should excuse the *Judenältester*. He demanded that your uncle request punishment in writing, i.e., that he be relieved of his position as cook and vacate his apartment. This would be an appropriate atonement for breaking the law. In this way, the *Judenältester* hoped to appease the German commandant.[8]

7. Religious marriages did take place in the ghetto. See entry September 22, 1942. Under Czech law, however, couples had to appear before a registrar's office. Gerta Beck was not yet entitled to change her name.
8. Note Redlich's concern in his own diary, March 30, 1944.

April 13, 1944. You are beginning to see, to see this world which is draping itself slowly in the green and warmth of spring. The world is casting off winter a little by little. The weather is still cold and there isn't enough coal.

We live a proletarian life. We have a small kitchen where we live, sleep and eat. In the hospital, we found bedbugs on you. All the surroundings are proletarian. But even here, there are great social differences. We have a small kitchen and live with your mother. Most of the families do not live together, a husband with his wife. There are separate barracks for men and women. There isn't enough food for everyone. We have a lot of advantages. There is no justification for this. Sometimes I am ashamed. But for you, they are very important.

A child died from among those whom the Germans permitted to be born. Just think of a mother's sorrow, who by a miracle gained a child only to lose it. It is true that: "The Lord giveth and the Lord taketh away." A great truth—but truth doesn't console.

April 13, 1944.[9] A strong bond exists among women with the same fate, similar to people who have endured a common experience. . . . Out of ten women, three children have died. One woman still has not given birth, but will do so shortly.

The mothers go for walks together. They talk to each other, sharing concerns, whether their children are drinking, growing, etc.

[From] a conversation: one mother, a gardener, boasts: "I'm already giving spinach to my son." (The child is three months old.)

Another mother asks: "How much do you give him?"

The mother answers: "A little—but if he wants, he could have a few kilos."[10]

The modesty is hilarious. It is legally impossible to get vegetables into the ghetto. Spinach is stolen, taken surreptitiously because if the spinach is handed over to our enemy, it isn't "stolen." "A thief of thieves is innocent. . . . " The boastfulness is ridiculous.

Yesterday, you reached the weight of three kilos. Your mother was as happy as a small child. She wanted the doctor to come in order to announce the happy news. I went to the doctor and humbly requested that he visit us. Everyone thought it funny to call a doctor for a healthy child. But the mother—who understands a mother's

9. Actually a continuation of Redlich's first entry of April 13.

10. As noted elsewhere, it was difficult, but not impossible, to bring vegetables into the ghetto. Teenagers worked in gardens (see entry in main diary, February 2–4, 1942), and their produce went to the Nazis and Prominents. Individuals who tried to smuggle such goods into the ghetto were punished. (Entry in main diary, May 1, 1942.) Whatever the case, the notion that an infant could down several pounds of spinach in one setting is patently absurd, and Redlich duly notes this bombast.

soul? I went humbly because I was a little embarrassed. Your mother was proud—so very proud.

April 13, 1944. Today we went out with you for the first time. We have a nice baby carriage, a product of the ghetto. Usually the craftmanship in the ghetto is second-rate, but this baby carriage is very pretty. It was made by two young men, relatives of your mother. It's made of wood, light as a feather, with springs.

Bright afternoons. In the city square, the Jewish orchestra played. A Jewish orchestra, as if a hard war full of blood was not being fought, a war of survival. Our enemies have new tactics—eye-catching, building a "Potemkin Village."[11] So the Jewish orchestra played in the ghetto when people were permitted to stroll. But the melody never blocked out the memory of the terrible sacrifice, the pogroms, the danger still ahead of us, the danger that only now has a new face.

May 1, 1944. Yesterday, your mother was in the nursery. She spoke with great compassion about an infant who lies there without a mother, without much care, because the mother who has consumption isn't in the nursery, but the hospital instead. His mother is a woman whose husband has been in a concentration camp for four years. The child is another [man's]. A few days ago, you caught a cold. Your mother was quite concerned! She circled your bed like a tigress. And there in the nursery a child with a sick mother is alone.

May 4, 1944. "And ye shall be circumcised in the flesh of your foreskin; and it shall be a token of a covenant betwixt Me and you. And he that is eight days old shall be circumcised among you, every male. . . . " [Genesis 17:11-12.] Eight days old. . . . You were seven weeks old before we circumcised you. We feared for your health and so we waited till you gained weight. Your mother waited nervously and with fear for your circumcision for she worries about you constantly, as if she felt your pain. She knew that my decision to bring you into Abraham's covenant was strong and it was impossible to argue with me. Don't think that all the boys born here are circumcised. There is a child here who is several years old. The doctor recommended circumcision, but the parents wouldn't hear of it, because circumcision is a Jewish custom and they hate themselves and their Jewish brethren. In general, there are uncircumcised Jews, children of mixed marriages, and "modern Jews." Their parents view ritual,

11. See entries in main diary, September 12, 1942, May 3–4, 1944, and June 19, 1944.

especially circumcision, as barbaric. But this is also a blessing. Before *Pesach*, there really wasn't a *goy* [Gentile] to whom you could sell *hametz* [leavened bread].[12] God forbid there should be *hametz* with a religious Jew! Who knows if a crumb of forgotten bread might not be found among their belongings. This is a great sin, a pity for the believer! But there aren't any *goyim* here. What to do? Our wise ones say: The uncircumcised isn't a Jew, even if he is from Jewish stock." So they sell their *hametz* to the uncircumcised Jew before *Pesach* and buy it back after *Pesach*. Deceit you say. Possibly! Deceit in a new way. Of course there is a little barbarity in the custom of circumcision. I remember the binding of Isaac when I saw you lying on the bench. Your eyes were as frightened as the eyes of a sacrifice upon the altar. But logically, the custom of circumcision is healthy, good, and praiseworthy. One other remark: circumcision is the first encounter between a small Jew and the outside world. The first time he feels that the great world is his enemy: contact with this world brings about the flow of his blood. A sign or redemption? We hope that for you and your generation, there will be a redemption from suffering.

May 7, 1944. Your mother isn't so nervous now, but she still is afraid all the time. Yesterday she felt a tiny sore on your head and thought it was a terrible disease.

Another thing I wanted to tell you about your mother: when she returned from the hospital and you did not nurse well, it was necessary to draw out the milk from her breasts. She sent the milk to the nursery. Two hours after I brought the milk there, she began to cry and complain that she didn't have enough milk. She asked that I return to the nursery and ask for the milk back. I laughed and did not go back. I knew: she had enough milk. Your mother got angry at me and said that I was cruel and lacked feelings of fatherhood.

May 10, 1944. Your aunt gave birth to a son. I don't know why they say that when a son is born: "a son, on top of everything, a son," as if a daughter or a woman was not God's creation.

May 11, 1944. The sun is shining, and the orchestra is playing. They have plastered the fronts of the houses, improvement of the city. *Stadtverschönerung*—someone in Berlin decided: seventy-five hundred Jews will go eastward also; there will be enough space for the *Stadtverschönerung*.[13]

12. Some European Jews would transfer their leavened bread to Gentile neighbors for the span of the Passover holiday, then repurchase same for a token price afterward.
13. For these transports, see entry in main diary for June 1, 1944.

Listen Dan! "A wanderer will you be over the earth. . . . " It's the worst curse.

June 2, 1944. One week: for you it means you have grown in weight a few grams. One week: seventy-five hundred Jews left the ghetto and went somewhere unknown, to greet an uncertain future. They went in order to make space. Now the [International Red Cross] Commission will come, inspect the city and express its opinion: everything is fine, the city is beautiful, full of children's houses, coffee houses, beautiful halls and gardens, Jews living in spacious quarters.

They ordered us to vacate the ground floor of these houses. The first floors won't be seen by members of the commission at all. In the houses they shall visit everything will be ready and prepared. There won't be any reason to object.

Our enemies are merciful, full of compassion. They will send the sick, the weak, orphans, old people eastward in boxcars. But they have commanded that we change a picture on a wall of a tiger with a small tiger in its mouth, lest it frighten small children. The orchestra is to perform only light music. They want us to be cheerful. They want to show that the Jewish city is happy. They are the merciful ones.[14]

Yesterday, I was at the chicken house. There is a small chicken house. The fowl are raised for the Germans. For the first time in my life I saw a hen turkey, sitting with its young. It reminded me of your mother.

Your baby carriage disappeared. Maybe someone took it and will bring it back later.

Yes, after a few hours the "thief" returned the carriage.

June 11, 1944. Two years ago, your mother took sick. They operated on her and removed her appendix.[15] I was in the ghetto for six months, and she was in Prague. The only communication [between us] during this time were two postcards with thirty words that passed the censor. For this reason, their content was meaningless and unimportant. Beside this, I wrote three other forbidden letters that endangered us too much. I heard the sad report of your mother's illness. My state became even more anxious. They made lists of families whose husbands were in the ghetto in order to send them here. My wish was for mother to come. But it was difficult to get her on the list. I feared they would send her too soon after the operation and that it

14. Redlich exudes sarcasm toward the Germans in view of the May deportations of seventy-five hundred Jews to prepare the ghetto for the Embellishment.
15. See entry in main diary, June 22, 1942.

would be dangerous to her health. In the end, she was not sent. At that time she was a clerk for the community and they were not sent, even if their names were appended to the lists.

June 23, 1944. The first movement that you have made with your hands. You already play with your hands and feel everything around you. The first sounds are also heard from your mouth.

Meanwhile, many things have occurred in the great world. The invasion has started.[16] German armies have retreated on all fronts, and here in the ghetto (it is forbidden to use "ghetto"), we play a big game. They built a Potemkin Village. The Red Cross Committee inspected it. They visited us and saw the wonderful children, houses, post office, hospitals, and nice schools. The ban on teaching has not been lifted, but we have schools. . . . It's enough if there is a sign "school" and magically, overnight, one appears. Jews are laughing, content with their fate. . . . Thus the committee has looked around and then they left. . . . The only question is: did they really believe what they were shown?[17]

July 20, 1944. Your eyes are as blue as heaven. This is no poetic exaggeration. Your eyes stand out the most. Everyone praises them.

Your mother fears that you will have long, drooping ears. Why? Don't ask. Every mother must have the most beautiful, the smartest, the healthiest child.

I wanted to give your mother a gift on her birthday: a picture of you. I asked an artist to draw your picture. Today they arrested the artist and took him to an unknown place. What was his crime? Along with others, he sketched realistic drawings of the ghetto (funerals, hospitals), drawings that served no purpose in the beautification of the city. These drawings were found in the possession of a collector.[18]

16. Redlich is referring here to the Allied invasion of Normandy.

17. Subsequently Dr. Frants Hvass of Denmark would concede that he exaggerated his praise of Terezin so the Nazis would permit the continued flow of food and supplies into the ghetto.

18. Redlich does not specify the artist, but he must have been among the group employed by the *Ältestenrat* for the purpose of sign-making and design. The Nazis permitted some of these men to offer exhibitions of their work. One of their patrons in the ghetto was a merchant named Frantisek Strass. About the time the Red Cross Commission visited Terezin, the Nazis intercepted some graphic sketches of ghetto inhumanity that Strass had sent to Gentile in-laws in Prague. Other drawings were smuggled to Switzerland by the artists. On July 17, the leaders of the group were summoned before Eichmann, Hans Günther, Möhs, and Rahm for interrogation. Charged with *Greuelpropaganda*, several were taken to the Little Fortress where they were tortured. Otto Ungar's fingers were crushed, and he died following liberation from Buchenwald in 1945. Bedrich Fritta died in Auschwitz in August 1944. Felix Bloch never

July 26, 1944. You can already turn onto your back and then onto your stomach. A wonderful sight: you are lying supine and suddenly you use your elbows to crawl. At first you don't succeed. You pull and groan like a puppy. The third time you lift up your head—another small push and you succeed. After much work, you get the hang of it and you lie on your belly, satisfied. After a while, you sleep sweetly.

When you were born, you weighed 2.50 kilos. Now you have reached the weight of 6 kilos. This last week, your mother was in despair because your weight gain for the last week was only 20 grams. I told her the scale was broken and did not show the correct weight. I turned it in for repair and, see, you grew not 20 grams, but 200 grams last week. Your mother laughed and was as happy as a little girl.

August 4, 1944. Yesterday, a child four months older than you died in a horrible way. He was playing with a small toy which had a thin rope. The rope wrapped around his neck and within two minutes, he choked to death. His mother was unable to save him.

Your first picture: in other times, we would go out to take pictures. But here we have to draw a picture. The artist drew you patiently. Most of the time you lay there without moving as if you knew the picture was a present for your mother as if you wanted the artist to do well. After an hour, you fell asleep. But the blue of your eyes was still in the mind of the artist and he made it the right color, even when your eyes were closed.

August 26, 1944. The end of summer is approaching and we can feel it. The days are still hot, but in the evening, there is a strange smell, the smell of leaves decaying and smoke, the smell of autumn. On Shabbat, I go walking with you on the city ramparts. There are three rows of trees there. You can only walk between the second row, because the third row is on the edge of the wall. From there, you can see the countryside, grass, fields, mountains, far away, freedom. No, there still is no freedom there. Not yet.

Frequently, you hear a sharp whistle, straight to the bone, the whistle of a siren. Within a few minutes, the walls empty out. Air raids. Everyone knows they never attack the ghetto, but it's an order, a military order, since the walls might look like the walls of any other city during an attack. The planes soar overhead at several hundred meters, like a flock of storks. The engines roar as if they were very

made it out of the Little Fortress. For a dramatic telling of the fate of these courageous men, see Green 98-114.

angry—a huge and terrible anger. But here, below, the big noise becomes a mere growling. Is there freedom under their grey wings? Yes, they bring freedom without the birthpangs of the messiah.

Jews have arrived from Holland.[19] There were bombings there as well, especially of the Jewish camps. Naturally, this was not intended. Perhaps the many barracks caused the British to err. even so, bombs fell and Jews were killed. Many Jews were wounded. A mistake—Jews paid for the mistake in blood and with their lives.

October 6, 1944. [Final Entry.][20] One of your games! I lift your body and you flutter with your legs like a fish on dry land. Afterwards, I bring my face to yours and you look at me with such surprise. Learn, my son, to read the face of a man, because everything is written in the countenance of a man: his wisdom and his folly, his anger and his calmness, his happiness and his sadness, his honesty and his falsehood—everything, everything.

They are making a movie of the ghetto, a nice movie.[21] They ordered the evacuation of two beautified youth homes. But before they did it, they filmed the "happy" children's houses. A movie on ghetto life which will show the happy life of the Jews, without worry, "with praises and celebrations." (Indeed, they filmed Jews dancing parlor dances.) They wanted to film you, in order to show a happy family. Luckily, it did not work out. This film would have been a nice reminder of your infancy in place of a photo. In spite of this, it was depressing and degrading. Even the kings of Egypt did not film the children they wanted to kill.

19. Two hundred fourteen Dutch Jews arrived during the first week of August. They were followed by 2,081 more on September 6. The influx of these people to the Hamburg barracks created another problem in housing. With the ghetto's population once more hovering near 30,000, rumors began to circulate about impending transports to the East. The people's worst fears were realized on September 23, when Eppstein was summoned to SS headquarters and instructed that 2,500 able-bodied men were to leave Terezin. Under the direction of Otto Zucker, they were to set up another labor camp beyond Dresden. Exemptions were to be granted to Danes, special Dutch Jews from Barneveld, Prominents, veterans, etc. Lederer (146) and Adler (188-89) both agreed that Nazi authoritities hoped to prevent a recreation of the Warsaw Ghetto uprising by depleting the able-bodied youth who might lead such a rebellion. The scheme also offered an opportunity to dispose of the strong-willed Zucker, who was led away in handcuffs on September 28, the same day that transport Ek took 2,500 persons to Auschwitz. Three hundred seventy-one survived. There would be ten more transports, totaling 16,000 persons that fall.

20. The month (though not the date) for this entry is unclear in the original manuscript. Ruth Bondy cites September 6. This seems unlikely as the Nazis did not resume deportations until the end of September.

21. On Günther's film, see entries in main diary for November 9, 1942, and June 25, 1944.

We bought a new baby carriage for you. The seller was one of my clerks and wanted to bribe me by giving me the carriage free.[22] We paid one kilo of sugar, one kilo of margarine, and two cans of sardines.

What is going to happen? Tomorrow, we travel my son. We will travel on a transport like thousands before us. As usual, we did not register for the transport. They put us in without a reason.[23] But never mind, my son, it is nothing. All of our family already left in the last weeks. Your uncle went, your aunt, and also your beloved grandmother. Your grandmother who worked from morning to evening for you and us. Parting with her was especially difficult. We hope to see her there.

It seems they want to eliminate the ghetto and leave only the elderly and people of mixed origin. In our generation, the enemy is not only cruel but also full of cunning and malice. They promise [something] but do not fulfill their promise. They send small children, and their prams are left here. Separated families. On one transport a father goes. On another, a son. And on a third, the mother.[24]

Tomorrow we go, too, my son. Hopefully, the time of our redemption is near.

22. In October, Rahm and Möhs did away with their own categories of exemption. Selections were made arbitrarily, alphabetically. Those previously immune to deportation (the sick, tuberculars, aged over sixty-five) were sent, along with leaders of the *Ältestenrat*. On October 11, seventy Jewish officers and their families were loaded into two trucks, which took them directly to the local gas chamber (Lederer, 155-57).

23. Although Redlich still hoped there might truly be another camp somewhere, he must have called the aged and sick first and advised the healthy that they need not take with them washbowls, water containers, or tools. See order signed by Rudolf Prochnik, October 20, 1944 (Transport File, II, Beit Terezin Archive).

24. When one woman asked Adolf Eichmann if she could voluntarily accompany her spouse, the response was: "Selbstverständlich. Your husband is in a new camp" (Ornstein report, Beit Terezin Archive, p. 11).

Editor's Postscript

If the SS leadership worried about Terezin becoming another source of armed resistance like the ghettos of Vilna and Warsaw, the deportations in the fall of 1944 headed off such a threat. At the end of October, there were eleven thousand persons in the ghetto, more than 70 percent of them female. Their numbers were swollen again to thirty thousand in the first months of 1945, when the Germans, retreating before the Russian army, were forced to evacuate the major concentration camps in Poland. As a handful of deportees returned to Terezin, those who remained behind discovered the grisly truth about Auschwitz.

When the cattle cars opened up, "what came to life was hardly human."[1] The survivors were "heavily infested with typhus, full of vermin, half and completely starved, human ruins."[2] Some were writhing with convulsions, "their bodies burning in heavy fever."[3] They were "emaciated, starving, half-dead, wild animals [who] begrudged their fellow man of his bread and hit each other for a little bit of food."[4] Concluded Dr. Edith Ornstein, "The impression was that all was lost."[5]

In the last weeks of the war, high-ranking Nazi officials worked at cross-purposes with one another. Eichmann and *Sicherheitsdienst* chief Ernst Kaltenbrunner tried to protect themselves by hosting a second Red Cross Commission, permitting the Danish Jews to leave for Sweden in April, and ordering the burning of records of the Main Security Office in one of Terezin's courtyards. Meanwhile, the Günthers and Karl Rahm were proceeding with a scheme to dig a huge pit near the Litomerice Gate. Once completed, the pit would have been larger than those in Buchenwald where 10,000 Jews were shot to death days before liberation by Patton's Third Army. Rahm also dispatched workmen from the ghetto joinery to seal off doors and ventilation ducts in underground passages near the Litomerice and Bohusovice

1. Starke, 160.
2. Leo Holzer Report, 1945, Feuerwerk File, Beit Terezin Archives, 2.
3. Zdenka Fantlova, "Modernes Mittelälter, 29-page memoir, Beit Terezin Archives, Microfilm Roll III, May 15, 1945, p. 23.
4. Rosenberger Memoir, Beit Terezin Archives, 27.
5. Ornstein Report, Beit Terezin Archives, 13.

gates. Once completed, the passages could have held four thousand people at a given moment. Said Rena Rosenberger: "The Germans planned to gasify all of the inhabitants of the ghetto."[6]

On April 6 and 21, 1945, Paul Dunant of the International Red Cross visited Terezin and promised Dr. Murmelstein assistance with what was then an epidemic of spotted typhus. As German soldiers abandoned their posts in the first week of May, Heydrich's "paradise ghetto" officially came under the protection of the IRC. At 7:45 P.M., May 8, 1945, the first Soviet tanks reached the gates of Theresienstadt. Before liberation, more than 140,000 persons had passed through the fortress ghetto, but as Len Holzer put it, "Unsere Anghehörigen kamen nicht mehr zurück. (Our companions never came back)."[7]

6. Rosenberger Memoir, 27. When the Russians entered Terezin, they discovered 7,600 Hungarians, 6,600 Germans, 3,800 Czechs, 3,500 Poles, 840 Hollanders, 200 Frenchmen, and thousands more from 35 different countries. Kulišova, 101.

7. Holzer report, 2.

A Bibliographic Note

Of the major scholars who have written on the Holocaust (Raul Hilberg, Lucy Dawidowicz, Yehuda Bauer, Nora Levin, Gerald Reitlinger, and Leon Poliakov), the one who offered the most cogent analysis of Terezin was Nora Levin. Her fifteen-page essay in *The Holocaust: The Destruction of European Jewry, 1933–1945* (New York: Schocken, 1973 edition), surpassed the flimsy, single-page treatment offered by Dawidowicz or Poliakov. Levin tracked the evolution of the transit ghetto from its origins as Heydrich's so-called "paradise ghetto" for the elderly to its liberation by the Red Army in May 1945. In the process, Levin revealed the private torment of Rabbi Leo Baeck and other *Ältestenrat* like Fredy Hirsch, the ingenuousness of Danish Red Cross officials who participated in the sham tour of June 1944, and the incredible arrogance of Heinrich Himmler who as late as April 1945 fantasized that the few remaining Jews in Terezin would provide him with "a passport to respectability." As with all of her work, Levin's writing on Terezin was incisive, accurate, complete. Her death in October 1989 left a void in scholarship that will never be filled.

A number of excellent volumes are available to those who seek more information on Jews in Czechoslovakia and/or Terezin. The most comprehensive overview of the Jewish experience in Bohemia and Slovakia may be found in the three-volume Avigdor Dagan, ed., *Jews of Czechoslovakia: Historical Studies and Surveys*, (New York: Society for History of Czechoslovak Jews, 1984; and Philadelphia: Jewish Publication Society of America). For information on the prewar period, consult Hillel Kieval's *The Making of Czech Jewry: National Conflict and Jewish Society in Bohemia, 1870–1918* (New York: Oxford Univ. Press, 1988), and *The Precious Legacy: Judaic Treasures from the Czechoslovak State Collection* (New York: Summit, 1983.). On the Holocaust, see Livia Rothkirchen, *Khurban Ya'hadut Slovakia* (Jerusalem: Yad Vashem, 1961); Gerhard Jacoby, *The Common Fate of Czech and Jew: Czechoslovak Jewry Past and Future* (New York: Institute of Jewish Affairs, 1943); and Joan Campion, *In the Lion's Mouth: Gisi Fleischmann and the Jewish Fight for Survival* (Lanham, Md.: Univ. Press of America, 1987).

Terezin has been the subject of memoirs, poetry, and novels in more than a dozen languages. Within a year of liberation these included Jacob Jacobson, *Terezin: The Daily Life, 1943–1945* (London: Jewish Central Information Office, 1946); Max Mannheimer, *From Theresienstadt to Auschwitz* (London: Jewish Central Information Office, 1945); Max Friediger, *Theresienstadt* (London and Copenhagen: Clausen: 1946); Mirko Toma, *Ghetto našich dnů* [*The Ghetto of Our Time*] (Prague, 1946); B. Curda-Lipovsky, *Terezinske katakomby* (Prague: Dielnicke nakladatelstvi, 1946); Anna Aurednickova, *Tři léta v Terezíně* [*Three Years in Terezin*] (Prague, 1946); Else Dormitzer, *Theresienstädter Bilder* (Hilversum: De Boekenvriend, 1945); and Gerty Spies, *Theresienstadt* (Munich: Freitag Verlag, 1946). Subsequent publications included Richard Feder, *Židovská tragedie—dějství poslední* [*The Jewish Tragedy: The Final Act*], (Kolin: Lusk, 1947); Ralph Oppenheim, *The Door of Death: Theresienstadt Diary* (London, 1948); Jirmejahu Oskar Neumann, *Im Schatten des Todes. Ein Tatsachen bericht vom Schicksalskampft des Slovakischen Judentums* [*In the Shadow of Death: A Factual Report on the Fateful Struggle of Slovak Jewry*] (Tel Aviv: Olamenu, 1956); T. Kulisova and O. Tyl, *Terezín: Malá pevnost-ghetto* (Terezin: The Little Fortress Ghetto, Prague, 1960); Benjamin Murmelstein, *Terezin, Il ghetto modello di Eichmann* (Milan, 1961); Joseph Bor, *Opuštěná panenka* [*The Deserted Doll*] (Prague: SNPL, 1961) and *The Terezin Requiem* (London: Heinemann, 1963); Arnost Lustig, *Night and Hope, Day and Night* (London: Dutton, 1963); Karel Lagus and Josef Polak, *Město za mřížemi* [*City Behind Bars*] (Prague: Nase vojsko, 1964); Oliva Pechova, ed., *Arts in Terezin, 1941–1945*, Hana Kvicalova, trans. (Memorial Exhibition, 1973); Joiza Karas, *Music in Terezin, 1941–1945* (New York: Pendragon, 1985); Inge Auerbacher, *I Am a Star-Child of the Holocaust* (New York: Prentice-Hall, 1986).

Terezin produced some of the most dramatic examples of art of the Holocaust. Among them are Gerald Green's *The Artists of Terezin* (New York: Hawthorn, 1969); *The Book of Alfred Kantor* (New York: McGraw-Hill, 1971); and Norbert Troller's recently published *Theresienstadt: Hitler's Gift to the Jews* (Chapel Hill: Univ. of North Carolina Press). One volume, however, may be the most emotionally wrenching collection of the Holocaust. Hana Volavkova, ed., *I Never Saw Another Butterfly* (State Museum in Prague, 1971), conveys incomprehensible horror in the innocent drawings and words of the fourteen thousand children who passed through Terezin. Perhaps one hundred survived.

Especially noteworthy are monographs based on eyewitness testimony and objective research. The best, most readable, and probably least arguable study of this kind is Zdenek Lederer's *Ghetto Theresienstadt* (rpt.; New York: Howard Fertig, 1983). It ought to be cited as the standard on Terezin. Others that merit praise include Frantisek Ehrmann, Otta Heitlinger, and Rudolf Iltis, *Terezín* (Prague:

Council of the Jewish Communities, 1965); Käthe Starke, *Der Führer schenkt den Juden eine Stadt* (Berlin: Haude and Spenersche, 1975); Ruth Bondy, *The Elder of the Jews: Jacob Edelstein of Theresienstadt* (New York: Grove, 1989), and Margareta Glas-Larson, *Ich Will Reden,* edited by Professor Gerhard Botz (Vienna: Verlag Fritz Molden, 1980). Victor Adler's 800-page study *Theresienstadt, 1941–1945: Das Antlitz einer Zwangsgemeinschaft. Geschichte, Soziologie, Psychologie* (Tubingen: Mohr, 1960) is replete with accurate statistics, but the author, a trained psychologist, permits his personal biases to influence his interpretation of individuals and events.

Finally a word about documentary repositories. Over the past two decades, many survivors of Terezin have transcribed their experiences as a lasting legacy. One such repository is the multilingual archive on microfilm available through Beit Terezin in Israel. Listing more than seven hundred major headings and multiple subentries, the archive contains files on every major office in the Jewish administration, works by artists, programs, and autobiographies written by survivors after their liberation. Similar work was done by Hebrew University through its Contemporary Oral History Program. These transcriptions are also available on microfilm titled "The Holocaust: Resistance and Rescue," (Glen Rock, N.J.: *New York Times* and Microfilming Corporation of America, 1975). Other resources are available through the Terezin Museum in Czechoslovakia and Yad Vashem in Israel.

Index